# THE RED CHIEF

*Ion L. Idriess*

**BOLINDA PRESS**
Melbourne, Australia

Copyright © Idriess Enterprises Pty Ltd

First published by Angus & Robertson Publishers, Australia, 1953.

This edition is published in 1998 by Bolinda Press a division of Australian Large Print Audio & Video Pty Ltd with permission of ETT Imprint, Sydney, Australia

All rights reserved.

**Australian Cataloguing in Publication Data**

Idriess, Ion L. (Ion Llewellyn), 1890-1979.
    The red chief / Ion L. Idriess.
    ISBN 1864423056
    1. Large print books.
    2. Aborigines, Australian – New South
       Wales – Gunnedah Region – Legends.
    I. Title.
    A823.2

# THE LAST OF HIS TRIBE

*He crouches, and buries his face on his knees,*
  *And hides in the dark of his hair;*
*For he cannot look up to the storm-smitten trees,*
  *Or think of the loneliness there—*
  *Of the loss and the loneliness there.*

*The wallaroos grope through the tufts of the grass,*
  *And turn to their coverts for fear*
*But he sits in the ashes and lets them pass*
  *Where the boomerangs sleep with the spear—*
  *With the mullah, the sling, and the spear.*

*Uloola, behold him! The thunder that breaks*
  *On the tops of the rocks with the rain,*
*And the wind which drives up with the salt of the lakes,*
  *Have made him a hunter again—*
  *A hunter and fisher again.*

*For his eyes have been full with a smouldering thought;*
  *But he dreams of the hunts of yore,*

*And of foes that he sought, and of fights that he fought*
  *With those who will battle no more—*
  *Who will go to the battle no more.*

*It is well that the water which tumbles and fills*
  *Goes moaning and moaning along;*
*For an echo rolls out from the sides of the hills,*
  *And he starts at a wonderful song—*
  *At the sound of a wonderful song.*

*And he sees through the rents of the scattering fogs*
  *The corroboree warlike and grim,*
*And the lubra who sat by the fire on the logs,*
  *To watch like a mourner, for him—*
  *Like a mother and mourner for him.*

*Will he go in his sleep from these desolate lands,*
  *Like a chief, to the rest of his race,*
*With the honey-voiced woman who beckons and stands,*
  *And gleams like a dream in his face—*
  *Like a marvellous dream in his face?*
                    —HENRY KENDALL.

# AUTHOR'S PREFACE

To those readers who care not for introductory notes, I suggest starting straight away at Chapter I, and you are into the story.

This story needs an explanatory note, otherwise many readers could be forgiven for doubting that it is a factual story, for the character of the Australian aboriginal here portrayed is quite different to the general idea of him. I believe the reader will see the aboriginals depicted here, their beliefs and hopes, joys and sorrows, ambitions and hates, good points and general cussedness, as surprisingly like ourselves.

I did not wish to write this book. In fact, for twelve months I tried to forget it. Half a dozen times I addressed the notes back to Mr Russell McDonagh, then hesitated to post them. I wished to write my next book on any subject other than the Australian aboriginal, for I'd had enough of him for the time being.

However, there remained the haunting knowledge of a good story in those notes of bygone years, a story from a fast dying race, a whisper from the primitive past, that never would be written if not tackled now. And this story was unusual for two reasons. Firstly, it was coming from the dead. Secondly, it was a straight-out story from an aboriginal—and told so clearly and sensibly, so very different from the fairy-tales and stories for children that the aboriginal has given the white man so often. I have wondered at times whether the old abo. believed the white man was not intelligent enough to absorb a real story of fact and grown-up life, when he obliged us so frequently with his fairy-tales.

Unwillingly at last I began to write the book. The notes were lent me—or rather forced upon me in such a nice way that I had to grudgingly promise, "Oh well, I'll have a look at them!"—by Mr Russell McDonagh, of McDonagh Proprietary Limited, Gunnedah, New South Wales.

Mr Russell McDonagh is very keen on recording the old pioneering records of his district. He has an interesting collection, painstakingly gathered through the years. Among these were notes, actually the aboriginal story in straight-out form of far and away the best-remembered chief of the now extinct Gunnedah tribe. This story was written down word by word years ago by another well-known Gunnedah identity, the late Mr Stan Ewing. The story was from the lips of old Bungaree, last full-blood aboriginal of the tribe.

The late Stan Ewing was the son of Senior Sergeant John P. Ewing, who was in charge of the Gunnedah Police District of those days. Sergeant Ewing, like J. J. Smyth, T. B. Roberts, Doctor Hayne the Government Medical Officer at Gunnedah, and others, was a keen collector of aboriginal stories and relics. Stanley and his brother Ernest, with their schoolboy mates in those happy old bush days, grew up to play with and know the last of the local aboriginal youngsters as well as they did their own mates. And young Ewing reached manhood imbued with a great sympathy towards the last of the local tribesmen. The brothers were respected, but above all trusted, by them—as was the father, though they were always in awe of his official position.

Time slowly passed, and the old sergeant

was ageing, too. It was fitting then, that young Stan Ewing, long after he had reached manhood, in the presence of the old sergeant and the old aboriginal, should receive this story he had long been curious to hear from the lips of the last of the tribe—but only after the very remnants of the tribe had faded away and old "King" Bungaree knew that he was going, too. Yes, just as the wind blows into dust the last stem of dried grass that was once upstanding and rich and green and "covered all the earth"—as the aboriginals believed they did, long before the white man came.

And now for Stan Ewing's own written description of old Bungaree, the real teller of this tale.

> At time of the digging up of the old chief's grave there were only forty people in the Blacks' Camp I take this from the notes my father made at the time. The majority were half-castes, but there were still a few full-bloods amongst them, mostly middle-aged or old. Bungaree was "king" of the tribe, but there is no Namoi River tribe at Gunnedah now.

Bungaree was a full-blooded aboriginal about seveny years old, and a very active man in his movements. He had a well-formed massive head. His face was large and round, enhanced greatly by a long and wide growth of beard that adorned it. His was a smiling face, given to hearty laughter. He was about five feet seven in height, a broad and deep chest, wide shoulders, good eyes, teeth, and hearing, with a decidedly poddy or Falstaffian stomach, while in talking to him one realized he was an intelligent man. Bungaree, from many years' association with white people, could talk a very fair type of English. I have always found that the Australian aboriginal will quickly learn to talk a good class of English if you teach him, and talk that way to him.

So much for the teller of the tale. It would never have been told but for the professional interest and the curiosity of a hunter after relics. But let Stan Ewing carry on.

It all came about because of the Blackfellow's Tree.

Even before 1865 the Black Fellow's Tree was well known in the little township, very different then to the Gunnedah of today. The "tree" then was only a huge box-tree stump some twelve feet high, carved from base to top with intricate totemic designs, the work done by a stone tomahawk. The stump stood opposite the old Wesleyan Parsonage, well back from the roadside of Poe Street (later Abbot Street). All knew the stump as the burial site of some great aboriginal chief and warrior, the stump carved with his totemic designs when the tree was hale and hearty in the long-gone days when the tribe had its favourite camping site where Gunnedah is today. Numbers of white women for a Sunday afternoon stroll used to walk to the Blackfellow's Tree. Even by 1865 it had weathered and been blown down and rotted and eaten to a shell by white ants. It was then only a twelve-foot stump. In that year Mr Arthur Turner, following tracks of his straying horses across Bloomfield Street, examined it. All around him then was virgin bush heavily timbered with box-trees, wilga, pine, belah, and patches of scrub. Big box-trees grew where the Wesleyan Church grounds are now.

Years slipped away. Gunnedah slowly grew. When Dr Hayne came to reside in Gunnedah he was an enthusiast on collecting ancient aboriginal weapons of war and domestic implements, such as stone grinding mills, needles from fish-bones, kangaroo and emu bones and kangaroo teeth. He found here some keen collectors in J. J. Smyth, T. B. Roberts, and my father, J. P. Ewing. But the doctor was keenest about getting possession of fine types of aboriginal skulls. The others preferred something extra in a boomerang, or in the material, shape, and fixings of a stone tomahawk, or in the shape and carvings of a nulla-nulla, heilamon (shield), or wommera.

My father was Senior Sergeant in

Charge of Gunnedah Station and lived in the same quarters as the Officer in Charge of Gunnedah does today. One Friday afternoon Dr Hayne came to the Police Barracks to get my father to arrange a meeting between the doctor and Bungaree, the King of the Namoi River Tribe at Gunnedah—for so the brass half-moon swung by a cord about Bungaree's neck was inscribed. Arriving just at this time from school, I was given a message to deliver to Bundaar, the tracker, down at the police stables, telling him to saddle his horse and come quickly to the office. Bundaar was then told to ride down to the Blacks' Camp and tell Bungaree to come to the Police Station by half past nine next morning, and that Dr Hayne had left a plug of Conqueror tobacco at the Police Station for him.

Doctor Hayne said, "Sergeant, if you are not too busy, come over to the old carved stump with me to have a look about the job. Afterwards I'll drive down and arrange with Mr Ashby about his job tomorrow."

Next morning at 8 a.m. Bungaree, accompanied by a one-eyed and much younger aboriginal known as Jacob Painter, arrived at the Police Station. Very soon their pipes were going full blast on the doctor's Conqueror tobacco.

On seeing Bungaree and Jacob Painter squatted down at the stable talking to Bundaar, the tracker, as any other schoolboy would I joined them, carrying the bull-roarer Bundaar had made for me. The three of them took it in turn to whirl the bull-roarer round, producing roaring, buzzing noises. During a lull in the whirling Warder Neil, on sentry-go along the promenade on top of the jail wall, shouted to Bundaar to take the bull-roarer and his friends too down into the far end of the horse paddock, and make his blinking noise there! Just at this time Dr Hayne drove into the Police Station yard, and he and my father walked down to where we were.

"Bungaree," said Dad, "this is Dr Hayne, he wants you to tell him all you know about the old carved stump, and what the carvings mean, and tell the doctor all you can about the great warrior chief of your tribe who lived here long, long time ago. Will you go with the doctor now?"

My father went back to his office work. A constable went with the doctor and Bungaree. Jacob Painter wasn't a Namoi River tribesman, he walked on the centre of the road, keeping off the burial-ground site. My brother Ernest, who had been seated with Mr Ashby on a log on the other side of the street amongst a clump of box-trees alongside Roache's two-rail fence, came running to join us. He and some other boys told me that Mr Ashby carried a pick and shovel to dig a blackfellow out of a grave for Doctor Hayne. At that time my interest was centred on Dr Hayne and Bungaree— and I write now of only those things I saw with my own eyes, and heard with my own ears. Coming to the old carved stump, Dr Hayne said to Bungaree, "Why was this stump carved like this?"

Bungaree put his hands on his head and said, "Stump long, long time ago was tall, live tree. Blackfellow come, carve him plenty, make all about bury ground for my tribe. That time long, long ago… Great warrior chief of Namoi River tribe, him die, and him sit down close up this stump—all blackfellows look it, this stump, know great warrior chief sit down close up"—meaning that from the totems carved on the stump any aboriginal would know that a great warrior chief of the Namoi River tribe was buried near by and, according to the customs of this tribe, buried in a sitting position.

At this time those present at the carved stump were Doctor Hayne, Constable Lambert, Bungaree, and we four schoolboys. Mr Ashby was standing near Roache's fence talking to Mr S. Turner, who had not long arrived. This small group gathered near the old marked stump had aroused the curiosity of half a dozen people who wended their way down from off Conadilly Street towards us.

Dr Hayne said, "Bungaree, this great warrior chief buried here, what name that one?"

Bungaree put his hands over his mouth and shook his head from side to side.

"Come, come," the doctor urged, "tell him name if you know that one."

Bungaree answered, "I bin know that name—I no tell name him!"

"Why not, why not?" the doctor said a bit angrily.

Bungaree replied, "Bad talk, blackfeller speakin' a name of dead alonga burial ground."

"Oh, all right, Bungaree, I don't want you any longer, you can go," said the doctor.

Bungaree started to walk slowly away. The doctor beckoned Mr Ashby to come to him.

"Here, Ashby, dig there."

There was a slight mound in the ground that looked like an old abandoned red ants' nest. It stood not far away from the stump. It was the grave of the warrior chief of this

Namoi River tribe. "Thud!" The pick struck the ground. Bungaree, just thirty feet away, turned round to see the pick thud down for the second time into the grave. He let out a pitiful, wailing cry and ran, waving his hands about his head. In front of him down past the Wesleyan Church grounds and round the corner into Bloomfield Street also ran Jacob Painter, wailing loudly. They ran on to their camp near the lagoon. There was not an aboriginal in the town or camp that night except Bundaar the police tracker. It was a month before a few resumed to a new camp above the Burrell waterhole. But most of them drifted down river to Narrabri and Wee Waa.

Dr Hayne said, "Go carefully, Ashby, and only use the shovel. Ah, that's a skull, give it to me." The doctor shook the damp earth off the skull and wiped it all over with a handkerchief.

"This is a very fine skull!" he said, holding it out to the townspeople standing round the grave, for about twenty more had joined us since Mr Ashby started to dig. The doctor said, "This man had a perfect set of teeth—none decayed—not even a crack in any. Of course, the missing tooth in the front jaw was knocked out when this man was a youth undergoing all the endurance tests of the Bora ceremonies to prove him fit to be a warrior."

Mr Ashby was kept going handing the doctor human bones out of the grave. The doctor kept saying the names of these bones, but said nothing else about them until he got an arm bone.

"Ah, now! This is a fine exhibit! See, it was broken here, and a very bad break it was, too. And though there was no Gunnedah Hospital here then, there was, nevertheless, a clever surgeon doctor in the tribe who did his job excellently. It is a fine job to look at."

Numbers of other bones were handed out of the grave to the doctor, but he never made any remark about any of them having been broken. Mr

Ashby cleaned the narrow and shallow grave of all loose earth. Dr Hayne said to various men present, "It's a strange thing there are no war weapons buried with such a great warrior chief."

No one present at the graveside saw any war weapon taken from the grave. Dr Hayne remained at the graveside until Mr Ashby had scraped it clean of all loose earth, then he wrapped the skull and the broken arm in some sacking—told Mr Ashby to put all the other bones in a packing bag and tie up in a bundle and take them over to the Police Stable and leave in the forage store-room. Then to get a cross-cut saw and a good thick slab of wood from top to bottom of the old carved box tree stump, making a cut across the stump above the ground grass line to get the totems of the Warrior Chief, and the stone tomahawk carved into the stump. Then to fill in and flatten the old grave down again.

The doctor took the skull and

broken arm away with him. The small gathering about the grave dispersed, leaving when Mr Ashby began to fill in the old grave. I went home by the stable-yard front gate and, seeing Bundaar the tracker outside the stable clean-sanding the stirrup irons, I went down to tell him about the digging up of the old grave. But Bundaar, who was generally very keen to hear any news, said, "Now, don't tell me nothing—I won't listen to you and won't look at anything you got from that place."

"Well," I replied, "Mr Ashby is carrying most of the bones from that grave rolled up in sacking, and he is going to put them in the forage store-room where you sleep. There he is now coming in the front gate!"

Bundaar ran for the stable door, sprang inside for the key and was out in a flash, locked the door and raced for the Police Office where my father was. He burst into the room with eyes staring from his head and cried out, "Sarjun, sarjun, I clear out dreckly, this minute! I no stand this. I sack myself—Government can keep my last two week pay. When I roll my swag I will bring you the key of the stable. I go back horse-breaking for Mr Mosely on Tibbereena."

"Sit down, Bundaar," ordered my father, "and tell me what's the trouble. Have those two young constables been playing more larks up at the stable?" They had mixed brown sugar in the sand Bundaar used to polish the stirrup irons, buckles, bits, etc., and had caused him to have a stickiness on his hands and the stable gear.

"No, sarjun, it is not them," answered Bundaar urgently. "It is that Dr Hayne and Jim Ashby! They dig up the old warrior chief's grave. Old Bungaree nearly die from fright—everyone in camp clear out Boggabri way. No, Jim Ashby bring a bundle of that old warrior chief's bones for Dr Hayne to leave in forage store-room where I sleep. I leave, sarjun, can't stand that! I no Namoi River tribe man, but I blackfellow and tonight I can't stop in my bed in forage room along that old warrior chief's bones. Tonight I know, him ghost sit on bundle of bones and look and look at me for not bury him bones in his grave now all his tribe run away frightened. And I know ghost will blame *me* now!"

"Light up your pipe, Bundaar," said my father soothingly. "Don't worry, no one is going to put the old warrior chief's remains in the forage room with you. I'll go and tell Ashby to take them away from here. And while you are waiting here, sweep this room out for me."

Down at the stable Jim Ashby was waiting for the key, but went along with my father to the gaol, and took the bones to the tower up on the wall. Bundaar the tracker was too good a man with sick or injured horses to lose, and had given proof of being able to track over stony land away from a road, or upon soft ground, or over animal pads. And father was not going to lose him if he could help it. At a later date Dr Hayne cleaned and packed the remains of the old warrior chief and sent them to the Australian Museum in College Street, Sydney, and also the sawn-off slab from the old box-tree carved stump. Some years ago the old sawn-off box stump slab was still there amongst other aboriginal tree carvings. The set up skeleton of the old warrior chief may be there also.

So that was that, as told by Stan Ewing.

Watching the digging up of the old chief's skeleton, the wailing despair of Bungaree, the horror of Bundaar the tracker, the immediate fly-away reaction of his friends the blacks, made a lasting impression on the white boy's mind. Years later when he reached manhood, and the ageing Bungaree had confided to the "sarjun", "Me go soon!" young Ewing got the old aboriginal and the old sergeant together. Bungaree was now the last of his tribe. And the young man asked his father to try hard, before it was too late, to get the story of that long dead warrior chief from old Bungaree.

At first, quietly they smoked the pipe of fellowship, of long years of understanding.

Presently the old sergeant said, "Bungaree, are you allowed now to speak the name of that dead old warrior chief of your tribe, that one that was buried by the carved box tree stump?"

Bungaree was sitting down by the sergeant's feet. Slowly he arose, took the pipe from his mouth, turned to face the west. He stood silently for a while, then turned to the sergeant.

"I can tell you here, sarjun, now. That old warrior chief of the Namoi River tribe was name of Red Kangaroo the Red Chief!"

"Now why, Bungaree," said the sergeant gently, "why couldn't you tell his name to Dr Hayne that day years ago when he asked you?"

Bungaree's old form straightened, a gleam came to his eyes.

"Because," he answered defiantly, "we stood upon my tribal burying ground. No one of my tribe must ever speak aloud the name of the dead when standing upon the tribal burying ground, because the ghost of the dead is called back to the burying ground. Then someone in the tribe must die, to allow the ghost to go away again. In my tribe anyone was killed quick, no matter who he was, if two of the tribe heard him speak the name of the dead on the tribe's burying ground!"

"I see," said the sergeant slowly.

"Yes. *That* why I no tell Dr Hayne name of old warrior chief. But Dr Hayne no understand. He get more angry. He tell me to go! Then he do very bad thing—he get Mr Ashby to dig grave of one of my tribe when I still on my tribal burying ground!"

"I see," said the sergeant. And there was silence for a while.

"Bungaree," asked the sergeant quietly, "did you ever hear of any great deeds, of raids or battles, in which that Red Chief led your Namoi River tribe?"

"Ah, yes!" breathed Bungaree, and he seemed to have grown in stature. "In every tribe there are men trained to remember. And so my father trained me!"

And thus Bungaree, with feelings and memory unleashed, started on his long, continuous story, a goodly feat of memory. As much of it as I could have used, almost just as Sergeant Ewing's son years ago wrote it down from the mouth of old Bungaree.

With but slight deviations to help make the story more plain every here and there, this book is, in the main, practically word for word as handed down by the legend-memory of the Gunn-e-darr-tribe. I have had help from a little book, *Kamilaroi and Other Australian Languages*, by the Rev. William Ridley, M.A., published in Sydney in 1875.

Ridley, way back in the eighteen-fifties, was working among the then numerous aboriginal tribes along the Namoi, Barwon, and other New South Wales rivers. Later he worked over the Liverpool Plains, along the Barwon, Darling, Macintyre, Moonie, Condamine, and Bundarra. In 1871 he again visited the Barwon and Namoi on behalf of the Government to obtain further information of the Kamilaroi tribes, their languages, traditions, songs, habits and manners, institutions and laws.

And the information in this little book, painstakingly compiled from the aboriginals themselves while many of the

Kamilaroi were still in their wild state, was one of those lucky finds. It has helped me to relieve slightly the "straight-out" story of old Bungaree, confined as it mostly is to jealousies, raids, fears, hunting and fighting.

I have also been glad to refer, for reasons of clarity upon several subjects, to several short articles luckily preserved from the pens of two old-timers, W. A. Squires and Rev. C. C. Greenway.

Names of aboriginal characters mentioned are nearly all as given by Bungaree. Where he or Stan Ewing, who took down his story, missed out a name I have taken an appropriate name from Ridley's vocabulary of the Kamilaroi, strictly, in so far as I was able, fitting the name to the character's totem.

Some of the names given by Bungaree are those of Jerrabri, war chief of the Gunn-e-darr tribe, Red Kangaroo's uncle Tulumi, the warriors Burradella, Boobuk, and Kuribri, Red Kangaroo's friend Giluram, the boys Gilwanand, Tuki, the girls Weetah, Nareen, and Naroo, Kulki of the Coonabarabran tribe, Ilpara of the

Goonoo Goonoo, Mooti of the Manellae, and Kibbi of the Bundarra.

The accounts of the strength of tribes and of their losses in raids and fights are as given by Bungaree. The losses given here will surprise many people. In our very incomplete knowledge of the aboriginal, a straight-out fight is believed to mean a shower of spears until a man is killed or wounded, when the fight is over. In general, this is correct. But before the whites came tribes here and there over the continent were again and again wiped out. The fighting and losses then must have been far more severe than has generally come to the latter knowledge of the whites. In his story I have given Bungaree's own figures. All through his long narrative he was explicit in figures, to every man, woman, and child, and their ages, in a tribe. And his account of the various fightings and losses are exactly as he gave them to Sergeant Ewing and his son.

Red Kangaroo's speech before the chief, Jerrabri, and the tribe complaining of the injustices of the chief and the council of the elders is practically as given in Bungaree's own words, as also is his speech on his return with his captive girls, Naroo and Nareen. The capture and escape back to the tribe are told in Bungaree's own words also. So is the duel with Jerrabri, and other duels.

The capture of women and the use of the strangling cord were according to custom, and are set down as Bungaree described them. The spying by the girl Weetah and her little brother, Tuki, on the enemy scouts and the fighting along the Porcupine Ridges and the Wallaby Trap also follow Bungaree's account. The Red Chief's address to the discontented guards and the instructions to the lads who were to creep to the Secret Camp are in Bungaree's own words.

The little love story of Giluram and Weetah is fact, though enlarged by me, the subject obviously being considered as of little account by Bungaree, except for convenient mention here and there. To many of us it would come as a surprise to be told that the aboriginal man and wife, young fellow and girl, can "love", more or less in the sense of the term as we use it.

The wild aboriginal man or woman can

be as fiercely jealous, faithful, or unfaithful, can "put up with it" or simply "just not care", as we can. In my wandering days in the far north I've known young couples in the "hot-house" stage, who, in utter despair at the tribal laws that would hold them apart for ever, made a run for it in the face of almost certain death just to snatch a few precious hours of love to carry into eternity.

It may surprise some readers, too, that wild Australian aboriginals, among the last Stone Age men remaining upon earth, should put into words the sentiments, "I love you" *("kurridu zinundun inda"),* and "You are my love" *("Da zinda gulirdul").* In this case the actual aboriginal words used have been taken from Ridley, just as he took them down from tribesmen of the Kamilaroi, in his translation of the language

Ideas of Baia-me, too, and of the Bora have been taken from this source. Although, in my experience, belief in the Great Spirit, and the meaning and action of the Bora ceremonies, are practically the same all over Australia, here I have stuck to the conscientious, though incomplete, account of the man who put these beliefs of the Kamilaroi on paper, from the lips of the Kamilaroi themselves.

As mentioned before, the substance of this book is, in various chapters, almost word for word as old Bungaree, the aboriginal teller, spoke to Stanley Ewing, who wrote the story down years ago. The reader may think, and correctly also, "But there are words and meanings here that surely could not have been used in what must have been a very limited aboriginal language!"

Words, yes, but not *meanings*. Perhaps the reader could solve this question to his satisfaction by remembering Ewing's own description of Bungaree's grasp of language—"in talking to him one realized he was an intelligent man ... Bungaree, from many years' association with white people, could talk a very fair type of English."

As to the language of the aboriginals before the white man came, it varied in scope and richness according to the aridity or richness of their tribal country just as their physique and knowledge did, but, generally speaking, it had just the same command of expression and range of subjects as did the wild aboriginals of the north not many years back.

Their vocabulary was naturally limited by their life and environment, by nature, and their own imaginings. But in their own life they could and did express themselves as lucidly as we do within our own immeasurably greater range of subjects and vocabulary.

If the reader has been patient enough to read so far this plodding explanation of the book it may help him understand the characters and subject a little better. And it may explain that the wild Australian aboriginal, though a true Stone Age man is not, and never has been, the brainless, brutal primitive that many of us believe him to be—I believed it myself for quite a time, though actually living amongst them. The wild aboriginal and his wife and youngsters have always been human beings very much like ourselves.

And now to the writer—and, I frankly admit, the not-too-expert writer—of this book. Perhaps the experiences of half a lifetime of wandering throughout vast portions of this continent during years when wild aboriginals were still numbered in thousands, and of being in intimate contact with them, should help me in writing a fairly accurate picture of this now vanished tribe. Thanks to the story of Bungaree, the understanding of the old sergeant, the painstaking notes of Stanley Ewing, and at that enthusiastic, dogged perserverance possessed by all those good folk who so painstakingly collect and treasure material from our past—in this case Russell McDonagh, who forced these notes upon me.

So here is the last corroboree to the Red Chief. I wish it were only worthy of the man he must have been.

# POSTSCRIPT

As mentioned above, Stan Ewing and several of the old hands refer to the Red Chief's skeleton, and part of the carved burial tree, as having been forwarded to the Museum in Sydney. My publishers and I were anxious to verify this, though we realized that it would be difficult to do so, since the objects would have been transported many years ago, during pioneering days in a very young and undeveloped country. We asked the Australian Museum if it would be possible to make a search.

Under considerable difficulties a search was made, but unfortunately it yielded no trace of the skeleton of the Red Chief. But the officials got very close, a remarkable achievement, considering the lapse of years and the very small, sparsely staffed, and struggling organization the Museum must have been at the time the skeleton was sent.

Here is an extract from the report the Australian Museum officials forwarded to my publishers:

The tree mentioned by Mr Idriess is listed in a Memoir (Geological Survey of N.S.W., Ethnological Ser. 3, 1918) on the Carved Trees of N.S.W., as 48 in the Taphoglyphs, and the following quotation is given on p. 50.

"48. Gunnedah, Liverpool Plains. The 'City of the Dry Plains', or the 'Home of the Fatherless and Motherless', as the name is said to imply in the Kamilaroi dialect. The grave of Cumbo Gunerah, by tradition a great old warrior of these parts at, or rather before, the white man's arrival in Port Jackson, tradition says about 1745, was located, and traditional history collected by Dr Edward Hayne *(Sydney Mail,* 1891, No. 1622, Aug. 8th). 'In front of the Wesleyan Church, and near the Courthouse, on the street crossing the main street of Gunnedah, stood a peculiarly-marked old stump. There was a boomerang cut on each side with a yeliman at the bottom. The tree seemed to have been down for years. The carvings were in the bark, but the second growth around it showed the growth of many years' development in the tree since the engraver had been there.' Cumbo appears to have been particularly successful in his attacks on the Coombri blacks about Terri-Hi-Hi and the Walleri or Big River blacks."

Etheridge did not illustrate this tree, but he figured several others from the Gunnedah district in plate viii, fig. 4, and pl. xxxvi, figs 2-3, and describes their situation on pages 49 and 50.

F. D. McCARTHY
E. Le G. TROUGHTON

I can only say, "Thanks," to the Australian Museum officials for their painstaking, long and arduous search.

ION L. IDRIESS.

# CONTENTS

| I. | THE WARRIOR LAD | 1 |
|---|---|---|
| II. | AN UNEASY CAMP | 11 |
| III. | THE LIFE OF STONE AGE MAN | 24 |
| IV. | THE TRIBE TRAINS ITS FUTURE WARRIORS | 38 |
| V. | THE LONE LOOK-OUT | 53 |
| VI. | EVERY WOMAN TEACHES WHILE SHE HUNTS | 63 |
| VII. | THE NEW WEAPON | 77 |
| VIII. | MAN MUST FIND FOOD TO LIVE | 99 |
| IX. | THE WOMAN-STEALERS | 113 |
| X. | THE TROUBLES OF BOOBUK | 126 |
| XI. | THE DEADLY BLACK SNAKE | 136 |
| XII. | THE VENGEANCE PARTY | 149 |
| XIII. | THE FALSE ALARM | 158 |
| XIV. | THE CORD | 166 |
| XV. | HE TREADS ALONE IN ENEMY COUNTRY | 172 |
| XVI. | THE MENACE | 183 |
| XVII. | WOMAN AND THE CLUB | 192 |
| XVIII. | THE MASTER | 204 |

# CONTENTS

| XIX. | RUNAWAYS IN THE NIGHT | 218 |
| XX. | THE FIGHT | 230 |
| XXI. | RED KANGAROO RETURNS HOME | 241 |
| XXII. | THE CHALLENGE | 252 |
| XXIII. | THE DUEL | 262 |
| XXIV. | THE WALLABY TRAP | 281 |
| XXV. | THE SPEECH OF THE RED CHIEF | 296 |
| XXVI. | MAKING MEN STRONG | 306 |
| XXVII. | THE LOST DILLY-BAG | 324 |
| XXVIII. | ABANDON CAMP | 337 |
| XXIX. | DANGER COMES FAST | 351 |
| XXX. | THE TRIBE IN DESPERATE STRAITS | 367 |
| XXXI. | THE GREAT PLAN | 380 |
| XXXII. | THE TRAP IS BAITED | 393 |
| XXXIII. | THE DEATH TRAP | 404 |
| XXXIV. | FRIENDS, MY TRIBAL LANDS, FAREWELL | 424 |
| XXXV. | THE RED CHIEF | 436 |
|  | APPENDIX | 442 |

# CHAPTER I

## THE WARRIOR LAD

All gazed at Red Kangaroo, youngest warrior of the tribe. Upon his seventeenth birthday proudly wearing the Bor, belt of manhood, unflinchingly he stood there in challenge to any full-grown warrior who cared to come against him. This was only practice—yes, but a mistake could mean a severe wound, even death.

Facing him one hundred yards distant a bearded warrior stood quietly fitting spear to wommera. Suddenly he leapt forward and the long spear was hurtling towards the lad, who twisted sideways with a lightning flick of his shield that turned the spear quivering harmlessly into the earth.

Again the warrior stepped back, leapt forward, and the spear was coming with bewildering speed as the lad sprang aside with a twist of his wommera that sent the spear skidding along the ground. The warrior fitted the third spear to wommera while the boy stood, left hand holding the wooden shield before him, right hand clenching his wommera, the spear-throwing stick, much as a Roman centurion with shield and short sword might have awaited the charge of a foeman.

An exceptionally fine specimen of the wild Australian aboriginal, this warrior lad. Tall, broad-shouldered, alert, he was to grow into the most powerful and agile warrior of his tribe. But it was his shrewd thinking that made many predict a great future for him. And now he watched unwaveringly the warrior opposed to him.

Again the spear came, but this time with a puzzling, jerky movement, low down and difficult to follow. The boy leapt straight upwards, striking downwards with his wommera, and the deflected spear bit into the earth.

A shout of acclaim greeted this most difficult parry, the men uttering loud "Wahs!" of praise, led by the warrior Burradella and old Bungadoon, and the women and children shrilling their delight. Easy to see that Red Kangaroo was a favourite with the tribe.

This took place on the corroboree ground, in the quiet of approaching sundown. Shadows from the big box-trees reaching out towards the camp, wisps of smoke by each gunyah where the good food was roasting for the family's evening meal. Gossipy screech of cockatoo and galah away down on the lagoon tree-tops, "Cark! Cark!" of crows, whirr of bronzewing pigeons, telling that many birds were congregating for their sundown drink. Up here upon the corroboree ground all of the Gunn-e-darr tribe were squatting out to both flanks of the spear-throwers, except those absent on look-out duty. To the youngest piccaninny in the tribe all others were there, the toddlers quiet for once, boys and girls all eyes on the defence made by their boy hero. This practice was in deadly earnest, continued training through which every lad must go when he reached warrior degree so that he would be ever fit and ready to help defend and fight for his tribe. But within memory of the oldest living warrior no boy who had but just passed his initiation through the final grim Bora rites into the young warriorhood of the Kubara had ever been able to thus stand up unscathed against the best that the seasoned warriors could do.

Young Gilwan squatted there with his

soul in his eyes, and often his heart in his mouth, in hero-worship of the lad warrior. Gilwan was twelve years of age, and squatting round him were all other boys of his age, sitting quietly apart from everyone, in charge of two old men. For these lads were now entering their first year's training for the Bora. Those lads of from seventeen to twenty who recently had passed the last initiation into Kubara warriorhood sat close by the tribesmen, as behoves proud warriors who had just passed through the dreaded Bora. And to these lads, too, Red Kangaroo was the hero of heroes. Especially so to Giluram, his mate.

But not only to the lads of these groups was Red Kangaroo an example of a hunter and a warrior, but to the younger boys still, even to boys of from five to eight years who still sat with their mothers. To young Tuki, for instance, only five years old. Alas, Tuki's mother was dead, so he sat beside his sister Weetah with the women. Weetah was only ten years old, but an aboriginal girl of that age will soon be a young woman. Little brother Tuki's big, solemn black eyes were all for the young warrior, Red Kangaroo, as he parried spear after spear. Tonight by the campfires young Tuki and all the boys would be boasting that one day they, too, would grow up to be hunters and warriors as mighty as Red Kangaroo. Weetah's girl friends also were gazing at Red Kangaroo. But it was at Giluram, Red Kangaroo's stalwart but somewhat sulky-looking mate, that Weetah was gazing with adoration in her limpid brown eyes.

The warrior had thrown his three spears. Suddenly he snatched a boomerang from his belt and threw. The whirling missile sped upward, then dived straight for Red Kangaroo's ankles as he sprang high. On the instant another boomerang came whining and another was following it as the first smacked down, but the lad had fallen flat and the boomerang whizzed up over his body as the next came ricochetting at his legs, which jerked apart to allow it to pass between. There was a shout of approval, in which the warrior joined good-humouredly as he walked away.

That would have been the satisfying finish of this day's test for any other of the lads. But this fledgeling warrior had had the audacity to challenge any and as *many* who cared to come against him—a challenge that had been greeted with deep, good-humoured laughter by the warriors, a rousing huzzah from old Bungadoon, laughing encouragement from the women, awed smiles from the girls.

But now silence fell as three elderly warriors stood up from beside the chief, Jerrabri. Deeply scarred, stern-faced men these, ominously fingering their weapons. The first warrior took his stand, staring across at Red Kangaroo from fierce, shaggy eyes. Suddenly he leapt forward and, with a vicious grunt, launched his spear.

Like lightning Red Kangaroo parried it. A deep breath rose up from the crowd. The boy warrior was tensely crouching, watching this opponent almost as if he were a real foe. Again the warrior threw. And again. And now, no shout of applause from the tribe as narrowly Red Kangaroo avoided each vicious spear—only a deep breath of thankfulness.

With dazzling speed the warrior threw his three boomerangs. Then with frowning brow he walked away and sat beside the chief. A low murmur from the tribe died down as a deep-chested warrior took his place. This warrior also launched his weapons with vicious intent, as did the third. And the boy warrior either dodged or parried them.

And now the chief, Jerrabri, stood up and, fingering his weapons, walked to the throwing place. His heavy black beard hid the scowl of his mouth, but could not hide his frowning brow.

The tribe gazed uneasily. The usually calm eyes of the warrior Burradella now were fiercely gleaming, hands twitching upon his weapons; he would leap up and fight should the chief dare kill Red Kangaroo. Young Gilwan was nearly crying out aloud to stop it, while little Tuki clung to Weetah's hand, nearly weeping. Old Bungadoon was frowning for once, growling deep down in his chest as if about to jump up and take a hand in the game, a game that now looked like death.

Red Kangaroo drew a deep breath as he crouched, his eyes above the shield, staring towards the fierce eyes of the chief. Instantly then he felt he knew what Jerrabri would try to do with his first spear. Split the shield—leaving Red Kangaroo with no protection but his eyes and agile legs and the thin stick of his wommera. The chief knew that the lad's body, but particularly his eyes, must be feeling the strain by now. A powerful warrior, if he is expert enough, can with a heavy war spear split even a hard shield in half—but only if that shield is held firmly straight on towards him. But Red Kangaroo had learnt this, so, as an inexperienced man would, steadily, tautly, he held the shield straight towards the chief. If he had guessed the chief's intentions wrongly he might suffer.

The chief stepped back, then hurled himself forward and threw with terrific force. The spear sped up into the air and straight down at Red Kangaroo, who had instantly twisted both shield and body just a wee bit aslant. The spear point zipped hard at the shield, which turned it flying aside at an angle.

Jerrabri had thrown to split the shield!

A moment's silence, then a deep sigh seemed to rise from the earth. It rose to a muttering growl, ceasing as the angry chief fitted the second spear to his wommera. Red Kangaroo gritted his teeth in a derisive grin; already he had learnt that anger can cause even an expert to miss his aim. Tensely, though, he watched the chief.

The next spear came apparently straight for Red Kangaroo's shoulder, but he guessed the deceptive throw and leapt back and upwards with legs thrust apart as the spear sped viciously between them.

A roar of acclaim from the crowd, for had Red Kangaroo stood and tried to shield his shoulder the spear would have pierced down into his thigh. The chief was now so fuming with rage that Red Kangaroo easily dodged his third spear. But the final boomerang came within an inch of breaking his ankle.

At the throwing of the last boomerang the tribe jumped up with cries of praise and relief and hurried back to the cooking fires where they squatted down for the evening meal. Red Kangaroo was shaken by his ordeal as Giluram and his friends crowded round him. In subdued excitement they walked to the camp while the furious chief rejoined his council and friends.

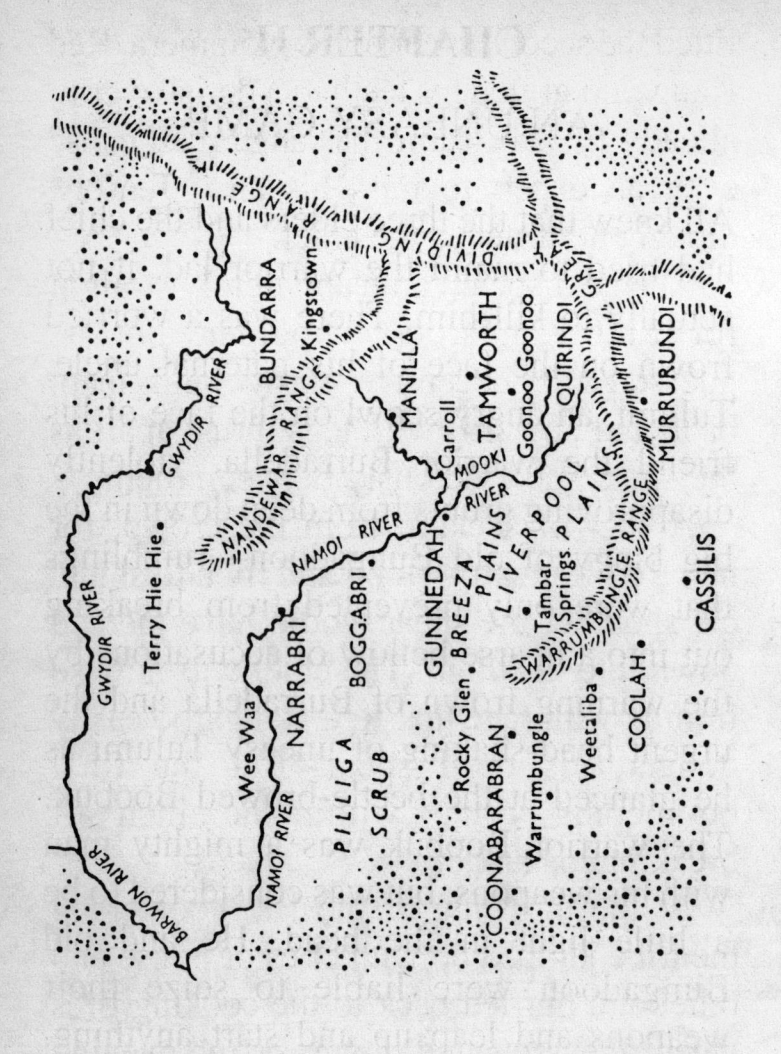

The area of country over which the events narrated took place. Present-day names are used.

# CHAPTER II

## AN UNEASY CAMP

All knew that the three elders and the chief had tried to maim the warrior lad, if not actually to kill him. There was a worried frown on the face of his paternal uncle, Tulumi, an angry scowl on the face of his friend the warrior Burradella, violently disapproving grunts from deep down in the big bingy of old Bungadoon—rumblings that were only prevented from breaking out into a hoarse bellow of accusations by the warning frown of Burradella and the urgent head-shaking of uneasy Tulumi as he glanced at the beetle-browed Boobuk. The warrior Boobuk was a mighty man with his weapons, but was considered to be a little light in the head. He and old Bungadoon were liable to seize their weapons and leap up and start anything, any time. And the time was not ripe.

A troubled silence, or indignant mutterings from others of the lad's friends. A shrill protesting from some among the women, barely silenced by their menfolk.

## Aboriginal Tribes of New South Wales

1. Anaiwan
2. Arakwal
3. Awabakal
4. Badjelang
5. Badjiri
6. Barkendji
7. Banbai
8. Baranbinja
9. Barindji
10. Baraparapa
11. Bidawal
12. Bigambul
13. Birpai
14. Dainggati
15. Danggali
16. Darkinung
17. Daruk
18. Gandangara
19. Geawegal
20. Jiegera

21. Jita-jita
22. Joti-jota
23. Jukambal
24. Kalibal
25. Kambuwal
26. Eora
    (Pt Jackson)
27. Kamilaroi
28. Karenggapa
29. Kitabal
30. Koamu
31. Koinberi
32. Kula
33. Kumbainggiri
34. Kureinji
35. Kwiambal
36. Maljangapa
37. Maraura
38. Minjangbal
39. Morowari
40. Muthimuthi
41. Naualko
42. Narinari
43. Ngaku
44. Ngamba
45. Ngarigo
46. Ngemba
47. Ngunawal
48. Pangerang
49. Parundji
50. Thaua
51. Turawal
52. Ualarai
53. Wadikali
54. Walbanga
55. Wandandian
56. Wanjiwalku
57. Wati-wati
58. Weilwan
59. Wembawemba
60. Weraerai
61. Widjabal
62. Wiljakali
63. Wiradjuri
64. Wodiwodi
65. Wolgal
66. Wonarua
67. Wongaibon
68. Worimi

—*From F.D. McCarthy*

Walcha the sun was sinking to rest, shadows merging into evening. Small fires now crackled brightly, laughing voices of the younger children chasing one another round the gunyahs, Kerior[1] tripping his yelling sister and belting her over the head with a carpet snake, the snake that mother had brought home for breakfast. A young girl's voice calling to her friend, a burst of shrill accusation from Kapota's gunyah— and the whole tribe knew again that big Boobuk had done again something he should not have done, or much more likely had not done something he should have done. Exasperated growls from Boobuk as he scratched his shaggy chest. Rumbling growls, too, still coming from old Bungadoon squatting by his fire while his placid wife Pumbul[2] chided him gently and, as always, in vain. Bungadoon was never afraid of making a noise, whether right or wrong, and he did not care who heard him. All the same Bungadoon's gunyah was known as Keringle, which means "happy home". Any stranger would have thought

*1 Kerior means "crayfish".*
*2 Pumbul means "wild orange".*

Bedlam a better name just then, for added to Bungadoon's growls were the yells of eight children of all ages urging him on, while wrestling with one another right to the very coals of the cooking fire. Bungadoon and Pumbul had no children, so long since they had insisted upon adopting the tribe's orphans. Many was the kindly joke at the expense of stout old Pumbul and Bungadoon, some declaring they had had more children than all the rest of the tribe put together. Not only did Keringle have a dozen squabbling children to feed and shelter, but numbers of the young women and men had cause for grateful memory of that same Keringle.

The evening hush was settling upon the bush. Those birds that are the last to roost were drowsily protesting from their leafy beds every here and there. In family and in friendly groups this Gunn-e-darr branch of the great Kamilaroi tribes ate hungrily while discussing the events of the day— the day's hunt and the game speared by each good hunter, the fish caught by trap and line by the women and children, the wild ducks snared by the crafty wildfowl hunters, the yams and bulbs and berries gathered by the girls, the mussels and yabbies found and caught by the children. And hearty was the praise given by every family and group to those children who had done something to add to the food of the tribe, or to the stock of gums and resins used as cements in the making of weapons and utensils. There was grave talk, too, upon the training progress of the elder boys, leading of course to the hunting exploits and the promise of great warriorhood of Red Kangaroo.

Every here and there low-toned voices discussed the growing jealousy of the chief and his council of elders and their friends and supporters towards the warrior lad. Certainly he was talking a little too much, questioning among the young warriors as to whether the chief and tribal council were doing their full duty towards the tribe and towards the young warriors. But then, it was ever the way of youth to murmur thus. He would grow out of it. Meanwhile he had already proved himself the equal of the best hunters amongst them all and, as all knew, except for its leading fighting warrior, the leading hunter is the most valuable man in any tribe.

Friendly greetings broke out here and there as the shadowy forms of men came chattering into camp. Squatting amongst his young friends by a small fire, Red Kangaroo frowned as his piercing eyes watched all over the camp, his keen ears heard a great distance away. These new-comers were the watchers from the hills, who through the day kept a look-out for possible enemies advancing across the low country. They were now reporting to Jerrabri, "No sign of an enemy all day." Presently the camp would rest in slumber—in false security, so Red Kangaroo believed. For this boy warrior was a deep thinker, and the safety of his tribe was very dear to him. Often he had thought that if he were an enemy seeking to attack this camp he would conceal his men in the scrub and rest all day out of sight of the look-outs on the hilltops, then advance across the more open country by night, and attack the sleeping camp at dawn.

He believed that at night, when the day watchers came in, then always night watchers should steal out and watch round the camp until after dawn, no matter how safe the camp might appear to be. Already he had made bold to suggest this safeguard to the tribal council. He had been told that a boy's place was to hold his tongue.

He, who had passed the degrees into the Kubara, he who was an initiated warrior!

There were two things lacking before he could demand his voice be heard in the councils of the tribe. Age—or else he must kill his man in defence of the tribe. In the meantime he must be thankful that some, at least, of the older warriors were his friends. His frown lifted as he looked across at Bungadoon.

Old Bungadoon was a favourite with the tribe. An old warrior, yet he was not old, for he could stand up against the best with spear, shield, and nulla. Could hunt with the best, could last out with the best in any long raid where speed and endurance were demanded—could do it, too, with good cheer as if it were a great joke, while much younger warriors were pushing doggedly on near to the limit of their endurance. And yet Bungadoon was seventy years old—with the heart of a lion; the laughter of a boy.

And that body of his—the great big head, the bushy black beard that the youngsters swore the crows nested in! A charcoal-black beard—not a single grey hair could the pawing youngsters find in it as they searched it for "goanna eggs". Big, laughing eyes set in sockets deep as a dried-up waterhole, and a nose so broad and flat that an emu could scratch gravel on it— so the children swore. Massive jaws from which gleamed perfect teeth as he chuckled at the least little thing—the youngsters proudly claimed that when he really laughed his mouth was as big as a pelican's, and his teeth like a deep-river cod's. His barrel of a chest made him look a monster when swimming. His paunch—tremendous! When he was squatting down "his children" would take in turn a kick at it to make it sound like a drum. They loved to see that paunch quiver and shake as rollicking laughter came from deep down there. And all was firmly set upon unusually thick legs that, despite his age, had never yet failed to carry him as far and fast as the toughest warrior could go. And yet with all his bulk he could hear the faintest sigh in the breeze; the faint gurglings and squawkings and guzzlings of greedy baby birds being fed by their mother high up in the nest of a tall tree would bring from him hearty bellows of sympathy as he patted his ever-hungry stomach.

Yes, old Bungadoon and Pumbul were loved not only by their "own children" but by sick people, too, for, despite the hungry mouths to be fed at Keringle, Bungadoon would pick up his spears and fish-traps and Pumbul her digging stick and coolamon and fishing-lines and away they'd stride into the bush and hunt from dawn to dark to bring home delicacies for the sick people.

The warrior lad Red Kangaroo was fast becoming the hero of the tribe, but old Bungadoon would always be its mascot—with Pumbul his kindly old wife. Like him she was of ample proportions, yet with never a complaint of bone or body, and seemingly tireless, too. She was as quiet as Bungadoon was noisy, and a great worker, with all that "family" to look after, yet so easy going about it all that you would think she never did a thing. It was she who really ran the show, without seeming to take a hand in anything, and it was her quiet diplomacy that saved the situation when Bungadoon's ready tongue and "I-don't-give-a-hang-for-any-of-them" attitude would have got him into difficulties. Yes, old Bungadoon would have been greatly surprised had he known who really managed Keringle.

From away across camp by the warrior Boobuk's gunyah again shrilled Kapota's voice, followed by a roar as Boobuk leapt up and came striding among the gunyahs to throw himself down by Bungadoon's fire. The ugly warrior's battle-scarred face was fiercely twitching, hairy chest heaving, eyes under those beetling brows glaring at the fire. Old Bungadoon's belly began rumbling as he laughed.

"What's she doing to you now, little boy?"

"Wah!" growled the shaggy giant.

"But what did she *do?*" demanded Bungadoon.

"Sat on hot coals!" sneered Boobuk.

"What did she do that for?" asked Bungadoon in surprise.

"Because she didn't know they were there!"

"Why didn't she know?"

"How do *I* know!" snarled Boobuk. "She just sat! That's all."

"How did the coals come to be where she was going to sit?" broke in Pumbul quietly.

"I put them there," growled Boobuk. "She was away gossiping. I was hardening a spear-head. I pulled the coals out of the fire, threw a few ashes over them, pushed in the spear-head, then went into the gunyah for my tying string. She came back and flopped down where she always sits and sat on the coals."

"And she blamed you?" inquired Bungadoon.

"Of course she did!" snarled Boobuk. "She always does!"

"But it wasn't *you* who sat on the hot coals," said the interested Bungadoon, "so what did you kick up such a fuss about?"

"Because she threw my spear-head into the fire," snarled Boobuk.

Old Bungadoon threw back his head in a roar of laughter.

"Laugh your guts out! You don't have to live with her!"

"You don't know how to manage her, that's all."

"Manage her!" exploded Boobuk. "You're just like the other fools!"

"What other fools?" demanded Bungadoon.

"These brats of boys who are howling that they can't get a wife. A wife! They can have mine any old time and everything in the gunyah to go with her. Wait until they *do* get a wife, the fools! They'll wish they'd never been born!"

"Still, you must find her handy to have around the place," said Bungadoon soothingly. "She always seems to be doing *something*. What was the row about last night, when you woke the whole camp?"

"She whanged me over the head with my own nulla!" growled Boobuk.

Old Bungadoon gazed meditatively at this muscular brute who in fight had killed seven men.

"Why did she hit you over the head with the club?" he asked.

"Because I trod on her stomach."

"*Why* did you tread on her stomach?"

"Because I had to get out of the gunyah to make water!" snapped Boobuk. "I trod on her stomach and fell over her and she snatched a nulla and clouted me one!"

"But what did you make such a fuss about?" demanded Bungadoon.

"Because she said I was the tail-end of last night's dream!" howled Boobuk.

"But that didn't hurt you," said Bungadoon.

"No, but the next clout did!" snarled Boobuk.

# CHAPTER III

## THE LIFE OF STONE AGE MAN

As for a thousand years, perhaps ever since the Dream Time, the winds sighed gently over the pine forests luxuriating among the foothills and the thousand valleys edging the vast plains,[1] loved homelands of the tribes of the Kamilaroi.

*1 The Liverpool Plains.*

In the chill before a cloudy dawn Red Kangaroo awoke, yawned, threw off his possum rug, sleepily reached for his weapons, crawled out of his gunyah entrance, stood up, gazed round, listened. The camp, except for an uneasy snore here and there, was silent in sleep. Red Kangaroo woke four of the lads of his own age—two he had to kick in the ribs—whose turn it was for duty on Ydire[2] look-out. Sleepily they awoke, shivering as they stood up despite their possum skin capes. At a grown warrior's command, yes, but for no one their own age except Red Kangaroo would they have arisen at this dreary hour. For it is towards dawn that the aboriginal sleeps as if drugged.

Red Kangaroo made them drop their capes, despite the chill, for he believed that on duty he who is clad the lightest fights unhampered and travels the fastest. He stood by to see that no sleepy lad left a weapon behind—to each his three war

[2] *Nobby Rock. The road to the settlement of Kelvin now passes not far from Nobby Rock, which is noted for its view of the surrounding countryside.*

spears, two hunting spears, two war boomerangs and one hunting boomerang, his fighting club, the nulla-nulla, also the throwing stick to break the legs of game or wings of flying birds at close quarters, his shield, his stone knife or blade of mussel shell and short-handled stone tomahawk secure within the hide thongs attached to the belt of human hair or twisted possum-fur tight round his waist. With a masterful grin Red Kangaroo saw to it that the hard, cold head of each sleepy-eyed boy's tomahawk was resting snugly at the small of its owner's back. Thus with ease he could use his weapons or run, or on the instant whip hand to back, snatch out the tomahawk, and fight. Also, with the tomahawk placed thus he could with ease "walk up" a tall tree, hold on with toes and one hand, reach behind him, pull out the tomahawk and chop out a possum, a wild bees' nest, a goanna, or those birds that nest deep within hollow trunk or branch. In the belt also were two feather-light fire-making sticks. On such duties as this the Stone Age men, heavily armed, had a load to carry.

Satisfied, Red Kangaroo nodded, and

taking the lead, the patrol walked silently out of camp. Other lads on look-out duty on other posts would not start out until Kukuburra the laughing jackass woke the camp with his ringing peals, not until all the tribe one by one awoke, the women sleepily lit the fires, and all had breakfast. But Red Kangaroo believed in his look-out men being well away from camp before dawn.

He frowned as quietly they walked away amongst the tall white and yellow box-trees, the knee-high blue-grass clammy with dew, the soft twittering of those first-dawn birds that awake with the earliest shivery grey coming to lighten the eastern sky. How easy for a stealthy enemy to creep into the sleeping camp on any morning like this! Not only should there be night watchers posted round the camp every night, but they should stay there until well after dawn, until well after the day look-out men had marched out past them to their posts in the hills. Once it had been so. But now the chief and the elders had grown lax. A time would surely come when the tribe would suffer because of this.

Birds in earnest were now waking with

whistle and chirrup and song. From away back on the plains came the happy trumpet-call of brolgas dancing to the new-born sun. Red Kangaroo frowned towards the rosy dawn as his long legs took him effortlessly over the ground, his men all out to keep up. He loved his tribe as all did, but he was a thoughtful member, whereas most of his tribesmen were content to leave the thinking to Jerrabri and his council. The lads forded the cold Namoi[3], waters and strode swiftly on, as if stepping up into a rising ball of gold that awoke the majestic bush into brimful life of tree and bird, plant and animal, insect and reptile, and brought, too, light and warmth to the velvety, chocolate-brown skins of these sons of the wild. From shadowed forest timbers and dark scrub edges wallabies every here and there came cautiously hopping out with their families for their early morning meal upon the open bushland grasses.

The warrior lads eagerly spread out while keeping straight on for the big hill

*3 The name Namoi is thought to be derived from Njamai Ornj, "place of the njamai-trees".*

looming up with its towering crest seemingly afire from the sun. They must spear food for the day as they walked along or else go hungry. For their leader would not allow time for the hunt, he would hurry them straight on to the big hill and away up to the top of Ydire, from which they would watch over the country for the safety of the tribe.

Back at the camp smoke was coiling up as yawning women tended the cooking fires. The men still sprawled on their possum rugs within the warm bark gunyahs. They came crawling out to the yells of piccaninnies as their women called that the morning meal was ready.

After a lazy breakfast the men for look-out duty at the big look-out rock called Booroobil strolled away from camp, two for duty at the Porcupine Ridge smoke-signal outpost strolling away in the opposite direction. As the sun grew in warmth the chattering camp gradually picked up weapons or utensils and, forming into groups, strolled in different directions out into the bush. The big-game hunters went through the forest towards the Breeza Plains and sweetly grassed flats where mobs of kangaroos would be browsing, emus stalking sedately along followed by their striped chicks. The fat plain turkey would be there, too, his snakelike head peering up above the grass. A few family groups were strolling away to seek their food elsewhere, the husband alert for whatever might fall to his spear, the wife and children keen-eyed for roots, bulbs, berries, carpet snakes, edible lizards and grubs and sugar cuts, wild bees' nests, wildfowl eggs and birds.

Most of the women, the girls and boys up to five and six years of age, started off on their chattering way to the big swamp, which, with the scattered lagoons and billabongs, was now alive with foodstuffs of fish, plant, and bird—wild geese, swans, pelicans, teal, black duck, wood duck, whistling duck, red duck, musk duck, with spoonbills and water hens and white and blue herons, and numerous varieties of bushland birds. Different kinds of fish, too, and tortoises, shrimps and yabbies, and shellfish on the bottom, and luscious varieties of vegetable foods in which a big swamp so often abounds. This was a particularly good season, but even so the Gunn-e-darr tribe of the Kamilaroi were blessed in that their wide tribal grounds were all good and well-watered country, and in places such as this swamp and the larger billabongs abounded in food of every kind. No wonder the people were fat and contented and lazy. Only during rare times of big drought did they really go hungry.

As the women made their way to the swamp a cloud of parrots dived down over them and up to a deafening, screeching whirr of wings, a flash of orange and scarlet and green. Presently half a dozen warriors picked up their weapons and strolled after the women. These men were guards, to watch over and protect the women. For the people never knew when a lurking enemy might pounce on a dawdling young woman and steal her away. Always girls and young women lived in danger from women-stealers, and young boys also, for all tribes sought to steal boys from other tribes to rear them up to become warriors of their own. The spoils to him who can take them has ever been a law of the wild.

Still remaining quietly sitting in camp,

listening intently to the quiet voice of the warrior Burradella, were Gilwan and the boys of from ten to fourteen. The older ones amongst them had already gone through twelve months' training in preparation for the Bora.

Burradella, the middle-aged warrior, friend of Red Kangaroo, had charge of these young boys for the next fortnight. Gravely he was telling them that he was going to put to the test, day by day, what each had learnt, or failed to learn, during his training so far. The first to be tested would be two of the twelve-year-old boys, Gilwan and Wanawah. They were to imagine that enemies had taken the camp by surprise in the dawn. The warriors had snatched weapons, the mothers their babies, and they had fled in all directions into the scrub—men, women, and children. And now the scattered warriors were trying to come together again, each group desperately fighting to drive away superior numbers of victorious enemies. The fight had been dragging on for three days. Meanwhile, Gilwan and Wanawah were guards, they alone in charge of a frightened group of women and children hidden deep within dense scrub. They dared not move from there, for inevitably some track would be found and they all then would be tracked down by the enemy and killed or captured. The babies now were whimpering for milk, the young children growing weaker, the mothers nearly frantic, all were starving. Gilwan and Wanawah must venture from the scrub out into the open bush and bring their starving people food. The outside bush was thick with prowling enemies. If Gilwan or Wanawah or their tracks were seen they would be hunted to death, then their careless tracks would be followed back into the scrub and the women and children found, killed, and captured. Such careless work on the part of Gilwan and Wanawah, the guards, would bring great loss and sorrow to the tribe.

Gilwan and Wanawah had also to imagine that in the alarm of the dawn surprise they had fled without weapons or hunting gear of any kind. How were they to secure food for the women and childen with only their thoughts and bushcraft and naked bodies to do it with? And furthermore, if they succeeded, how were they to get that food back to the women without the prowling enemy discovering them or their tracks?

"Now is that all clear?" asked Burradella. The boys nodded.

"Right. Now come along and show us how you will manage it."

As Burradella strode out into the bush the boys followed him. And now remaining in camp were only a few old men and women and several mothers with very young babies, squatting round the smouldering fires. The old men patiently toiled at the laborious though skilled tasks of repairing weapons and making cooking utensils and preparing materials for ceremonial work, while old Mullionkale the play-maker sat musing of the songs and dances and play-acting he would dream up for the next big corroboree. The deeply lined face of the old corroboree maker was broodingly peaceful as he sat there in the shadowed sunlight dreaming, a little smile now and then playing with the "fairies" dancing in his mind. Mullionkale means "flight of the eagle", and old Mullionkale had been an eagle in his day. But long since his flights in war and chase had gone into song and the joy he put into dancing feet.

Beside him now sat his middle-aged assistant Kayari, quietly grinding differently coloured ochres and pipeclays into powders to be used as paints by the actors and dancers in the next corroboree. Kayari means "will take tomorrow", and when Baia-me[4] the Great Spirit, "He Who Built all Things", should call old Mullionkale to his new home in Star Land then Kayari would take his place.

Oh, and poor Bilar sat there, too, apart from the others beside his gunyah, bent over his labours. Yes, Bilar the spear-maker, reckoned not only the best spear-maker in the Gunn-e-darr tribe but excelling all the tribes around. And now he was bent over a long slender heft of myall wood, using scraper of mussel shell and rasp of stone, with sand and water, with heat of ashes and infinite labour and patience thinning it

*4 Baia-me or B'Hai-me, "The Great Builder". The aboriginals believed thunder to be his voice.*

down, straightening it, shaping it, hardening it, strengthening it, working into it perfect balance. It would be a beautiful, a prized, an envied weapon when finally finished. Bilar the spear-maker was putting all his craft into it, but not his heart. For Bilar toiled for old Kuluman from whom, at great price, he had bought his wife Gille[5] and Kuluman was a hard taskmaster.

The old women, with a chuckle of gossip now and then, were cunningly weaving and plaiting cocoon-like mats for carrying very young babies, dilly-bags for carrying foods and belongings, fish-nets and traps, and bird-nets from cane, grass, vine and bark fibres and long thongs cut from animal skins. The young mothers, in between fondling their new-born babes, were grinding grass-seed into flour between their grinding stones. Under warm sunlight, with an eagle in the sky and a dreamy crooning from high up among the branches of the big old trees, it was a peaceful scene, a happy day.

Ah, but with a snake in the grass. The voices hushed as from a gunyah apart a

*5 Gille means "the moon".*

wizened old man emerged, his face a maze of wrinkles, his half-closed eyelids disguising piercing eyes sinister as a snake's. Around his skinny neck hung a necklet of yellowed human knuckle-bones and shrivelled eagle claws, and suspended by the human-hair belt at his waist the smoke-dried hand of a child.

This dangerous relic was Nundoba the witchdoctor, the rain-maker and medicine man. In clawlike hand he carried his bag of charms—queer musty things, and with them his Kuradyi, his doctor's spirit stones. He hobbled quietly away in the direction of Porcupine Ridge. He would climb up to the big scrub and within its gloomy depths hunt for secret herbs for medicines, and poisons of sap and evil-tasting berries, and fungus that glowed sickly green and blue upon rotted logs in the dripping gloom on a dark night.

The witchdoctor with his herbs, his magic stones, his mumbling spells and auto-suggestion can cure, but—he can more definitely kill. From under lowered eyes the people watched his hunched back as he went. Feared indeed was Nundoba the witchdoctor, whose name means "the deadly black snake with the red belly"!

"The Black Snake moves early towards the Poison Scrub," murmured Mullionkale the play-maker to his assistant.

But Kayari only grunted softly as he bent over his work, fearful lest an evil spirit overhear indiscreet words and carry them to the ready ear of the witchdoctor. For all knew that witchdoctors encourage their familiars, those spiteful ones among the evil spirits that listen in to the conversation of humans, then fly to the ear of the witchdoctor when unhappily they overhear something whispered against him.

# CHAPTER IV

## THE TRIBE TRAINS ITS FUTURE WARRIORS

The bush was alive with bird calls as Burradella led his boys away from the camp. A few little white clouds far away up were playing chasings with the wind, some vagrant wind not felt down here upon earth. Under a gnarled old blue-gum Burradella halted.

"We shall imagine," he said gravely to Gilwan and Wanawah, "that you both have now crept out to the edge of the scrub in which the women are hidden. Before you is the open bush. Enemy scouts are prowling somewhere—anywhere! You have no hunting gear of any sort. You must bring back food to the women, must not be seen or leave betraying tracks. Now go!"

Gilwan and Wanawah jumped ahead and, bending low, seemed to vanish amongst the bushes and grasses.

"Come!" ordered Burradella, and strode forward while the other boys followed eagerly, leaping into the air to try to fault the two hunters by keeping them in sight. They caught an occasional glimpse of the dark head of Gilwan or the buttocks of Wanawah as he vanished down into a depression or beside a fallen tree. Then they disappeared.

Burradella stopped. The boys gathered round him, craning their necks, listening.

But there came only the hoarse, booming call of a swamp pheasant, the rustle of a pademelon through the kangaroo grass, the sigh of the breeze, the distant call of waterfowl, the drone of insects.

"Well?" asked Burradella quietly.

For some moments the boys pondered, trying hard to reason out the direction the two had taken, and why.

Young Gurah spoke softly. "Not the way we are looking, for there is a butcher-bird watching in the wilga-tree and he has seen no more than a snake."

"Wah!" Burradella nodded approvingly.

Had the hunters passed that wilga-tree the keen-eyed butcher-bird would probably have raised a shrill alarm. Then, had there been real enemies within hearing they would have come to see what had alarmed the butcher-bird. Thus the hunters had not only to advance unobserved to enemies, not only to hunt while leaving no visible track, but also to keep their eyes on the branches ahead, on the ground near their feet, the grass beside them, and the bushes around them, down into and along the gullies, among the tree-trunks all around, and through the bush ahead. For to startle a wallaby from the grasses or an alarm bird in a tree could cause a lurking enemy scout to come and investigate.

"Well," said Burradella, "our hunters have proved too smart for us, as they would have, so far, for enemy scouts. But we know their intentions, and we know every inch of this country. Now, where do you believe they would make for?"

"The swamp of the big oaks!" they answered.

"Good. We shall see whether you have guessed right. Come."

And at the full run he set off, the boys following. As they passed the wilga-tree the butcher-bird shrilled his alarm. Presently luxuriant swamp oaks with mighty gums appeared before them, a tang of water-weeds was in the air. As they dodged amongst the tree-trunks they heard plainly the muffled calls of many wildfowl. They emerged from the timber at a narrow neck of the swamp, the banks golden-green with tall grasses and reeds, the water gleaming clear and cool.

Hidden among the reeds by the water's

edge, Gilwan and Wanawah bobbed up smiling as Burradella and the boys came running. No word was spoken. Wanawah vanished amongst the tall grasses, working his way up along the swamp edge. Gilwan, again invisible amongst the reeds to any but those actually watching, was carefully pulling up a length of long-leafed, trailing water-vine. Cunningly he began to entwine this round his head until his black hair seemed but a bunch of leaves. Then he drooped long trailers of the vine over his shoulders and back until his crouching body was indistinguishable among the surrounding reeds. The expressive eyes of the watching boys told they had guessed his plan.

Gilwan squirmed slowly out into the water. The sharpest enemy scout, even from the near-by bank, could hardly have noticed him as inch by inch he crawled out into deeper water. No sign of a body, no ripples, only a bunch of water-weed gently, naturally drifting out into the narrow stream. As the water grew deeper so Gilwan gradually straightened up until he had waded out into midstream, which here was but a very narrow neck of the swamp, barely the width of a street, hemmed in by tall reeds, and only neck-deep in midstream. And now Gilwan stood there motionless, facing upstream, but invisible. There was only that loose bunch of water-weed, its tendrils idly drifting back with the stream. Under the weed his nostrils were just above water, his sharp eyes staring upstream through the leaves.

A heavy silence over the bush just here, just a murmurous cackling, squawking, crooning of wildfowl upstream.

Burradella took his boys back and up along the bank and soon the swamp opened to them in a wide sheet of water, cluttered here and there with flocks of ducks, the white of solemn pelicans, jet black of the cruising swan, blue and white of crane and egret. Plainly now came the call of many wildfowl, the carefree, brazen trumpet-call of the dancing brolga, and from the trees screech of cockatoos and galahs and parrots, whirring flocks of bronzewing pigeons, whistling, cooing, and twittering of many bush birds. The water edges were hemmed in by reeds that stretched away back into long grasses walled in by the oaks and gums; the broad sheet of calm water gleamed under the sunlit blue of sky.

Cautiously, so as not to startle game, Burradella's boys climbed trees in an endeavour to overlook the speck of water-weed that was Gilwan, and watch if possible the progress of Wanawah. But never once did Wanawah betray himself. Hostile tribesmen could have passed within yards without detecting him. He was in trouble, all the same. Crouching amongst the long grass, almost staring into the questing eyes of a swamp wallaby now sitting uneasily back on its tail, its pretty eyes staring inquiringly, its ears twitching this way and that to catch any hostile sound, its nostrils sniffing the air from this direction, then that. The animal sensed that danger hovered near, yet it could see nothing suspicious, could hear nothing but the peaceful sounds of the bush, could smell no tang of enemy.

Wanawah lay motionless. He knew that if he startled the wallaby it would bound away and the agitated *thud! thud! thud!* of its feet, the urgency of its going, would cause any hostile scouts to pause, then walk back along its tracks to find out what had alarmed it. And in that case Wanawah would have failed in his test.

Uneasily the wallaby hopped a few yards away, then sat back again, watching, listening, sniffing. After a while a vagrant air current brought it a tang of wild blackboy. It sniffed a moment longer. There was no sound, no hostile movement, but again it got a faint whiff of blackboy. Uneasily it hopped away.

Wanawah breathed again. A wallaby hopping casually along would raise no suspicions in the mind or eye of a hostile scout. Cautiously he crept along again.

Presently he stopped. It was not that the grass ahead grew so much shorter; it was at sight of a sunlit white flower perched high up on a red-gum branch leaning out over the water's edge.

That white flower was a cockatoo on sentry duty, overlooking the richly grassed portion of the swamp shore where its friends were hungrily foraging for grass seeds or enjoying a morning's bath by the clear water's edge, pluming their feathers with gurgling clucks of pleasure. Any suspicious movement down below or round the edge of the swamp would cause the sentry to screech questioningly and alert other sentry birds watching from other trees, those white flowers that were cockatoos, and those pink flowers that were galahs. Any further movement, and a score of yellow crests would arise, piercing screeches would warn every bird all along the swamp shore—animals also, while if man were within hearing he would pause and turn to gaze questioningly back to where those white flowers would now stand out upon the highest tree-tops, yellow crests raised, each bird peering down upon and along the shore from its strategic perch, each bird seeming to have grown larger.

The next step would be for urgent screeches to sound an alarm piercingly taken up by hundreds of disgusted birds below, as in a cloud of shuffling wings they would rise to the trees to clothe the branches in their thousands with white or rosy blossoms as their now deafening cries alarmed the whole swamp. And this would tell the warrior Burradella and his listening boys that Wanawah had failed.

Wanawah turned aside towards the timber, squirmed through the grass, then rose up behind a tree-trunk and made his way cautiously on from tree to tree. Presently, when again the grasses were tall enough to hide him from those feathered sentinels, he crawled stealthily back to the swamp shore. Peering from behind the grass he saw what he sought, a small mob of fat teal lazily swimming close beside the swamp edge. His job was now to drive those ducks away down along the swamp bank to the narrow outlet where Gilwan was waiting—a task requiring caution, skill, and patience.

The leading duck became aware of a "something" amongst the grasses at the swamp edge, a "something" that vaguely appeared to threaten. The duck could not distinguish a human form about to throw a weapon; it could not quite get a glimpse of what "it" was, but it sensed the urge to move along. With a soft "cluck-cluck!" to its flock it began to swim quietly down along the swamp edge. Obediently the flock followed. Again and again as that flock dawdled on the way a rustling, a hissing, or a shadowy "something" from the reeds at the swamp edge urged the leader on.

Taking their time in their own ducky way, now and again one or two sped out of line to chase an agitated frog or some darting water beetle, bobbing up to paddle back to line with a gobble of satisfaction or complaining "cluck-cluck" of disappointment. Ever and anon they went bobbing down, neck deep, tail up, webbed feet kicking skyward while a swift glance under water spied out possible prey.

The leader, piloting his flock down the narrow laneway of water, spied a floating patch of water-weed directly ahead. He speeded up a little, keen to bob down head and neck and investigate, for there would probably be a fat, juicy shrimp, a prawn or two feeding under and amongst that fresh green weed, a morsel for his ever-gluttonous beak. He came to the weed, bobbed down head and neck, tail to the sky. He must have spied something tasty, for he continued his dive straight down—and vanished! A lean black hand had been waiting, had instantly gripped the duck's neck and pulled it straight under. Its neck was broken under water, limp head and neck were tucked under Gilwan's belt as his hand crept out ready for the next. So swift the act that the duck merely appeared to have continued its dive; not the faintest flutter or unusual water movement had shown that anything was wrong.

The following duck, seeing the leader dive, immediately concluded there could be a shrimp under that water-weed for him also so he came speeding on, bobbed down his head and—dived. A third duck guessed there must be good pickings under that water-weed and he greedily followed the leaders—as did no less than seven of his mates, one after the other, making ten in all. Dived—but did not reappear! Ten of them, before some deep instinct warned the remainder. With uneasy cluckings the swimming mob divided out from that water-weed and swam on down the channel.

They were gone. Slowly the patch of water-weed began drifting back towards the shore reeds. Had any enemy happened to be passing by he would hardly have given that weed a second glance.

Gilwan returned to the sheltering reeds with ten fat ducks at his belt. Burradella and the boys came, and soon afterward Wanawah appeared. In grave tones the warrior Burradella complimented the two proud lads on the work. So far, without weapons or hunting tools, they had secured ten fat ducks for the starving women and children, and had done it without giving a sign that could have roused the suspicions of any prowling enemy. In the same way, they still had to get those ducks back to the women and children supposedly waiting in the scrub. Completion of the test would come after the mid-sun meal.

"Go and get food!" ordered Burradella, and immediately a chattering broke out among the boys as they scurried out along the swamp and began wading for mussels, crayfish and turtle, water goanna or some unlucky fish sleeping within a hollow log or under ledge or bank. Soon each was returning with his catch to throw it on the fire of coals Burradella had already spread out. Soon the shellfish were pop-popping as they opened their shells to the heat, cooking in their own juice, soon to be hungrily gobbled up by the boys. After the meal Burradella questioned each boy as to what he had learnt from the morning's test, examining him as to his observation and memory, then questioning him as to whether he could suggest any improvement in the performance of Gilwan and Wanawah.

During the warm afternoon the remainder of the day's test would be strictly carried out. After this all would return happy and hungry to camp at sundown, to the hilarious laughter of the kookaburras, the musical warbling of the magpies, the sweet chirping of the lively little willy-wagtails. After the evening meal the men and boys and girls, even to the toddlers, would gather round the warrior Burradella's fire. The boys would sit silently while the warrior would tell the chief and the council just how the boys had carried out the test. Gravely then the elders would congratulate the boys, or explain where mistakes had been made or any precaution overlooked, or suggest how even better work might have been done. And the boys and the children also would listen earnestly and remember. For this was serious work; it was training them to grow up to be hunters and warriors for the tribe. And the tribe was all one, so every boy must become a hunter or warrior or both, or at least an expert in the making of weapons, of traps and nets, or in fashioning those stone mazes across the shallows of a watercourse that are such efficient fish-traps on a large scale. He *must* be able to play his part in some imperatively necessary task, otherwise the tribe could not continue to exist. And every girl must do her part, too.

The next day another highly trained warrior would put these boys through a quite different test. And so it would go on until finally they passed through the dreaded Bora rites and become fully initiated warriors like Red Kangaroo and Giluram, Guru, Keri, Duri, Kerran, and those others of the envied Kubara, the lads who had gone through this year's Bora ceremonies and were now entitled to wear the Bor, belt of manhood—until in time to come they, too, would be doing their share in training the boys of the tribe.

# CHAPTER V

## THE LONE LOOK-OUT

Long since, nine miles eastward across the Namoi, Red Kangaroo and his warrior lads, one now with a wallaby over his shoulder, had climbed the big hill and scaled the windy summit of Ydire and been welcomed by the look-out band awaiting relief.

Having reported no sign of an enemy, these lads gleefully picked up their weapons and, yelling carefree war-cries, clambered down the great rock, then "kangaroo-hopped", leapt, and ran down the hill to cross the river and hunt their happy-go-lucky way back to the tribe.

This look-out post of the Gunn-e-darr tribe, a landmark far and wide, was situated upon an isolated spur of the Nandewar Range.[1] Along most of the range the valleys and foothills were beautiful under forests of cypress pine,

*1 A spur of the Great Dividing Range, dividing the waters of the Namoi and Gwydir.*

while many of the ridges were densely clothed under dark-green masses of hoop-vine and other scrubs. The great rock of Ydire, which white men call Nobby Rock, stands out boldly by the summit of one of the highest peaks on its southern side of the Nandewars, towering like a gigantic lighthouse upon an island peak. It was named Ydire because away down the spur grew a prized forest of Ydire or gidgee-trees, from which particular timber the tribe made its boomerangs. And, because of a "something" in the soil, the boomerangs fashioned from this particular grove of timber were prized far and wide.

From the summit of Ydire Red Kangaroo could spy away out over the valley of the Namoi as it flowed northward, out over far distance of the great plains, could see solitary scattered peaks near and far, could spy out over hill and silvery watercourses, over forest and dark scrub and sunlit bushlands towards ranges hazy under distance. But the greatest advantage of this particular look-out post was that it overlooked distant tracts of quite open country, long, broad, open spaces every here and there separating the scrubby patches from the timbered lands. Any enemy incautiously crossing any such open space by day would be seen by the eagle-eyed watchers upon Ydire. In the same way another large area was overlooked from the towering height of Booroobil Rock some miles distant. If enemies were seen, a signal smoke from either look-out would warn the tribe wherever they might be. By night a hollow tree would be set ablaze, a flaming beacon in the sky.

Other look-outs, such as Carrowreer,[2] overlooking country that was destined to be called the Black Jack, offered more localized protection to favourite camping grounds. The towering look-outs on the Nandewar Range had saved the nomadic tribe from surprise many a time, but Red Kangaroo knew that in the legendary past cunning enemies had occasionally

*2 Carrowreer was the aboriginal name for Black Jack Mountain, a landmark in the Black Jack Range, about four miles from the present-day town of Gunnedah.*

outwitted the watchers on the mountains by sleeping through daylight within sheltering scrubs, then crossing the open country by night. And he believed that such enemies would try again, that they were only awaiting a cunning leader to come in large numbers and strike when least expected.

Red Kangaroo ordered his friends away to widely placed vantage points along the crest from which they could see the skyline of the range behind. He gazed far out over their tribal country in front, meanwhile attending to cooking the wallaby down in a deep crevice from which no prying eyes could see signs of smoke. Any enemies coming to raid the tribal lands from that direction would be spied by the watchers as they came creeping up over the crest.

Away back in the big ranges[3] lived fierce tribes, such as those of Bundarra and Kingston,[4] and the Goonoo Goonoo

*3 Now known as the New England Ranges.*
*4 Some of these names of course, cover areas named since white occupation.*

tribe eastward[5] under the fighting chief Ilpara. There were also the Barraba men to the north and the more peaceful Manellae or Manilla tribe to the nor'-east in the valley of the Manilla River under the chief Mooti, who, however, preferred peace to fighting. Other foes westwards were the Coonabarabran tribe under the warrior Kulki, their legendary enemies being the Walleri, the Big River tribes, and the Coombri tribesmen around Terri-Hi-Hi. And they had to be ever alert against woman-stealing raids by the Boggabri and Narrabri men to the north-east, and the Quirindi and Murrurundi men south-east. But their most dreaded foes, though they came but seldom, were the distant and dreaded Cassilis men, away over the range to the south.

Happily for the survival of the Gunn-e-darr tribe the fierce mountain tribes, in time snatched between their constant hunting and strict ceremonial periods, were ever watching, raiding, or fighting one another.

*5 Near where Tamworth now is.*

The Bundarra and Kingston tribes seemed never happier than when raiding the Goonoo Goonoo and Manellae, their pet enemies or prey as the case might be. It was the same with other tribes. Thus for long past they had only been able to spare time for an occasional lightning woman-stealing raid against the Gunn-e-darr tribe. Had the fierce tribes known how weak the Gunn-e-darr tribe now really was their tactics would have been very different.

Thus the life of the Stone Age aboriginal was more than one happy nomadic round of hunting from season to season. That was certainly part of it—during the good times, and during good seasons. But with it went the severest training for both hunting and warfare, a careful learning also of various ceremonies and age-old beliefs that made up their deep inner life—and ceaseless vigilance against both Nature and tribal enemies. So that these Stone Age humans were up against worries and problems strangely akin to our own. But then it has been ever so, since the Dream Time of all of us. How often have our own ancestors sat high upon a rock and watched and drowsed and pondered as Red Kangaroo was pondering!

Why did not the Kamilaroi tribes combine—the "mighty Kamilaroi" as they loved to call themselves? They believed they were one. The same language, the same beliefs, and every warrior among them proud to boast, "I am a warrior of the Kamilaroi!"

With its sub-tribes, the Kamilaroi tribe was the second largest in numbers and lands in all that big land which many years later white men were to call New South Wales. There was only one slightly larger tribe, or rather tribe of tribes, the Wiradjuri. The Kamilaroi lands included the great plains now known as the Liverpool Plains, of some ten million acres, and extended northward almost to where the Queensland border was to be. Their southernmost limits were roughly level with a point on the coast midway between the present cities of Sydney and Newcastle. These rich, well-watered lands were an animal, vegetable, and bird paradise; the waters, too, teemed with fish.

The slightly larger lands of the Wiradjuri reached south-west from the Kamilaroi boundary, beyond the Murrumbidgee and almost to the Murray. Thus the lands of these two great tribes stretched in a broad strip across New South Wales from south to north.

Hedging in both these tribes right along the coast and pressing against them from the west were numerous much smaller tribes. Some were fiercely aggressive, others raided whenever they saw an opportunity and fought back when they had to, others were more or less peaceful, the smaller tribes of these battling for existence as best they could.

All the warlike of these smaller tribes within raiding distance were jealous of the rich lands of the Kamilaroi. It was the numbers of the Kamilaroi, and the fact that most of them were fighters, that kept them back within their own tribal lands.

But the Kamilaroi themselves were only a loose conglomeration of sub-tribes, friendly in the main to one another, but each distinct unit looking after itself. Thus, if one of these units suffered from a disastrous raid then it was "just too bad". Friendly units would be indignant, might even offer help when it was too late, would certainly come and drive back the enemy should they seek to hold the precious land after they had annihilated the sub-tribe, but this was of small comfort to the little group of people directly concerned.

At this period the Gunn-e-darr tribe of the Kamilaroi had been gradually weakened in fighting men because of the bad leadership of two succeeding chiefs, and was in grave danger from warlike tribes hemming them in to the east and west, south-east and south-west, north-east and north-west.

"If only all the Kamilaroi would combine," sighed Red Kangaroo, "like the ants in the one anthill."

But no reply came from the majesty of the vast blue sky, the far-flung rays of Walcha the sun. Maybe an answer came from far across the quiet lands, that whispering sigh from the pine forests along the valleys of the Nandewars—those lovely forests that in time coming were to crash to the bite of the white man's axe.

Red Kangaroo sighed, rested his chin on his knees, clasped his arms round them and gazed far out, glad again that no enemy knew how weak his beloved Gunn-e-darr really was. Glad indeed that the restless tribesmen of Moonbi far out there did not know, nor the warrior tribe of the Wallabadah, nor those aggressive "ants" of the Coolah, Bomera, Weetaliba, Deringulla, Ulamambri, right to the fighting tribes of the Warrumbungle Ranges, and further north through the Great Pillaga Scrubs to the aggressive men of Narrabri.

How fortunate for Gunn-e-darr that all these "ants" were kept so busy biting one another!

Red Kangaroo little knew that but for these "idle" thoughts of his the Gunn-e-darr tribe would in time to come have been wiped off the lands of the Kamilaroi to the last man.

# CHAPTER VI

# EVERY WOMAN TEACHES WHILE SHE HUNTS

The spurs of the Nandewars, the bastions of the Warrumbungles were clothed in gold of wattle, sweet-scented by the honeyed flowers of countless trees. So ever since the Dream Time that loveliness had come and gone. As the seasons come and go, and come again. As the floods come and go. As men come and go. And tribes. And nations.

Yet again Walcha the sun had risen from far over the mountains bringing light and warmth and life to the Gunn-e-darr men, and to the world they did not dream of. The look-out men had gone away to their duties; the people had eaten. Casually the warriors picked up their hunting weapons and, idly talking, strolled away in small groups in different directions, followed by boys of from ten to twelve proudly carrying their first real hunting weapons, light weapons, lethal enough for small game. Should a pademelon or bandicoot or kangaroo-rat fall to a boy's spear then a happy hunter he would be, his skill the envy of his comrades.

Meanwhile the women and girls, with the younger boys, in three chattering groups were leaving camp. One group was making for the big swamp, one to Connewarri, "place of the black swans", one to Gulligal, "place of the long grass", where the blue-grass flat was rich in grass seeds, carrying their grass-woven dilly-bags and their coolamons. Each woman had also her long, fire-hardened, sharp-pointed digging stick and her stone tomahawk.

Strolling along at their rear and flank went a few elderly guards to watch that no incautious or mischievous girls strayed from the others. For as the groups spread out in the hunting there were bound to be stragglers, usually chattering young girls, often with one or two amongst them daringly contemptuous of the danger of being ambushed and hurried away by raiding parties of hostile women-stealers.

The mother of Weetah and her baby brother, Tuki, had been carried away thus on one bright morning just twelve moons ago. She and a young girl, busy at their yam-digging, had dawdled behind, not noticing that the women ahead were now strolling in amongst a patch of brigalow-trees, the unobservant guards disappearing with them. Lurking woman-stealers from the Goonoo Goonoo tribe had pounced upon them and forced them to run with them for many miles until they had got them clear away.

Since then Weetah had been a mother to baby Tuki. And now the young girl spoke reproachfully.

"Oh, Tuki! Where *are* your eyes?"

Tuki gazed hard all around, then triumphantly pointed at a mark on the soft earth so small and faint it seemed a miracle that his sister had noticed it.

"What is it?" questioned Weetah.

Tuki bent down on hands and knees, looked carefully, crawled along, found a following track then exclaimed, "Possum!"

"Right! Now which way is it going?"

Carefully Tuki examined the faint little marks, then pointed.

"Good boy!" said Weetah. "That naughty possum has been out all night.

With the coming of Walcha the sun he has hurried home to sleep. Follow him."

And Tuki did so, his plump little body bent low to earth, his big, solemn eyes to the ground. Slowly he crawled on, noting just here and there the imprint of a tiny paw upon soft earth. And then he quite lost the track. No matter how carefully he searched, no matter how his little brow furrowed in thought, he simply could not pick up the track again. No wonder, for fallen leaves lay upon the grass-strewn earth, vines trailed over fallen branches, big logs lay every here and there. How then was it possible for a little boy to follow the delicate imprints of a small animal that hours before had made its way over all this litter of the great bush?

"Now," said Weetah patiently, "come back here. No, right back, well back from where you saw the last track. Now, look carefully ahead of you. Then tell me what you see."

Carefully Tuki gazed, peering this way and that. But no matter how hard he tried all he could see was a brown snake slithering over a fallen kurrajong-tree, and the short, thick, green grass.

"I see grass," he said at last.

"Right. Now stand a little this way—bend a little—so that the sun shines upon the grass ahead. Keep bending a little—sweep your eyes slowly along a little ahead of you—keep bending your head a little—this way and that—up and down—*make the sun shine just where you want it to!*"

For a long time Tuki tried, a growing disappointment on his face.

"Never mind, you'll soon learn." Weetah smiled. "This is a really difficult track to follow, only a grown-up man hunter, as you will be some day, could do it. But stand peering, just as you are now." And she walked a few yards ahead then bent down. "Now," she said, "what do you see—right under my finger?"

For quite a time Tuki peered, this way and that, but all he could see was soft green grass. Then slowly the glum disappointment lifted from his face, his big eyes shone.

"The grass has been pressed down," he said uncertainly. "He has crawled over the grass there."

"Now you have it!" Weetah laughed.

"He has no bare ground to walk upon, so now he makes his way over the soft, dewy grass. It bends under him, and only slowly rises up after he has passed by. It has not quite risen right up. That tender grass under these shady trees will not rise quite level with its neighbour grass until the sun warms it and drinks up all its dew. So when you use your eyes the right way you can still faintly see the impression of our possum's ambling body on the grass. Now carry on."

Tuki did so, as intently almost as if his life depended upon it, which in a way it did. For he must learn to do a hunter's work for the tribe, must grow up to be a warrior also. Seriously indeed do the wild aboriginal children absorb their daily lessons from their Book of Life.

Tuki tracked the possum across the grass until all trace of track ended at a tree butt. He gazed closely at the bark, but it showed no tell-tale scratches, no sign of sharp little claws. So the possum had not climbed up there!

Tuki started to puzzle out which way the tracks could have gone, until Weetah laughed.

"Come round the tree and look, silly. If you do not see a bandicoot down one end of a log, you go round and try to look down the other end, don't you? See, *there* are his claw marks where he has climbed up to his home. See, from this side the tree leans a little way towards where you were looking. And, as this side is the easiest way to climb, the possum has used his eyes and his head—not like a little hunter called Tuki, who would even seek to climb a tree the hard way. You watch me climb this tree. And then we'll have possum for dinner."

And as she spoke Weetah was climbing straight up the tree, really walking up it with her wonderful hands and feet. She did not even have to follow the claw marks, her keen eyes had already marked the hollow up there in which deep down the possum would be coiled up asleep. She was pleased she did not have to use her stone tomahawk to chop him out. She peered down into the dark hollow a moment and smelt, to make sure no snake had recently followed the possum down into his home. Then, reaching in her hand

and arm right down to the shoulder, she could just touch the warm little body. She gripped its neck and drew the now awakened, helplessly fighting possum up out of the hollow. She held him wriggling and scratching and spitting into the air as she called down to Tuki.

"See, a fine fat possum! Very angry, too! The first possum that our hunter Tuki has ever tracked. Now won't we have a lovely dinner!" And, jamming the possum back into the entrance to the hollow, she broke its neck against the doorway of its own home. Dropping the warm, furry body to be caught by the eager Tuki, she slid straight down the tree with a laugh.

"Come quickly now," she said. 'We must rejoin our friends, for in tracking the possum we have fallen a long way behind. Who knows but that devil men of the Goonoo Goonoo from the bad chief Ilpara, or raiders of the terrible Cassilis warriors may be tracking *us!* Come!"

And Tuki, with a fearful glance round at the wild, silent bush, hurried on after his sister.

Thus all the women and elder girls

while daily seeking food for the tribe were teaching the younger children, while the men away on the hunt were teaching the older boys and picked warriors such as Burradella were teaching the lads soon to begin the long, arduous training that prepared them for the sternest school of all, the Bora. Even now, away out in a secret place in the bush, selected old men, fathers of the tribe, were training the grim-faced, hollow-eyed, silently huddled lads who must face this year's Bora. Well before sundown all the scattered parties except the lonely Bora initiates, came hurrying back to camp, for tonight the young warriors were to dance, and the people dearly loved dancing and chanting and play-acting. The women came heavy-laden into camp with dilly-bags bulging with yams and tubers and roots balanced on their heads, and sometimes with a baby clinging to back or hip. Their coolamons were loaded with seeds and berries and nuts, and also with small game and with goose eggs and other luxuries that thrive in good country during a good season.

If it were not for the patience and

labour, the marvellously developed hunting instinct of the women for vegetable foods and small game, the men would often go hungry. For there are times when the best hunters return tired and hungry to camp, empty-handed. This happens during the hot, dry times, when game is both scarce and very wary. In such times if it were not for the women and their vegetable foods and small things from the mud of drying river or swamp or waterhole, the men and children would go hungry indeed. A woman is therefore very valuable, both as a mother for the tribe, and as a food finder for the family.

Amidst expectant chattering the cooking fires were alight as the hunters came drifting in, throwing down their game at the fires. There were delighted acclamations as lucky ones came in carrying a big, fat kangaroo. Others had an emu slung across their shoulders, others brought wallaby, others massive jewfish and codfish. It had been a good hunt, and all would feast as they watched the dance.

Sunset came bringing a peaceful hush from the bush, except for her children chattering round the campfires. Dark night came and the trunks of the big old trees encircling the corroboree ground danced to leaping flames.

Just before moonrise the chief, Jerrabri, rose from his campfire and grandly walked to his place, followed by the council of the elders, then by the warriors, led by Burradella, all in their correct order of precedence.

Jerrabri squatted down, his council beside him, then the elder warriors down to the second degree. It was the first degree, the Kubara, the recently initiated warrior lads, who were to dance. Behind the men, in a semicircle, were the chattering women and children. Before them all lay the green sward, illumined by fire-glow that faded into the blackness of the trees.

Suddenly the tip of the silver moon rose far away out over the black country. Instantly boys ran to throw armfuls of kindling on the fires, which roared into leaping flame as a chanting arose with click of kylies and muffled drumming. From the darkness came leaping a tall young figure leading a line of comrades.

The leader's body shone bronze-red as he came bounding into the fire-glow; no other knew how to mix red ochre with phosphorescent oil of fish as did Red Kangaroo. Vivid white of cockatoo feathers in his jet-black hair, tufts of brilliantly hued parrot feathers seemed alive on his prancing limbs and broad chest; a plumage of pink galah feathers showed rosy in the firelight as he leapt and whirled to the clash of nulla-nulla against hardwood shield. A rising shout of "Wah! Wah! Wah!" arose from the warriors; shrill calls from the women and girls and children greeted their favourite, Red Kangaroo. The lads dancing with him had their admirers, too. Though little Tuki, sitting beside Weetah, had big round eyes only for Red Kangaroo, his sister's limpid brown eyes were all for Giluram, while to little Yulowirre the Rainbow the young warrior Keri was the only one in the dance. Brave the lads looked in their war-paint and feathers, their movements in perfect rhythm with the story actions of their leader, the sharp clicking of the kylies, chanting and drumming of the women, as scene after scene portrayed the life-story of the red kangaroo.

To a quickening of the drumming Giluram now came leaping into the dance. He turned on Red Kangaroo and they danced their parts as two old-man 'roos standing up to one another in snarling fight for possession of a demure young doe. The fire-gleam reddened the swaying, darting bodies as each leapt and bounded and kicked and clawed at his fiercely dancing antagonist. The people applauded in delight as the two kangaroos leapt in to attack with savage grunt and slash and parry of forepaws, instantly swaying to dodge the deadly ripping kick of the great clawed leg, only to fly aside and leap in again as if their toes had not touched the ground. Dancers, yes, and wrestlers too were these lads. Red Kangaroo was to remain unbeaten throughout a long life.

The sharp drumming and clapping of the women rolled out through the bush until far into the night, the musical clicking of the kylies, the rise and fall of the hunting song sweetly blending with the movements of the dancers as they acted the life-story of the red kangaroo until he finally falls to the spear of the hunter.

It was near dawn when the dance ended. Sighing, the people arose. Some yawned, as if just realizing that they were sleepy. With low laughter and talk they began straggling away towards their gunyahs.

Suddenly Weetah glanced up. Giluram was walking beside her, fierce desire in his eyes; she saw his chest rise and fall.

*"Kurridu zinunduninda!"* he hissed. "I love you!"

Weetah's hand tightened upon little Tuki's as she gazed up, hearing herself whispering, *"Da zinda gulirdul*—you are my love."

At the delight in Giluram's face tears welled to Weetah's eyes. She gazed straight ahead, her heart one dull ache.

"Ssh!" she whispered urgently. "Walk on! Someone may see! It could mean death to us!"

And it was so—for such was the law. Alas, Weetah was not for Giluram; she had been promised as a baby to old Tulduna. What mattered the breaking hearts of Stone Age lad and girl, all the more bitter in the knowledge that, but for the cold selfishness and the distorted laws of certain of the old men, it need not have been so?

## CHAPTER VII
## THE NEW WEAPON

Not all had acclaimed the dancing of Red Kangaroo. Jerrabri had glowered there with a scowl on his broad, bearded face, reflected on the deep-lined visages of the elders. Smouldering hostility, too, showed in the unfriendly eyes of some among the middle-aged warriors.

For the sayings of this overgrown pup had been repeated to the council of the elders, who deeply resented the stripling's criticism. He had had the temerity to declare that the chief and the elders were not administering the laws of the tribe in fairness. He had said even more—that not only were they administering the laws to their own selfish ends, but by so doing they were even endangering the very safety of the tribe! The chief and the elders bitterly resented such opinions, knowing in their secret hearts that they really had twisted several laws to their own selfish ends. This dangerous young firebrand must be watched; it might become necessary to quieten his tongue for ever. And the warrior Burradella also had better be careful, for it had come to the ears of the council that he had warned the lad to be more discreet.

Red Kangaroo was thinking on these same laws months later when he was on look-out duty again, this time up on Buriagala[1] or Booroobil Rock. Staring far out over river and plain and hill and bushland, he frowned at the injustice gradually, craftily done to the tribe. He understood now why Jerrabri and the two chiefs before him had twisted the laws to their own lasting advantage. For one twisted law gave them the right over every

*1 Buriagala means "brigalow". This rock is a landmark from the present-day township of Carrol.*

young girl in the tribe. They could sell her to any man they wished, and it was always to an older man, who had something with which to pay, whereas a young warrior had not.

Red Kangaroo frowned. This twisted law of the old men, how cunning it was! How deep it went! It made the young men slaves to the older warriors. Always, from far back in the Dream Time, that very beginning of things, the wise old men had been trusted and revered, the wise laws they had made were unquestioned.

But today several vital laws of the Gunn-e-darr tribe had been gradually twisted to benefit the elders and older warriors—even to the danger of the tribe! This fact worried Red Kangaroo, had set him thinking while still a mere boy—the danger to his beloved tribe.

For if the old men held the right over *all* the young girls, while the young warriors had to wait years perhaps for a much older wife, then there could not be enough children to keep the tribe strong and powerful; it would grow slowly weaker until at last a stronger tribe must overwhelm it. This once powerful tribe had now only fifty first-class spearmen with which to hold their rich, envied lands. Eighty warriors in all! But thirty were well beyond their prime, in time of stress only capable of a last-stand fight, or as guards for the women and children.

Red Kangaroo's thoughts flew south to the fierce tribe dwelling by the Cassilis River, who boasted that they could go to war with one hundred and fifty fighting warriors—three times the strength of the Gunn-e-darr Tribe. More so, for to start away on a long and dangerous raid with one hundred and fifty spearmen meant that a strong body of warriors must remain behind to protect their women and children lest enemies seize the chance to attack their home camps. Yet again Red Kangaroo was glad no enemy knew how weak the Gunn-e-darr Tribe now really was.

All the middle-aged warriors had two wives, some had three. The elders had three and four, even more. The young warriors had none. That was how the chief and council of the elders kept the older warriors with them, thought Red Kangaroo angrily. As soon as a warrior reached a certain age a wife was given him. Presently he would have two and could take things easily, sell a wife if he wanted to and buy good weapons with her, or fish-traps, or skin rugs already sewn, and other things—or sell on condition that the buyer should do his hunting for him when he was feeling too lazy to hunt for himself. That was often the price for a wife with the lazy ones. The hunter must work twice as hard, for he had then to hunt for two families, and if he had a poor day then it was *his* family who would go hungry, for he must hand over whatever game had fallen to his skill and patience to the grizzled tyrant from whom he had bought his wife.

Red Kangaroo frowned disgustedly and swore to himself that he would win power in the tribe and stop all this.

There were other ways in which a woman was valuable. Take Bilar the spear-maker, for instance. He had slaved at making spears for old Kuluman for years past now. Some years ago Kuluman had sold him a wife, and not a young one either, though Gille the Moon was not hard to look upon, was good-tempered, a good worker, too, and noted for her diligence in collecting surprising quantities of grass-seed even in a poor season, husking and winnowing it, and patiently grinding it into flour. These good qualities, of course, had helped old Kuluman put such a cunning price upon her—so many first-class spears a year. A stiff price that Bilar had eagerly accepted, not looking well ahead on the bargain. He of all people, the best spear-maker in the tribe, should have known that it takes time to make a good spear—time to roam the bush and carefully select the best timber in out-of-the-way places, much time and labour for the dozen and one processes before the rough stick was the finished, straightened, hardened, shaped, hafted, headed, pointed, barbed, beautifully balanced weapon.

Besides, he had to find time to do his own hunting, for he had no time now to make spears to sell to others for foods from their hunt. Bilar must work long, long hours at spear-making for old Kuluman. When the others were yarning round the campfires or taking things easy Bilar was bent over his spear-making, working, working, working, working for old Kuluman, who sold those spears to eager buyers, demanding and securing especially big prices from other tribes. For the Stone Age men had their recognized trade routes, "spider-webbing" over the continent for surprising distances. Bilar would be working for old Kuluman for as long as the old wretch lived, working at buying off his wife Gille the Moon.

Red Kangaroo angrily clenched his fists. By ancient law of the tribe Bilar should have been allowed a wife after he had passed through the Bora and won the Bor, his belt of manhood. He should have four piccaninnies by now, so doing his share to help strengthen the tribe. Instead of that he had but one baby girl, and instead of the excess from his hunt going to the tribe to help feed the sick, the injured, the old, or those engaged on other duties, he never had anything over at all—all his time being taken up in working for old Kuluman.

Angrily Red Kangaroo thought of the young warriors, too frightened to stand up beside him and demand their rights of the chief and council upon the council grounds before all the tribe. In awed silence his boyhood friends had listened to him when he suggested it. Uneasy faces, downcast eyes, heavy silence had been their answer. Only Giluram had offered to stand by him. Then his uncle, Tulumi, had come secretly to him by night with whispered warning to say no more against the chief and elders and the laws. For the matter had come to the ears of the chief, and the elders had muttered angrily in their beards.

Then one day, deep in the heart of the bush, his warrior friend Burradella had gravely warned him also, suggesting that he bide his time—just a few more years until he would be a fully accredited warrior in full confidence of the tribe and could much more safely state his case.

"If you do not keep a quieter tongue and bide your time," warned Burradella, "then one night you will wake up to feel the kiss of death."

Red Kangaroo sighed. He knew that Burradella's advice was good, but to youth, to wait seems long. He gazed out over his beloved tribal country, making sure no enemy was creeping over any of the widespread open areas visible from his eyrie.

This Booroobil Rock, commanding a wide stretch of country, was another great look-out post of the Gunn-e-darr Tribe. It is almost isolated, rising sheer near the bank of the Namoi. It was not only a look-out, but a revered spot too, for this great rock overlooked the sacred Bora grounds directly below. This was Baia-me's Ground, the Ground of the Great Spirit—"He who built all things".

It was at Baia-me's command, far back in the Dream Time that the First Bora for the First Tribe was held. And he commanded that every tribe ever to be born into the aboriginal world must ever hold the Bora. And it was so.[2]

And Baia-me gave to each tribe the magic wand Dhurumbulum, which was endowed with life. It was only shown to those initiates who, exhausted and half dead, were judged worthy after having

*2 Throughout unknown thousands of years—until the white man came.*

passed the long, painful trials. And it put a new life into them, which was one with the Life, life of the earth and all things therein, thus life of the tribe. Henceforth their life was only on loan to them, for their life belonged to the tribe. And the tribe belonged to Baia-me.

Each was then given the Bor, the belt of manhood. This had been touched with the Dhurumbulum and thus acquired some of its magical properties, of health to the wearer and immediate illness to an enemy. For if, as a last resort, the Bor was thrown at an enemy he would reel back in dire distress. But the Bor was sacred, too. It had to be hidden away by each initiate and only worn in case of great need, and then in secret. When the Builder had made all things and finally man, he left the earth, never to return. But to every Bora he sent his mediator, Turramulan, to represent him to his people. Turramulan is always present throughout the main ceremonies, though invisible. He in turn is visibly represented to the initiates by one of the old men in sacred costume, who, while training another to take his place, acts the part of Turramulan, representative of Baia-me, until he shall die and ascend to the Pleasant Lands far up in the Milky Way, there to receive life and rest and praise from Turramulan himself.

Red Kangaroo, sitting high up on Booroobil Rock and gazing down with troubled brow upon the Sacred Grounds of Baia-me, pondered upon the Bora, and how deeply its unbreakable bonds held and shaped the whole life of his tribe, from far back in the Dream Time right to this present, sunlit day. Even those who gave up the struggle and wished to return to Baia-me before their time were guided by its power. For it was to this place that a deeply troubled warrior or, more often, a broken-hearted woman or girl, sometimes stole away from the tribe, to stand on the rock and gaze a moment far down upon Baia-me's Ground—then jump.

Red Kangaroo was gazing down at the giant figure of a man lying flat out in the very centre of the Bora Ground. The figure had been modelled of sticks, bark, and bushes, then carefully covered with earth. As the earth settled down more had been added until the giant figure stood out in relief well above the perfectly levelled ground. The figure was twenty-five feet long, the outstretched arms twelve feet from hand to hand, the body four feet broad. Stretching out from the figure right to the giant trees that almost encircled the ground were carefully graded lines and laneways of stones ochred in different colours, with broad geometrical patterns here and there, all with deep symbolical meaning. Carved in the bark of one hundred and fifty great trees were the totems, animals, snakes, and birds, stretching twenty feet and more up the trunks. There were other carvings, too, of regular patterns, or eccentric curves, or simple angles, and carvings of the tracks of men and women and wild creatures. Stretching out towards the figure in the centre was a huge, leaning tree, bent so low to the ground that surely, many years ago—a hundred, two hundred, probably hundreds of years ago—it must have been trained to grow that way. Along this were deeply cut by tomahawk emu tracks. During one part of the ceremonies the initiates must lie under this tree in the posture of the giant figure while the old Emu Man with the stuffed emu walks along the tree over them, as if the emu were sedately stepping upon and over their line of bodies. Where the tree branches came to the ground the emu emblem steps down and, solemnly followed by other totem figures and the circle of seven walk round a circular path away out from the initiates—every figure, every sign, every movement, every chant holding meaning.

Mounds of various designs, some strangely like altars such as the prophets and Moses might have built out in the wilderness, stand here and there upon the Grounds. Other things and signs and designs also, all with a deep symbolical meaning merging into the whole. Deep indeed was the meaning of the Bora and its ceremonies and laws throughout all aboriginal life.

Red Kangaroo sighed, picked up his shield, and came back to daily life, the life that is but a span. Long and thoughtfully he gazed at the lower end of the shield. He was very proud of his shield; it had stood the test in many a hard fight. It had been his father's father's shield. When his father had at last been killed in fight, Red Kangaroo's uncle, Tulumi, by tribal etiquette, had gravely presented the lad with the shield.

"If only you can carry this shield as bravely as did your father," Tulumi had said, "then you will be sung in corroboree as a warrior before all the tribe." Prophetic words.

The lad hoped to carry that shield fearlessly, but never dreamed how famous it was to become. For his thoughts, "built into" this shield, were to give his people a new weapon, which would do its part in helping save the tribe from extinction.

This was the short shield, designed for easy handling on long travel and in squirming through thick vine scrubs during raids against surrounding tribes. Of toughened hardwood to withstand the heavy blows of clubs and the splintering impact of hardened spear-points, it was yet light to carry, easy to handle. The best shield-makers knew a great deal about Nature's secrets, and were skilled in selecting woods of particularly suitable trees—expert, too, in the secret arts of seasoning, toughening, and shaping the wood. Probably they are the only people in the world's history who have invented a weapon, both for hunting and fighting, that could be made to return to the thrower if it missed its mark, to be immediately used again.[3] The "come-back" of the boom-erang, the secret of its lifting power, intrigued our early experimenters working on the flying machine.

But on that sunny morning long ago when the warrior lad Red Kangaroo sat thoughtfully studying his shield high upon Booroobil Rock the white man had not yet come to this Great South Land. Only Baia-me could know of him, and of the time of his coming—Baia-me who sees, who knows all things.

> *3 Modern civilized man, for all his high-explosive and atomic horrors, has fortunately not yet invented a projectile which can be fired in such a way that, should it miss its mark, it would fly back to the gun to be immediately fired again.*

The top and bottom ends of Red Kangaroo's shield were smoothly rounded. But for some weeks past, as opportunity occurred, he, with stone axe, with stone rasp, water and sand had been carefully chipping and rubbing the rounded end to make it more wedge-shaped, and gradually sharpening it, particularly the lower edge, very carefully, lest he damage the prized shield. Only after long thought and study had he commenced the experiment. The idea in his mind had grown so definite that he was almost certain now it was good.

As he was carefully grinding yet a little more of the roundness off the lower end of the shield, sharpening it yet a little more, Giluram and four of his friends came up to the look-out carrying a half-roasted wallaby. Red Kangaroo welcomed them with an appreciative grin.

"And why is the Red Warrior carving the bottom of his shield?" asked Giluram.

"To make it a weapon of offence, as well as defence," replied Red Kangaroo.

They looked puzzled, suspecting a joke.

"The only way to use a shield as a

weapon," said Giluram slowly, "is to bash your enemy's face with it—if he lets you! That would not cripple him; it would only make him more savage."

"Ah," said Red Kangaroo, "but look! If I did *this*—" he held out the shield as if warding off an imaginary blow—"see—if he gave me the chance and instantly I—" and he jabbed downward but at an angle. "Don't you see?" he appealed to their blank faces. "The edge! The narrow, pointed edge would jab him sharply in the throat, knock his wind out, jerk him to his knees—"

"But there is *no* edge, and *no* point," objected Giluram doubtfully. "The end of the shield is broad and rounded. Even if you did attempt a blow like that it would strike down well below the chin—at the top of the chest. It would only make him cough. Hard, maybe," he added with a laugh.

"Yes," admitted Red Kangaroo, gazing thoughtfully at the shield. "I have not shaped the end long enough, nor narrow and sharp enough as yet. But let us try it out." And he jumped up and seized his nulla-nulla, while Giluram picked up shield and club.

Always, at these times, the lads wrestled for practice. The others were no match for Red Kangaroo, but this duel of shield against club should be different. The combatants circled one another warily, then suddenly leapt together to a clash of shield against shield, and smack of club against shield as they sprang aside, only to pounce at one another again. For swift minutes they struck at head and ankle and leg, then Giluram leapt well back and laughed.

"What have you done with your new weapon, Red Kangaroo? It has not cut my throat yet!"

At their good-humoured laughter Red Kangaroo gazed in puzzled fashion at Giluram.

"No," he said thoughtfully, "I had not thought of that. I did not think of making it so that it would *cut* an enemy's throat!"

"It has not even touched my throat," said Giluram, "let alone cut it!"

"No," agreed Red Kangaroo seriously. "I have been trying to make it, but it is very difficult. I have not yet made the end the right shape, not yet long and pointed enough—"

But Giluram had leapt straight at him, and only by lightning-like footwork did Red Kangaroo dodge the club. He laughed delightedly as he leapt aside.

"Serve me right," he said. "You almost caught me off guard. You would have cracked the skull of an enemy then."

"And would have needed no end-pointed shield to do it!" replied Giluram. "Now what about *this!*" and he smashed his shield straight at Red Kangaroo's face, while leaping in to swing his club low at his thigh. But at the very swing of the club he gave a startled grunt as his head was jerked back by Red Kanoaroo's shield end, jarring heavily against his throat and jerking him to his knees. His mouth gasping in agonized alarm, he rolled to his chest and over, clawing for breath.

A moment's silence, then Red Kangaroo was kneeling with Giluram's head on his knee.

"Giluram, Giluram!" he cried. "I didn't mean to do it—I didn't *know* I'd done it!"

Giluram's ghastly attempt to smile was convulsed by his gasps. It was some time before he recovered. The young men, sitting round quietly discussing the happening, for once forgot their look-out duties. Red Kangaroo was examining the end of the shield in a puzzled silence.

At last he said thoughtfully, "It could not have been the newly shaped end of the shield alone that did it. It was what I had in mind might happen if I could think out the shape, but you can see the shape is far from right. It was only by chance it happened; something must have helped it. Not the blow alone—perhaps one shield dragging down against the other—"

Abruptly he reached down and picked up Giluram's shield. For quite a time he experimented, Giluram's shield in his left hand, his own in his right, striking the two together as in a duel, trying to remember exactly how he had held his shield and what he had done against Giluram's shield as it came smashing at his face. Presently his piercing black eyes began to shine, boyish pleasure upon his face.

"I have it!" he exclaimed. "Look!

Giluram's own shield by the manner of his attack helped direct mine and added force to the blow." He used the two shields to illustrate his words. "See, I was warding off Giluram's blows while seeking a chance to strike his throat lightly with the bottom end of the shield. It couldn't be done; the end is still far too thick and rounded—until Giluram sprang upwards at me, at the same time striking with his shield in a downward blow to batter my shield against my face. But my shield thrust against his while his downward blow added weight to mine, and at the same time drove the shield downward and inward—outward from me—because I thrust against him, helping drive *my* shield in the right direction, straight in at his throat. As he was springing upward his neck was thrust out, and the end of my shield caught him on the throat! Yes that's it! Come on, we'll prove it!" And he leapt up eagerly.

They laughed sarcastically.

"So you'd cut our heads off, one by one," said Kerran.

"No, no, I couldn't, for the end is not nearly narrow enough yet, or nearly sharp enough. No. Just let us stand and slowly move the shields against one another, exactly as Giluram struck at me and I warded off his blow. Just to find out the right movement. Come on," he added coaxingly. "Come on, Kerran."

None too keenly Kerran picked up shield and nulla. In slow movement they tried to recapture those two lightning-quick movements, watched with puzzled interest by the others. And presently, to his delight, Red Kangaroo felt that his surmise had been correct. But Kerran and the other boys, though they humoured their mate, felt sure that the blow that had stretched Giluram flat was merely a fluke, just one of those things that happen.

"Well, you've got what you want," said Kerran, "and this work is too hot for me." He broke away and joined the other boys squatting on the sun-warmed rock.

"We have only to carve the correct shape upon the lower end of our shields," Red Kangaroo declared enthusiastically, "then practice the holding of it and those few movements to watch for, and seize the opportunity—and we have a terrible new weapon, one that an enemy will never suspect."

His comrades smiled and winked, except the still sick Giluram, propped up against a rock listening with watery eyes, not feeling like joking at all.

But in time to come that blow was to be known and dreaded far and wide as the "death-blow of the Red Chief", and was to do its part in helping to save the tribe.

## CHAPTER VIII

### MAN MUST FIND FOOD TO LIVE

A black night, and cold, too. Not a star—only blackness engulfing the earth. Came moaning wind bowing shivering tree-tops, and then near by, somewhere up in the night, tortured howls shudderingly dying away only to rise piercingly—two swaying branches these, writhing in agonised screeches as they were rubbed against one another by the wind. A demon thing, that wind, filling the night with moaning, rapidly swelling to a terrifying hum swiftly coming from far over the bush. Then all was roaring sound wherein the crash of falling trees was no more than a vanishing sigh. Thunder rocked the sky to roll in thunderous roars that pinned all live things against the shivering earth. Dazzling flame sizzled down as thunder roared again. In those blinding seconds the mushroom gunyahs of the Gunn-e-darr tribe shone vividly far down there upon the little clearing surrounded by moaning trees.

If modern man had witnessed that scene he would have marvelled that such flimsy things of bark could for a moment have sheltered the beings within from such a storm. But it was so. The end of each bark sheet making up the little, bell-shaped gunyahs was tucked so securely into the earth that there were neither corners nor edges that a jealous wind could get its teeth into and whirl away. The rounded bark was built over a light framework of bent saplings, and here and there each sheet was lashed to the framework with rope-like vine, the main points with thongs of kangaroo hide.

For this, the tribe's main camp, was built much more solidly than their hunting camps. Each doorway was but a rounded hole cut out of the bark at ground level. Through this hole the family crawled in and out of the gunyah. On cold nights they blocked it with a little sheet of bark from the inside. Each gunyah was built with its "back" to the prevailing winds, while the little space of ground upon which the scattered shelters stood had centuries ago been chosen for this camp because the nature of the surrounding country and timber sheltered it from all weathers.

Yes, that terrifying flash from the sky illuminated even these tiny gunyahs upon the vast earth. Truly, Baia-me sees *all* things. Just two seconds—but not only the gunyahs were visible, even every hair showed upon the dark forms lying cuddled there—in each gunyah the warrior, his wife, his children, silent as frightened mice, moveless as the granite rock, huddled tight together for warmth, but above all for the reassuring comfort of companionship. Eerie gleam of eyes of father staring into mother's eyes as again the voice of Baia-me thundered through the skies to roll around the earth. What had made Baia-me angry? Children's eyes shut tight as they clung to parents trying to shut out the storm and the moaning of the spirits of the night.

Under each family was a sheet of bark, over same a kangaroo or possum-skin rug partly sheltering the huddled bodies. There was a surprising warmth from glowing embers and closely packed bodies in the enclosed little space. Only live coals there now, but the fire had warmed the ground underneath. The lightning flash was gone, leaving pitch blackness within the gunyahs except for that dull glow, and for the occasional gleam of white as eye of man or woman moved at the crash of some great branch coming hurtling down to tear its path amongst its fellows and thump dully outside.

Then rain poured down in torrents, a fierce drumming on the rounded bark of the gunyahs. In moments the earth was a morass, to the howl of the wind, a hissing of water, a vast sighing from swishing branches, billions of rain-drenched leaves.

The huddled people felt glad that they were in their main camp. Otherwise, unless they had been sheltering in mountain caves, this night would have meant both misery and danger. But these cunningly built little gunyahs defied both wind and rain, and since they were built on rising ground that gave excellent natural drainage the water swiftly gurgled away.

Thus, in comparative security and comfort, these primitive folk heard the wild night howl itself away. Thus for unknown thousands of years the Stone Age man has survived against all the many terrors of Nature, of wild animals, and his own wild brothers. In every land he existed only because he had brains and used them in his ceaseless fight against Nature.

In a watery dawn the wind gradually dropped. Presently the sun shone out bright and warm as birds with drying feathers joyously greeted the freshly washed face of the bush. Happily the people, the women first, came crawling out of the gunyahs to light the cooking fires and prepare the morning meal for their lords and families. Old Bungadoon's rollicking voice was soon informing the whole camp how he had unwittingly shared his bed with a centipede. Of course it was the largest centipede in all the wide bush. The storm had driven it into the gunyah for shelter. It had huddled up between him and Pumbul, his wife, as she clung to him while he was shielding her and all "their youngsters" from the storm. She had clung to him so tight that it was a wonder the centipede had not been squashed between them. It must have been very warm. But that, of course, proved its good sense in squeezing into such a comfortable sheltering place. Of course, he had taken fine care that the centipede did not bite Pumbul.

Pumbul, now cooking Bungadoon's breakfast by the fire, had really noticed the hideous green-and-yellow centipede when she woke up. While Bungadoon still snored she had carefully, with a stick, edged it away from him. But she said nothing, whereas Bungadoon's booming voice would not rest until he got his teeth into his breakfast—and not for long even then.

It was a glorious morning when the tribe in chattering groups straggled away into the bush for the day's hunting. The long grasses, flattened by the night's downpour, were lifting up drooping heads to the sun. Broken branches, massive limbs of trees, here and there a forest giant littered the bush. The sodden ground was a picture book clearly portraying the tracks of every living thing that had crawled, walked, hopped, run, trodden, or settled upon it since the sun rose and the rain stopped, and every mother, every elder sister, seized the opportunity of teaching the children as they walked along.

"Who made that track?" Weetah asked her brother.

"Ibis," answered Tuki promptly.

"Good boy! His tracks are very plain in the mud, so you can read them clearly. Now what has he been doing?" And for Tuki the daily lesson was on again.

Farther along, by the bank of the lagoon, Wynar pointed out a fresh track to her poddy-bellied toddler.

"Now tell mother who made that track?"

Little Bigabilla gazed at the track with puckered brow. Never, he was sure, had he seen such a track. It was so big, and plain, and altogether unusual. With his eyes growing wider he gazed along those big plain tracks where a "something" had waddled across the mud flat and on into the water. Slowly Bigabilla's face grew solemn with fright. Could it be—it *must* be, the track of the terrible Bunyip.

Then Wynar laughed reassuringly, and pointed.

"What is that great big fat bird fishing away out on the lagoon?" she asked.

"Gulamooli the pelican," whispered Bigabilla.

"Well, it was only old Gulamooli the pelican that made the track. Old father pelican came ashore to visit his wife and children, and those are his tracks across the mud where he went back to the water again to fish for his breakfast, and his family's breakfast. Now, study those tracks carefully so that you will always know a pelican's tracks in the mud again. This mud is nice and fresh and squashy. The pelican is a big 'old man' and he was heavily laden with food, so his tracks in the squashy mud are much bigger and deeper than they generally are. But memorize them so that you will always recognize not only a big old father pelican's tracks, but his wife's and his babies' as well."

Away past a clump of wilga-trees five mothers, each with a toddler, made for a sandy patch, nice and fresh after the rain—and found what they wanted. They gathered the toddlers round, then a mother bent down and pointed.

"See!"

The babies gazed down, big-eyed. They saw a wriggly line of little points dotting the sand. Sharp eyes indeed were needed.

"What track is it?" asked a mother.

"Centipede!" replied a baby boy promptly.

"Good boy! You'll be a great hunter when you grow up. Now you children track that wandery old centipede to his home. He's up to no good, you'll find out!"

And the babies, on hands and knees, eagerly started tracking the wandering of the centipede until finally they would find him, some distance away, in his home under a log or stone or piece of bark.

Meanwhile the mothers set about finding and digging yams undisturbed by the babies. When they had finally tracked the centipede a mother would keep them busy again by finding them a beetle's track to follow, or the track of a lizard, or a frog, or a bush rat, or the wriggling impression a snake had left in crossing a sandy or dusty place—anything at all so that this day should not pass without each child's learning some little thing, no matter how small, about his great mother and feeder, the bush.

Meanwhile, some miles away by a tree-shaded billabong beside the Namoi, another group of women and children were busily hunting for edible water plants, for fish, yabbies, water-rats, eels, and tortoises. Some mothers had chubby babies clinging like little possums round their shoulders, sitting round their necks, chubby hands with a fast grip in their hair. Thus every tribal baby very soon began to learn the tense struggle for life, the hunting for food. Big eyes very solemn, staring at the bush as the mother glanced round, watching the water, the trees, the ground, a baby felt every movement, watched every action as the keen-eyed mother slowly walked along on her hunting. When she bent to dig up root or bulb the large black eyes peering down over her forehead solemny watched, listening and trying to memorize and understand as the mother held up the leaf of the plant as she dug with her digging stick, held up root or bulb or tuber before putting them in her dilly-bag.

Just within the edge of the billabong, upon clear white sand, a mother was slowly walking, her baby boy toddling beside her, the water up to his belly.

"See!" The mother pointed down into the clear water. "What track is that?"

For quite a time the toddler stared down at, then along that track. He was not going to be caught at fault if he could help it. The track was merely a long, thin little line along the sand, just as if someone had lightly dragged the point of a little stick over the sand. The line had no beginning and no end.

"Mussel," he declared.

"Good boy! That's a mussel track, all right. Now find the mussel."

But this had the baby beaten. Perhaps a big old-man fish had gobbled it up, or a big old crane might have flown away with it, or a water-rat might have dived down and gobbled it up—but no, there was no shell left. Perhaps one of the women or girls might have picked it up. Yet there were no tracks to tell him that any of these things had happened. The mussel's track was certainly there, but the mussel had gone, and there was neither sign nor track to show that someone or something had taken it.

Sombrely he shook his head. The mother laughed.

"We must find him," she said encouragingly, "or else go hungry. Now stand back at that end of the track and tell me what you see. Look carefully."

The toddler did so. He stared down long and hard. But there was no sign of anything but that thin little line along the sandy bottom. He bent down until his eyes were on a level with the water; he could see every grain of sand, but nothing more. He bent lower until his eyes were well below water, almost standing on his head. The mother was chuckling delightedly. He emerged with a great blowing and puff-ing, his face woebegone, for he had seen nothing.

"Never mind," consoled the mother. "Now come up to *this* end of the track, and look again. Look very carefully now."

The toddler waded up along the faint line, bent over, stared fixedly again. But this end of the track looked exactly like the other end, neither beginning nor end— nothing. To hide his disappointment he still kept on staring and then—

He tautened, stared harder. Had he— yes, there it came up again, a wee bubble prettily emerging from the end of the track to come drifting up and vanish in the water. Here was another one—he was staring very hard—and yet another was coming, just like a fairy pearl!

"What do you see?"

"Bubbles!"

"Ah ha! Good boy! Now, *something* must be making those bubbles. Dig down with your hands and see what it is."

The baby did so, scooping down into the sand, scratching deeper down until he stopped with nose at water level, one great big eye cocked sideways up at his mother. She could hardly refrain from laughing, for he seemed to be all one big eye and tail—she thought he would topple over, but he rose up fairly gasping with triumph as he held aloft in chubby fist a big fat mussel shell.

Throughout the ages, going back to the days of the Great Beasts, the Great Crocodiles, the Great Birds and Reptiles, how many, many times has thus a mother of the Children of the Bush taught her baby son or daughter how to find the first mussel, the shellfish that has helped feed innumerable generations of many, many tribes.

How very, very often has the great, quiet Bush listened sympathetically to that, "Good boy! Good girl! and so now we shall not go hungry this day."

# CHAPTER IX
## THE WOMAN-STEALERS

The moons came, and passed away, a summer and winter had come and gone since the lad Red Kangaroo had won his Bora warriorhood. Soon he was to be the tallest man in the tribe, broad-shouldered, deep-chested, lightning quick of movement, with long, powerful legs. No warrior could now wrestle and hold him down, nor throw a spear so straight and far, nor swim farther, nor stay under water longer. There was no man whose long-drawn, piercing cooee could be heard so far away over the bush. All this seems to make Red Kangaroo a superman of the wilds, but this description of him is just as it is handed down to us by the last of his tribe.

These feats of Red Kangaroo endeared him all the more to most of the tribe, for bushcraft, strength, agility, and above all endurance, were naturally greatly esteemed by these children of the bush. Some few men of every tribe, fortunate ones, excel in one, or perhaps two phases of bushcraft; few indeed excel in many. But he was liked for warmer reasons. Always willing to help man, woman or child, his happy laugh as welcome as old Bungadoon's in camp, on the hunt, or on a long, hard march, he was ever ready with praise for others who distinguished themselves in the hunt or with weapons or in the dance.

Very unusually also for a lad his age, he was quick to admire each new tribal baby, to the smiling content of the mother, who did not realize he was thinking of future warriors and mothers of the tribe. His ready tongue and appreciative smile, not to mention his sharp nose, brought him as a welcome guest to where anything tasty was cooking.

"He can smell a hunk of emu meat or a fat goanna on the coals a mile away," chuckled old Bungadoon. "Just as well I'm three men in one as a hunter or Pumbul and I and the family would go hungry many a day!"

At which Pumbul would smile her quiet, knowing old smile and urge Red Kangaroo to try yet another tasty morsel.

While Boobuk the warior would growl at Kapota, his long-suffering wife, "You always seem to like Red Kangaroo to come prowling along here and fill his belly. But you chuck my tucker at me as if I were a dog—it's always covered with lumps of charcoal, too! What has Red Kangaroo got that *I* haven't got?"

"Everything!" Kapota would snap.

"What's everything?" demanded Boobuk.

"A smile and a laugh and a good word for the food I cook and the way I cook it and the trouble I've taken to catch it!" Kapota would snap. "Whereas all you've got is the weather-beaten rump you squat down on, and the grunt you wolf your meat with! You've got nothing else—except the snore when you plop back to sleep it off!"

Such an answer would bring a surly growl and an unbelieving frown to Boobuk the warrior's corrugated brow, leaving the ever-ready Kapota with the satisfaction of the last word.

"And that's all I ever *have* got," she would complain bitterly to her friends, "from that hulking great guzzler. Just a growl, and guzzling noises, and a snore."

No wonder that poor Boobuk was so often bitterly puzzled. For he actually was that pride of every tribe—a man-killing warrior, no one so savagely fierce, such a ruthless batterer when it came to an all-in fight as he. Yet his own wife, Kapota, seemed the only person in his world who did not appreciate him.

Everyone, nearly everyone that is, liked Red Kangaroo, even the women. That smile, and cheerful voice of his were welcome—almost everywhere. There were times, though, when he sat quietly and thoughtfully, or stole away to brood with the bush and himself. But he was not brooding on this lovely morning as he strode through the bush, weapons in hand—only two war spears in case of emergency, for he was a hunter for today, and tomorrow, too, and tomorrow again. He was bound for Tambar Springs, home of the ibis, to join the warrior Kuribri, who with his young friends Giluram and Kerran, Burowa, Duri, and Keri, had sent him word there was such good hunting.

Twenty miles away, but he gloried in the walk; he would meet them easily by mid-sun. His noiseless step was light and springy as he trod the good earth, breathing in the early morning sweetness, keen eyes alert, ears drinking in the quiet, the whispering, the querulous or alarmed, the cocksure or distant voices of the bush that speak only to those attuned to hear. Striding on through a lovely grove of tall red and yellow gums, he emerged by a sunlit billabong with the blue-grass caressing his knees. He stopped inquiringly at a tinkle of girlish laughter somewhere on ahead, down by the water's edge amongst those reeds.

He frowned. Hugging the clear, gently sloping bank just here, only a little distance back from the water's edge grew a dark belt of hoop-vine scrub. Within that gloomy tangle of trees, shrubs, vine, and bracken fern a hundred enemies could lurk unperceived. And yet, though familiar with this menace from childhood there were—yes, tinkling laughter again—three young girls dawdling by the water close to that gloomy scrub. Despite all warning, advice, and command it had ever been so.

Three prized, valuable young girls lagging behind their hunting party—he frowned at the subdued laughter, the giggling coming from somewhere among those tall bullrushes along to his right. If *he* were chief of a tribe he would make certain that careless guards allowed no such opportunity to lurking woman-stealers. Anyway, he would make sure now that it would be a long time before *these* three girls dawdled thus again. With grim-set jaw he turned and strode on, clenching his wommera. He would spring out at the girls and land each a thump across the head that would send her spinning, he would push their heads under water until at their last choking gasp—and then he was flat upon the earth.

From out of the hoop-vine scrub had stepped two crouching, warriors, startling in their painted nakedness. In swift eagerness they ducked down the bank, then began to stalk up along the watercourse. Red Kangaroo thrilled to those sinewy bodies so stealthily, with such keen purpose, creeping along beside the bullrushes. Hunters these men, hunters now of women—his tribal women! He rose to a crouching position and began to hunt the hunters, tingling with a fiercely growing glee as his fingers twitched round his weapons, now deeply etched upon his face the Stone Age urge to hunt and kill. The raiders' attention was concentrated on creeping closer, ever closer towards the muffled laughter occasionally coming from the reeds. Red Kangaroo crept eagerly on, itching to get within spear-throw of those lean, muscular backs stealthily moving ahead. Coombri men from the Terri-Hi-Hi by their tribal scars and war-paint—noted woman-stealers, the Terri-Hi-Hi. That black-bearded, wall-eyed savage ahead was a warrior of an advanced degree. Both were heavily armed, while Red Kangaroo carried only two war spears. But with every step ahead his heart was beating faster in that terrible urge to kill.

From the billabong edge the raiders were half standing now, peering among the bulrushes out towards the shallow water. Red Kangaroo crept swiftly on, hearing now quick laughter as the girls splashed after a frantically dodging tortoise. And then, from slightly rising ground, he could see over the reed tops the three wading girls seeking by touch of feet to scare the tortoise from its hiding place. And he saw now why the woman-stealers remained watching, hesitating. For one girl was wading a little distant from the others. Not far, but just a little *too* far. Otherwise the raiders could have crept into the reeds, then suddenly leapt out and felled a girl each with a single blow of the club. But the third girl would have one startled moment in which to scream the alarm. Red Kangaroo grinned fiendishly as he crept stealthily on, knowing how those two raiders must be on edge waiting for the three girls to come close together. If there had been only two they would have been so completely at the raiders' mercy. But with three, each must be stunned on the instant to stifle any alarm, or it would be the raiders who would be running for their lives.

He was almost within spear-throw when a cry of delight urged him to bound forward, fitting war spear to wommera.

One girl had caught a good-sized fish under a log and was holding the flapping thing up for her comrades to come and admire; the raiders were creeping out through the reeds as the three girls waded together. Red Kangaroo drew back his arm for the throw just as Black-beard glanced round. Then the spear was in the air, aimed now for the other raider, who wheeled round to splash back with the spear deep in his chest. Black-beard was bounding back to the bank and his spear came hissing as Red Kangaroo sprang aside and threw again. Leaping towards him, the enemy warrior parried the spear, and now both advanced crouching, in little leaping runs coming closer together as another spear came and Red Kangaroo fell to his knees with the long spear hissing over him. He was upright and poised on the instant and threw a hunting spear, which the enemy disdainfully struck aside with his shield as he came crouching on, again fitting spear to wommera. Neither noticed the piercing, long-drawn warning scream of the girls as they raced away. The raider came leaping and dodging while hurling his weapons, knowing he must kill this man and run—in a race for life with the guards at his heels.

In a snarling rage he threw his last spear, and both men were crouching in erratic leaps, dodging the tricky, spinning boomerangs. One came near to breaking Red Kangaroo's leg; it struck the ground deceptively to the left and behind him where the force of impact jerked it straight back to gash his leg. Had that swiftly revolving blade struck fully it would have snapped his shin-bone like a carrot. It was the last boomerang, too.

Both maddened men rushed each other to the crash of shield against shield, the smack of club against warding shield. Leaping high and aside and around, to crouch low and spring while striking at head and thigh and low to the ankles in a fury of grunting bodies and jarring shield and club, Red Kangaroo was now feeling the strain of resisting this older warrior's maniacal struggle for life. Yet again the two fierce bodies plunged together as blazing eyes snarled into blazing eyes. In the shuddering pressure as the shields struck it was instinct that jerked Red Kangaroo's shield downward so that the end drove sickeningly into his enemy's throat, shocking him to his knees as Red Kangaroo struck hard down on his skull. He sprang back, panting, as his enemy rolled over with convulsive limbs agonizedly thrashing amongst the grasses.

Red Kangaroo stood trembling, panting down at the dying warrior as the women's guards came running. One glance at the fallen man, a glance then at the figure lying in the water with the long spear-haft sticking up above the reeds, and their expressive faces screwed up to astounded expressions in deep grunts of "Whough! Whough! Wah! Wah! Wah!" Then a warrior lifted his head and there rang out over the bush the long-drawn, wavering call of alarm, while several men ran for the nearest hill to summon the scattered hunters by a smoke signal. The tribe must be warned lest the two dead raiders had not come alone. Again, and yet again the call sounded. Then faintly, from away over towards the Whispering Belahs, came floating an answer. They laughed relievedly. That answer would be from Jerrabri's men hunting kangaroo on the big gum flats. They in turn would signal Kuribri's men at Tambar Springs, while those fishing down the Namoi would smoke-signal the look-outs on distant Ydire and on Booroobil Rock. Thus quickly over many square miles of country keen eyes would be eagerly watching and the man-hunt would be on.

Red Kangaroo, eager for action, raised his voice in a short, sharp call. The women and children hiding like frightened mice among the reeds and scrub came running back through the bush towards the call, eyes popping from their heads at sight of the dead raiders, the three girls who had been rescued excitedly jabbering as they pointed from one dead warrior to the other, screeching to the other women how narrowly they had escaped death or capture.

They grew bashfully silent as they noticed Red Kangaroo's glowering face, but he said nothing, realizing that had these three girls not dawdled behind he would not this day have made a great name for himself.

He grunted, then strode swiftly away

towards the main camp, the guards urging on the women and children who now were alert to scatter and fly at the least alarm.

But relieved laughter broke out when they saw the camp was safe, and the old people coming creeping out from their hiding-places at their reassuring cooees.

Red Kangaroo's task was now to help guard the camp until the scattered huntsmen could arrive. He put in time by running in a wide circle round the camp. And presently his quick eyes saw two tracks of foreign warriors who had run away from behind the camp. He followed, and saw on a clear patch where two more tracks joined, then two more. He stopped, and again his voice sent out the long-drawn signal cry.

Distantly through the trees came answering voices as running hunters turned in the direction of Red Kangaroo's voice. But those raiders were trained to the minute. They were four miles and more away by now, racing for life back to their own country, and they made it.

Before midday the tribe, except for the look-outs and distant scattered groups had congregated excitedly to read the story of the tracks. There had been twenty-six raiders all told. The two men killed by Red Kangaroo had been scouting well out from the camp and could not resist the temptation of trying to capture those three young girls. Thus they had ruined the whole raid. The other twenty-four had remained in hiding away behind the main camp waiting for late afternoon to bring the first party of women straggling back to camp. They would then have struck swiftly, and away. But for Red Kangaroo some among the Gunn-e-darr tribe would have slept their last sleep this night.

## CHAPTER X

### THE TROUBLES OF BOOBUK

Red Kangaroo was the tribal hero, plied round the campfires with the choicest morsels of the day's hunt. Proud he was when the chief and the elders, followed by his uncle Tulumi, and by the warriors

Burradella, Boobuk, and old Bungadoon, trying to be serious for once, came to his campfire and gravely congratulated him on his victory in a warrior's fight, and on saving not only the three girls—for it would have served them right had they been killed or captured—but some members at least of the tribe from the shower of spears that later would have been hurled into the camp. Jerrabri added that the tribe was proud of the fact that the warrior lad Red Kangaroo had so soon proved himself the warrior son of a warrior father. This pleased the lad greatly, for he had loved his father, but he was saddened when he saw that the chief's words had made his old mother cry.

Then the chief and the elders walked back to their own fires, leaving Red Kangaroo with his uncle and Burradella and Bungadoon and Boobuk, and the adoring group of warriors of his own age. Far into the night again and again old Bungadoon's hearty voice and rollicking laugh could be heard all over the camp extolling the deed of Red Kangaroo the warrior, prophesying great deeds ahead.

Not until the small hours did the camp

quieten into slumber. But Red Kangaroo slept not at all. Coiled by the warm ashes of his dull campfire he was fighting every movement of that great fight over and over again, concentrating on that last, that unexpected blow, that downward, slanting thrust of the sharpened shield—that fatal blow.

He knew now that he had been right; a shield could be made into a deadly offensive weapon. No foeman would dream that a defensive shield with one sharp blow could end a fight. On this occasion it had been partly good luck, of course, for the end still was not the right shape. In a fever of impatience he sat up and reached for his shield and sharpening stone. He would start now. It would take time and patience, another moon might even come and go before he had the shield ground down to that tapering shape and sharpness. Then in every fight where it came to the last final test of man to man, shield to shield, nulla to nulla, he would wield a secret weapon undreamt of by his enemy. He smiled as he worked. He would teach his fellow warriors of his own degree; they would be eager now to learn the blow and shape their own shields. And then, when he was a full-grown man, his warriors would be unbeatable in a close fight, a shield to themselves and to the tribe. His warriors——

He ceased work, staring out into the night. His warriors? Not his—yet. Slowly he put down shield and grinding stone. Unseeing, he stared out into the night, feeling some strange prompting of caution. He lay quietly back, thinking. Perhaps for the time being it might be best to say nothing more about that blow, about that shape to the shield end. No man had seen him strike that blow; all thought he had clubbed his man by greater strength and skill. No, perhaps it would be best for the time being to keep the secret, quietly to shape the end of his shield at such times when he would be quite alone.

When the first cold grey of dawn came stealing over the treetops he hardly felt the chill. He was still wide awake, trying to puzzle things out, groping into what the future might hold.

Steel-grey grew the sky above the dark

tree-tops. Slowly the grey merged into dull silver, slowly then into faint pink rippling into rosiness. Somewhere, far away over the mountains, Walcha the sun was rising from his night's sleep. A bird twittered sleepily, a new day was being born.

Red Kangaroo, the warrior lad, had grown into a man—a thinking man.

Not so Boobuk the warrior. Boobuk was a good man when pushed into action; at all other times he found it pleasant to hunt if the hunting was not too strenuous—pleasant, too, to loaf or eat or sleep, or just to drowse on the river bank while others did the fishing. Boobuk hardly knew what thought was; anyway, he had no time for thought, he had his worries instead. Kapota, his wife, of course—the only but greatest worry in the world to Boobuk, his nearest approach to a headache. She had spoilt even such a lovely night as this had been, just pleasantly warm, the bush a dreamy stillness, stars a-twinkle in the sky, happy groups round each little campfire, a momentary flame painting chocolate bodies into bronze. Subdued voices here and there, laughter here and there, tinkle of kylies, haunting chant of girlish voices in some age-old love song, the rumbling bellow of old Bungadoon laughing at his own joke—and then the shrill voice of Kapota, followed by a bull-like roar.

Silence had fallen on the camp at this particularly outrageous disturbance from the warrior Boobuk's gunyah; then he had come flying out, tearing away a sheet of bark as he landed backwards upon his campfire, leaping up with a howl, his roars followed by shrill abuse and the whiz of a nulla thrown by the irate Kapota. Growling furiously to the subdued laughter from the shadowy gunyahs, Boobuk came like a great shambling ape to throw himself down by old Bungadoon's campfire.

"Women!" snarled Boobuk. "Women! And those fools of cubs howling their eyes out for them! Wait till Red Kangaroo and his cub mates get their women! They'll wish they'd never been born!"

"What's wrong now?" chuckled Bungadoon.

"Women!" roared Boobuk as tenderly

he felt his buttocks where he had fallen back upon his own fire. "You heard, didn't you? Women! Red Kangaroo and his mob can have my Kapota and everything in my gunyah with her—if they'd only take her!"

Old Bungadoon gleefully caressed his paunch; he dearly loved to see Boobuk in a rage.

"You don't know how to handle her," he said soothingly. "Why don't you give her the father of a hiding?"

"Because she'd give me worse, you fool!" snapped Boobuk.

"Oh, indeed!" observed Bungadoon thoughtfully. "Have you ever given her a hiding—a *real* hiding?"

"Once," grunted Boobuk.

"Ah! And what did she do?"

"Ate me alive with bulldog ants!" snapped Boobuk.

Old Bungadoon's eyes opened wide, Pumbul gazed silently, all the "family youngsters" and their small friends listened entranced.

"How did she eat you alive with bulldog ants?" inquired Bundagoon wonderingly.

"She didn't, you fool!" growled Boobuk. "The ants ate *me!*"

"Why?" inquired Bungadoon.

"Because she threw them all over my belly!"

"What did she do that for?" asked the puzzled Bungadoon.

"To get even, of course."

"Then why did you let her do it?"

"I didn't!" howled Boobuk and sat straight up and glared at Bungadoon. "It was a hot day, and I was asleep—asleep out in the bush, under a shady kurrajong-tree. She sneaked up, found a bulldog ants' nest near by, cut up some raw pademelon meat and put it in the bottom of her coolamon, laid the coolamon beside the nest. When the coolamon was full of hungry ants she snatched it up and ran to me and emptied the ants all over me!"

"Well, well now!" exclaimed Bungadoon in astonishment. "And what did *you* do?"

"*I* do!" howled Boobuk with his murderous face glaring at Bungadoon. "What would *you* do if you woke up and found your fat paunch being torn to pieces by bulldog ants! Why, run, of course! Jump up and yell and race for the big timber and keep yelling, you fool! Keep yelling and leaping and running and rolling in the grass to wipe the cursed things off!"

"Yes," admitted Bungadoon thoughtfully, "I suppose I should do just that. But what a terrible thing for a woman to do—to her very own husband, too! But didn't you run back and kill her when you found out?"

"No," sighed Boobuk, and gazed gloomily at the fire. "I didn't know she'd done it; it was not until a long time afterward that I found out. I thought I'd just lain down near a bulldog ants' nest and the ants had swarmed over me while I slept."

"But didn't you give her the father of all hidings when you did find out?"

"No," answered Boobuk shortly.

"Why not?"

"Because I had time to think!"

Old Bungadoon looked his surprise.

"What are you gawking at, you fat owl?" demanded Boobuk.

"What did you think?" replied Bungadoon mildly.

The warrior Boobuk again sat up, gazing fiercely at Bungadoon.

"I thought what you would have thought," he replied sarcastically, "if you weren't sitting on your brains. I thought this, that if that woman could throw bulldog ants all over me just because I'd given her a hiding, then what might she do to me next time?"

"Yes," admitted Bungadoon, "there's something in that."

"There is," said Boobuk feelingly, "as you'll know if ever you wake up with your navel full of bulldog ants."

# CHAPTER XI
## THE DEADLY BLACK SNAKE

Happy days for Red Kangaroo, proved warrior but eighteen years of age. Giluram with shining eyes brought him news that old Mullionkale the play-maker was going to sing him in corroboree.

He, Red Kangaroo, to be sung by the tribe in corroboree, his deeds handed down by the tribe to generation after generation of its warriors to come, and learnt of by other tribes far away! For a successful corroboree was handed on or traded from tribe to tribe, creeping further and further across the great continent according to the popularity of its theme, songs, and dances.

Old Mullionkale the play-maker squatted quietly by the fire, his wrinkled face a cobweb of his thoughts as he planned this corroboree, celebrating a deed worthy of the tribal play-maker's best efforts. In the days that followed he went again and again over the ground of that now historic fight to absorb every detail of the story. Giluram acted the part of the too-bashful Red Kangaroo, and a young and a middle-aged warrior with square black beard were chosen to act as the two raiders. For the benefit of the play-maker the complete incident was rehearsed, the women strolling out of the camp on the morning's hunt, everyone acting, even to the eager children, every little thing that each one did on that morning. The three girls who had caused the trouble were the keenest actors of all.

Working with knit brow beside the play-maker was Mugille Bao-illna the song-maker. For Mullionkale would make the play, while Mugille Bao-illna[1] would make the songs that would describe the happenings of that day as the players acted their parts.

It was a night of the full moon when at last the eagerly awaited corroboree was first played. The people squatting in their family groups facing the corroboree ground impatiently awaited the chief, Jerrabri, and the council of the elders,

*1 Mugille means "make", and Bao-illna means "sing".*

coming now solemnly to take pride of place. Then beside them, as an honour of the occasion, the Kubara, those young men who had last passed through the Bora, Red Kangaroo and his band of young warriors. Beside them again were the Biribrau, those serious-faced lads brought in as a great treat from bush solitudes where they were undergoing the last tests before facing the Bora. Yes, serious indeed were these lads, and they must now study the example of warriorhood soon to be staged before them. As the moon rose a low chant of voices seemed to come welling up from the listening heart of the bush itself, echoed hauntingly from on high where under the moon a flight of wild geese passed swiftly overhead. For two hours Red Kangaroo lived that great morning all over again, lost in the mimicry, the descriptive song, the perfect acting in dance of all that had happened from start to finish.

The enthusiastic tribe, strolling back to their gunyahs to sleep for what remained of the night voted old Mullionkale's new corroboree, "The Making of a Warrior", to be the best ever. Red Kangaroo did not sleep at all.

So much did Red Kangaroo appear to be the idol of all, so pleased was he at having struck a hearty blow in defence of his beloved tribe, that it was some months before he realized that Jerrabri and the elders and some among the older warriors frowned at the mention of his deeds. This knowledge made him bitter—indiscreetly so.

One fine morning the young warrior unexpectedly found the warrior Burradella walking through the bush beside him. Red Kangaroo strode along in respectful silence, for the younger warrior waits for the elder to speak. Red Kangaroo had been going to the green flats alone, to hunt that fine big bird that falls only to the spear of the skilled huntsman, the plain turkey. They walked in silence through the red and spotted gums, the sunlit loveliness of the yellow and white box. It was not until they were passing the Valley of the Winds that Burradella spoke.

"You are talking too much again," he murmured.

"It does not seem to do me any good," replied Red Kangaroo sulkily.

"It does you harm that you know nothing about," said Burradella gravely. "Your tongue will yet spur others to action, then you will talk no more!"

They walked on in silence past thickets of wilga. Red Kangaroo felt a chill of dread. He whispered uneasily, "Has Nundoba the witchdoctor spoken?"

"No," said Burradella. "His thoughts lie as yet in his silence. So the elders dare not act—yet—because of that and because of your popularity. But you are becoming too rash, which again encourages the tribe to say big things too openly about you, some even praising you against the elders, foretelling great things for you."

"But they will not act with me," broke in Red Kangaroo bitterly, "not even for their own rights! Not even the Kubara who went through the Bora with me, none but Giluram will stand by me!"

"Which is just as well," replied Burradella meaningly, "for what you would say or do would upset the easy life of not only Jerrabri and the council of the elders, but of those older warriors who are now enjoying privileges which are not theirs, as we know, by right of law. And it would ruin the prospects of those other warriors who expect with time to enjoy those privileges also. If you would upset those laws that give power, even though unjust power, to the elders who guide the tribe, then you might make Nundoba the witchdoctor uneasy, and let any man who does that beware!" After a troubled silence Burradella resumed. "And now I shall let you into a tribal secret. It is Nundoba the witchdoctor who really controls our tribe!"

Burradella paused. Red Kangaroo gazed in surprise.

"It is Nundoba, who with but a glance sways the chief and the council of elders—when he wishes to interfere." Burradella paused again. "Now tell me, should you betray that I have told this secret to you, then what would happen to me?"

"The bone!" barely whispered Red Kangaroo, and now there was fear in his eyes.

"Ah!" murmured Burradella as they

walked on. The bush seemed hushed, though the birds still sang, though there came the thud of a wallaby bounding through the grass near by. A woodpecker, clinging away up a stringybark, was immersed in his own world as he pecked the bark, seeking insects, his beautifully hooked, needle-sharp claws helping him up and around the tree, his questing eyes like gleaming beads.

"The bone!" The most awful dread of any Australian aboriginal, the fear of the witchdoctor's "pointing the bone"!

Burradella was walking now towards the waterlily lagoon, beautifully shadowed by its grey and green and red and white timbers. Red Kangaroo followed mechanically, crushing the golden buttercups under his big black feet.

"Now understand," said Burradella softly, "that Nundoba controls the tribe as if from far away—Jerrabri, the council of the elders, of the seven—all of us! But he rarely interferes—unless something happens that interferes with *him*. Should he become really angry, he strikes—as death strikes in the night."

They walked on again in silence, nearing now the blue-gums and stately oaks fringing the lagoon.

"Should Red Kangaroo," said Burradella abruptly, "in his boyish haste start a big trouble that would upset Nundoba the witchdoctor, then what would happen to Red Kangaroo?"

"The bone!" whispered the lad.

Silently they walked on, and Red Kangaroo for all his pride in youth, his bravery, his truly great strength, trembled to this unexpected threat of death he could not fight. For he at whom the bone has been pointed must abandon hope.

Burradella noted how his ominous words sank in, then he said softly, "Yes, the bone. But he need not bother to use that! Just one glance, and your enemy Jerrabri would know that he could act. So then?"

"The strangling cord!" breathed Red Kangaroo swiftly. "And the people would never think of Nundoba!"

"You are learning!" said Burradella dryly. Then added, "How did you know about the cord?"

In new-born caution Red Kangaroo

glanced uneasily round, then almost whispered, "I keep my ears open, my eyes also."

"It seems so," agreed Burradella, "but there are things that you of the Kubara should not hear, should not see! you have to pass other degrees yet before you learn of these things. Be sure that you do not mention the cord, or other forbidden things that you may have learnt or guessed at, to your Kubara friends!"

In silence again they strode on, Red Kangaroo's mind now whispering of unguessed at dangers threatening him. How different seemed the morning to the dawn!

A pademelon sat up and gazed curiously at them from bright brown eyes, its long ears comically listening, its creamy-white little chest an inviting target under its russet neck. Red Kangaroo did not even notice it.

They could see now the young boys on the grassy lagoon bank patiently awaiting the coming of their teacher, Burradella. Their eyes would be sparkling now they saw their hero coming, too, each boy's heart would be beating with eagerness to excel in his lesson. But none would dream how troubled was the heart of Red Kangaroo.

How little those lads knew! How little Red Kangaroo had known until this morning!

"I have spoken to old Bungadoon," said Burradella abruptly. "I have told him to be careful of the words that big mouth of his shouts to all the camp."

"But Bungadoon is friendly to me, surely," protested Red Kangaroo miserably. "He has been loud in my praise."

"Too loud!" growled Burradella. "You have heard his voice booming round the campfires, 'And mark what I say! That warrior lad Red Kangaroo will one day be a great chief!'"

"Ah!" sighed Red Kangaroo. "He was condemning me to the strangling cord— and did not know! And I did not know."

"Correct," replied Burradella, "but—"

"But?" almost whispered Red Kangaroo.

"But even so, the witchdoctor Nundoba

still has given no sign. Thus Jerrabri still hesitates to act."

It took quite a time for this to sink in. "But then," whispered Red Kangaroo, "if Nundoba signs neither yes nor no, then perhaps he really may not be hostile to me!"

"He cannot be—yet!" replied Burradella. "But then, no man knows his mind. See to it that you do not make it up for him against you. I can do no more. I have given you the last warning and now—here are the boys."

Some thirty of them, all standing in silent respect for their teacher, the warrior Burradella, and in big-eyed adoration of Red Kangaroo. Gravely Burradella commenced the lesson, and all that day Red Kangaroo followed along with the lesson, to the delight of the boys. But they little guessed all that was behind his grave demeanour, his appreciative eyes, and encouraging smile. For all his towering height, youth, strength, and warriorhood, he now felt very small indeed. Frightened, too—and lonely. Never had he felt so before. Towards sundown they were strolling back to the camp. The old familiar sounds—never before had they come so clearly to his ears. A ringing "Coo-ee-eee!" floating through the bush, tidings of success from a returning hunting party; the soft voice of Turilawa the Waterlily talking to her son Kuliya as she led him back to camp by the hand, the toddler looking tired after the long day's hunting. Screech of cockatoos, shrill call of a girl, laughing reply from a friend returning to camp with dilly-bag laden with good things to eat, snatch of a hunting song in the warrior Kuribri's deep voice. Yell of children hurling reed spears in mimic warfare, old Bungadoon's boastful laughter as he threw down a wallaby to be admired by Pumbul and their appreciative "children". Hilarious laughter of kookaburras high up on a branch where one was killing a snake, dropping it and snatching it up just before it smacked upon the ground, dashing it against the branch. Ah, now their loud laughter broke into bird fury as far up in the branch half a dozen snatched the nearest portion in their powerful beaks and began a tug-of-war, three pulling back on the neck, three pulling back on the tail shaking their heads in fury while tugging against the others. Sooner or later they would tear the stretched out thing to pieces and fiercely fight to gobble whatever part was clenched in their beaks.

Ah yes, the familiar old sights and sounds of the camp. Now he could see the girls gossiping as they winnowed grass-seed; they were threshing it, separating the husk from the seed, grinding it between stones into flour to be baked in cakes on the coals. Some chatted as they worked, others sang a lilting song about the black swans' flight by night. How sweetly the haunting refrain now sounded to Red Kangaroo, how clearly he smelt the fresh smoke from newly lit fires!

He murmured to Burradella, "I thank you for opening my eyes, that I may see a little way ahead. You have taught me many things, but never so much as today. And," he added, "I promise to talk less, and think more."

"It is well!" replied the warrior Burradella gravely.

# CHAPTER XII

## THE VENGEANCE PARTY

He kept his word. And learnt other things—among them that his dignified uncle Tulumi was with him, too, though he did not—could not—mention these things when he had occasion to speak to the young warrior.

"There are others!" murmured Burradella one evening.

And Red Kangaroo thrilled to the knowledge that he had unknown friends among elder warriors of standing in the tribe. Why should it be so? Through Burradella they seemed to be protecting him against hitherto unrealized dangers— had even protected him against himself. Why?

Could it be because they believed in him? Or believed in his rashly spoken opinions that an injustice was being done to the tribe? They would never have allowed him to be told secrets—known only to the elder warriors had there not been some serious reason. Could it possibly be that they also believed the chief and the elders were working against the laws of the tribe?

The more he pondered the surer he became that he was not alone in his beliefs with frightened warrior lads as his only allies. If so, he was on the right track after all. With a pleasurable certainty he began to regain confidence. But how carefully now he watched his tongue, and how much more his eyes seemed to see, his ears to hear, his mind to think.

It was eventide some time later when the hunter Mobo came panting into camp to gasp out a story of tragedy. He and three others had been spearing fish along the banks of the Black Creek. He had climbed a tall tree to cut out a bees' nest. Suddenly a score of painted Terri-Hi-Hi warriors had dashed out from the timber and fallen upon his friends. They had not had a chance, and were transfixed by spears on the instant. Coolta had leapt into the creek with a long spear embedded in his leg, and as he splashed frantically about trying to break off the spear haft they had yelled in laughter from the bank and made him a target. Then they had slashed out the kidney fat of the fallen men and eaten it, gathered up the weapons and swiftly departed. Mobo had seen it all from the tree-top—in their excitement they had forgotten to count the tracks—and had never been so frightened in his life.

He had clung up there, sidling round the tree-top like a frightened goanna every time he thought they might glance up. He had stayed there a long time in case they were hiding and waiting for him to come down, just playing with him.

At last he had slid down the tree and run with all speed to the camp.

Silence, as Mobo poured out his tale to the chief and the elders. Then from the dead men's relations rose the death wail. The camp was in an uproar on the instant, warriors leaping into the air, rattling their weapons, chewing their beards in fury, howls from men, screams from women for vengeance. The camp became a den of human animals gone mad.

All through the night rose the mournful death wail, taken up again and again to slowly rise in a long, drawn-out wail that seemed to hang on the air, to moan slowly away through the night.

Next day relations went out to bring in the bodies for burial and the long, solemn death ceremonies. After this would come vengeance. An eye for an eye, a tooth for a tooth, a life for a life. The relations of the dead men must take up the blood feud, must kill three men at least of the Terri-Hi-Hi.

The warrior Burradella was chosen to lead the vengeance party. Red Kangaroo's heart leapt at the news, for he was certain now he would be one of the band chosen. Most of the tribe believed so, too, for not only was he related to one of the victims but, under experienced leadership, his endurance, skill with weapons, strength and quickness made him an ideal man for such an enterprise.

Boastful laughter broke out. The Terri-Hi-Hi would rue the day they had raided the Gunn-e-darr men.

Red Kangaroo was *not* chosen to be one of the vengeance party. The camp was very surprised, more so Red Kangaroo. Then he felt hurt. Then he sulked.

Several evenings later he overheard a remark, "Perhaps the elders did not pick Red Kangaroo because Jerrabri knew he would kill his man and not be killed himself."

"We know," came a growling answer, "the elders are jealous. They will never give Red Kangaroo a chance if they can help it."

Red Kangaroo passed on into the night, fiercely resentful.

Next day he was up on look-out duty at Ydire. At midday the warrior lads with him lit a fire and threw a porcupine and several possums on the glowing wood. They gossiped in low voices, but Red Kangaroo, sitting morosely aside, knew their voices were meant to carry to him. For a long time past he had not joined in their conversation when it affected themselves and the elders. He, who always had taken the lead in such subjects, had for long been strangely silent.

"It would have been such a wonderful vengeance party," one murmured, "with Burradella in the lead, Red Kangaroo in the rear."

"Nothing could have stopped their

success," broke in another. "And—they would all have returned."

After a silence, another murmured, "Should the warrior Burradella be killed—"

"Then Red Kangaroo will lose his best and strongest friend!" broke in the first speaker.

Red Kangaroo instantly perceived the implication of these words—that the chief and elders would not care if the warrior Burradella did *not* return! He had never dreamed of this, that his friend and protector might be killed.

Slowly his resentment against Burradella faded. By his death Red Kangaroo would truly lose his most powerful friend, while those others who only dared speak and secretly act through Burradella would in fear remain silent. Red Kangaroo would be all alone.

Fiercely, all his resentment returned and more, this time against Jerrabri and the elders. And he was anxious now, anxious for the safety of the warrior Burradella. Not only was he now afraid to talk, but helpless to act.

The seven men of the vengeance party were still in camp, carefully seeing to their weapons, greasing their bodies with animal oils, partly against possible cold and rain but chiefly so that a foeman's grip must slip from body and limbs. Gravely Burradella discussed plans with the others, the distances they had to travel, the time and manner of their surprise attack, and their get-away. The following dawn they had gone—stolen away in the night.

Four returned, one week later. Burradella, badly limping, had a broken-off spear-head deep in his thigh. They had killed their men, but on returning had run full into a war party returning from a heavy raid on a neighbouring tribe. They had fought their way through, but had lost three of their number. Again rose the death wail, mournful through the night and the next night and the following night again.

Morosely Red Kangaroo sat beside Burradella while Nundoba the witchdoctor cut the broken spear-head from his friend's thigh. Deeply embedded in the flesh, the barbed hardwood spike caused torture at the slightest movement of the leg. Only the sternest warrior could have fought and run those miles and miles with those burning fangs of pain biting deep in his flesh.

Slowly, unfeelingly, methodically, his face a maze of wrinkles, skinny old Nundoba proceeded to cut the awful thing out with cunningly fashioned knives of stone, bone, and shell. He was two hours working on it, his talon-like fingers, so slow, so definite, so sure. Burradella, his eyes closed, teeth biting on a stick of hardwood, quivered every now and then, but never a groan escaped him.

Red Kangaroo wiped away the sweat that poured from Burradella's forehead and temples as the knives began to bite deep. Now and then he gave him a long drink of cold, life-bringing water. At long last the witchdoctor had cut deeply enough to clear the way for withdrawal of the last barb. He grunted, signalling to Red Kangaroo with his bloody hands. Red Kangaroo knelt on Burradella with all his weight, put each big hand to the sides of the long cut, then pressed it open as deeply as he could. The witchdoctor, crouched down like a crow upon a carcass, fixed his teeth firmly in the broken off spear-head, then slowly, strongly, carefully began pulling out the thing while the sinews stood taut in his neck. The gory thing came out finally. Burradella shuddered, groaned.

The witchdoctor filled the deep wound with the fine ash of certain carefully prepared acacia leaves containing curative properties. Then he plastered it all over thickly, firmly, with mud, but it was not just ordinary mud, it was of dried powders of differing kaolin clays, mixed into the form of mud. And each prepared clay possessed some secret cooling or healing property. The warrior Burradella's wound would heal with surprising quickness. His wife would feed him well. He would walk again, hunt and fight again.

Sullenly, low-voiced, the people growled round the campfires at night again. Another vengeance party must be chosen, must prepare to go out to avenge the three dead men.

An eye for an eye. A life for a life.

# CHAPTER XIII

## THE FALSE ALARM

The tribe had barely commenced the mourning ceremonies when hunters brought news of tracks of Narrabri warriors who had crossed over their northernmost boundary by Kolorinbrai.[1] And the next evening Giluram came running into camp with news of Quirindi warriors having crossed the southern boundary near Buk-Kulla.[2]

All plans of vengeance against the Terri-Hi-Hi were forgotten for the time. Excitable warriors snatched weapons and leapt up in the war-dance. Soon they were all at it to the rumble of stamping feet and the frenzied chant of the women. Warriors rattled their spears and clashed their shields, with a roar to the chief demanding to be led against these invaders of their lands. Only then did Red Kangaroo seize his weapons and join in the call for action.

*1 "Place abounding in kolorin, the flowers of the kulaba (box-tree)."*
*2 "Pace of leopard-trees."*

But with a plan. These last few months had taught him how to think. The men of Narrabri coming down from the north, the men of Quirindi coming in from the south—two strong tribes against one! Probably they were only scouting parties, but if they were war parties, then the swifter the Gunn-e-darr tribe turned on one and destroyed it the sooner it could turn and face the other. But who was he to argue in the councils of the elders? There was much solemn talk among the elders, but nothing was decided.

Several days later the Gunn-e-darr tribe were badly frightened. From a friendly tribe a nervous messenger arrived with a warning. Chief Ilpara of the Goonoo Goonoo and Kibbi, war chief of the Bundarra, were both threatening war against the Gunn-e-darr, jealous of their lands and waters.

The messenger left apologetically after hurriedly delivering his message, murmuring to Jerrabri and the elders that his own people dared not be brought into the trouble lest their small numbers be wiped out.

Jerrabri and his council decided that the fastest runners amongst the first degree warriors should scout the southern boundary on the look-out for the Quirindi men, while another fast group would scout the north and race back with word should the Narrabri men come in from the north. Meanwhile the tribe must still carry on with hunting to live, while also guarding against the Goonoo Goonoo and Bundarra. All tribal groups would hunt in close reach near the centre of their lands. If big danger came then the tribe would rapidly congregate along the Porcupine Ridges by Mullibah Lagoon camp, for deep within the dense hoop-vine scrubs near there was hidden the Secret Camp, refuge for the women and children.

This plan seemed to Red Kangaroo a council of despair as, in charge of a party of the younger warriors, he hurried through the bush to patrol the tribe's northern boundary. A Stone Age patrol, but demanding extreme endurance, mobility, speed, initiative, and powers of observation.

Red Kangaroo, moving with long, easy

strides at Giluram's side, said with a sly smile, "Giluram is not glum, surely, at the thought of the wicked plans of Ilpara of the Goonoo Goonoo?"

The forlorn expression eased from Giluram's face as he smiled. "No. Wouldn't I love the chance to hurl this spear deep into his chest!"

"Ah!" grunted Red Kangaroo. Presently he remarked, "And is there not *another* chest you would like to bed that spear in?"

Giluram glanced at him as they hurried on, then muttered, "You know!"

And Red Kangaroo did know, for the other man was old Tulduna, to whom the elders had promised Weetah.

"Only two winters to come and go and she will he his," said Giluram morosely.

"In time you will be able to buy her from him," replied Red Kangaroo.

"Yes," answered Giluram savagely, "in a long time—and then hunt for the old dingo all the rest of my life."

"All the rest of *his* life," corrected Red Kangaroo.

They strode on in silence, until Giluram

said miserably, "I thought—we all thought you were going to do something for us, Red Kangaroo. But the chief and his council remain still unfair with the laws."

"None of you would stand beside me," answered Red Kangaroo shortly. "Good job, too, else I should have been food for the fishes before now."

Giluram glanced at him in surprise, but his grim face invited no question.

Suddenly wild, defiant yells ringing through the bush were answered away to the right and left. Red Kangaroo swiftly gathered his handful together, certain this was to be his one big, and last fight. The timber was ringing to the howls of many men.

A sheet of flame, then billowing smoke ahead, and in moments fire came crackling towards them, swiftly fanned into fury by a strong wind. Their enemies had set the bush afire. A mob of kangaroos bounded past in terrified leaps, birds sped agitatedly before the smoke and cinders.

Red Kangaroo's men turned and raced back a mile to plunge into a creek. The fire roared over them. But no enemies followed. They had retired under cover of the fire, believing the whole strength of the Gunn-e-darr tribe were coming against them. If they had only know how few that number really was! Tracks on the blackened earth proved them to be a combined party of Narrabri, Baan Baa, and Boggabri men.

For the next few weeks Red Kangaroo's young warriors patrolled their northern boundary with ceaseless vigilance, as away to the south the boundary was being patrolled against the Quirindi men. As to what safeguards Jerrabri was taking against the Goonoo Goonoo and Bundarra, the patrols did not know.

To such straits now was the Gunn-e-darr tribe reduced, with enemies apparently about to fall upon them from all sides. Had those enemies known the real strength of the Gunn-e-darr men at that time this story would never have been written. For the tribe would have been hunted and wiped out, or its remnants scattered and absorbed until perhaps not even the name in legend remained—a fate that has befallen many and many a tribe and nation since the Dawn of Man began.

Red Kangaroo's border look-out was a bold hilltop from which he could signal back to the main tribal look-outs. As the days passed without bad news from their rear or sign of danger from the north his scouts began to relax, and Red Kangaroo on his hilltop, watching more or less casually now for smoke signals, began thinking again.

This sudden danger had apparently passed. Their enemies seemed to have been acting but half-heartedly and—independently. But had they co-operated those four different enemies would have attacked from different directions at once. He drew a deep, fearful breath. Such an attack must have meant the end of his tribe. What an escape! But next time—!

He gazed out over hill and plain, gleam of water amongst the dense dark lines of river trees, the ramparts of distant ranges, all bathed in sunlight from a deep blue sky. How he loved this, his tribal land!

It was lost—if something were not

quickly done. The weakened tribe was dwindling—the young men not marrying, the loss by raids and in expeditions for vengeance. In this season alone how many able-bodied men had fallen in battle, or by accident or "mysterious causes"? His face was furrowed with concern as he began to count them and compare their replacement by children. And then there was the loss of stolen women and children!

No wonder the once powerful Gunn-e-darr Tribe had dwindled so alarmingly during the lifetime of its recent chiefs and elders. So very few in the tribe realized it. The tribe would do nothing. Could he, one man, barely more than a lad, do what the tribe was afraid to do? There must be some way, otherwise surely the witchdoctor would have allowed the elders to get rid of him as a nuisance to their peace.

He thought and thought, almost in despair. Only one little gleam of light began steadily to grow. If there was anything that could be done, then he must do it alone. Then suddenly his face lit up. At last he believed he could see the track ahead—the track he must follow to save the tribe.

# CHAPTER XIV
## THE CORD

As the campfire embers slowly dimmed the children of the wild huddled in sleep, wrapped in the slumbrous blanket of night. Yet not all things slept. Furtive things crept out in the living silence—a stealthy sound, a rustling in the grass. Somewhere glowed eyes of molten gold. Flash of green eyes, too—eyes that vanished. Deep, hoarse croak of the mopoke, lingering howl of a dingo in the hills, mournful call of the curlew, swish of the night hawk's wings. And other things were prowling in the breathless watchfulness of the night. Other things that did not sleep, the Spirits of the Night.

Dread thought! Should a human be forced to walk by night he might even meet Wunda, the white-skinned spirit.[1]

> [1] Many years later, when white men came to Australia, the advancing overlanders were called "Wunda", and were believed to be Wunda spirits.

Most spirits were good, but some were bad—very bad. Others again took no interest, or but a mildly passing interest in humans. Still others were mischievous imps, such as those who delighted in carrying tales to the ears of witchdoctors, or in whispering trouble into the ears of friend and foe, man and wife.

Brave with a fearful bravery were any warriors who ventured forth by night, clinging close together, swiftly urged by lust or necessity or the maddening thirst for vengeance—or fleeing, because Death raced at their heels. And the warrior who would travel *alone* by night, unless to escape certain death, was looked upon with awe as imbued with a bravery past understanding.

Red Kangaroo was wondering if he possessed this courage as he worked secretly while others slept. He was making twine of human hair and possum fur—thin, cord-like twine, such as was used for snaring the strongest of birds. Red Kangaroo was planning to snare something—but not birds.

He had prepared a number of long,

supple strings of fur or hair, and they were spread out neatly to hand as he squatted on his possum rug, intently working by touch and the light from the dull glow of coals. Sitting cross-legged he took two strings of hair and one of fur and laid the ends together on his thigh. Then, pressing with the warm palm of his hand, he began rolling them along his thigh. With each expert roll of the palm he twirled the strings against his leg, twisting the three strands into one. The result was a thin twine, very strong, springy and elastic. As he tested it a smile of satisfaction made his face very boyish.

The next night the real work commenced. Very serious was he, very secretive as he bent over his task in his gunyah when all the camp slept. He took long white threads of kangaroo sinew, which, skilfully treated, were almost unbreakable and felt like finest silk. These he laid lengthways, side by side, across his possum-skin rug. Alternately between them he placed, in equal lengths, the twine of fur and hair. Then he laid all the ends upon his thigh and carefully began to twist them together into the one cord. He was very particular. A long job, but time did not matter, it was the finished work that would count. Slowly the white of the pliable sinews began to merge with the blue-grey of fur and the black of hair into one thin cord, an extremely strong, pliable, springy cord of an ominous finish and neatness. As one end began to form and grow longer it seemed to live and writhe under the warmth of his hand and thigh as slowly, very carefully now, with rolling pressure he twisted the strands.

The night came when this cord was completed, except for the two ends. With one end he now took especial care, making it into a tiny loop, as a sailor might splice an eyelet in the end of a rope. The other end he finished off into what a sailor would call a "Turk's head". Then he squeezed the Turk's head through the loop.

He now had a running noose—and such an elastic, slinky, dangerous little noose! Smiling his delight, he began to splice the Turk's head end of the cord round a grooved stick six inches long. This formed the handle; the other end was the running noose. He tested the finished work on the possum rug. With but a touch on the handle the noose seemed to run together.

With a half-smile he tried it round his own neck. The thin, pliant cord seemed to caress his strong young neck, until he gently pulled back on the handle. The noose bit viciously into his neck; if he pulled harder he knew he would feel it like a burning wire choking out his life. Now he could understand how, if this noose were slipped in earnest round his neck, a man could never escape.

He eased the cord and the noose fell away as if by itself. It was a perfect job—just the slightest pull and the cord gripped the neck and bit into the throat, slightly relax the cord and the pressure immediately eased.

Red Kangaroo held the noose in his hands as a girl might hold a prized necklace. He was very proud of this "necklace"; he had won the materials and made it himself, and not a soul knew about it. He really had made a "strangling cord".

The tribe believed that only old Muga

Tulle, the expert, had the skill to make such cords. Muga Tulle means "blind and deaf and tongue-tied". He seemed a very quiet man, but he was none of these three—except when it came to anything at all connected with a strangling cord. Red Kangaroo with the other lads had often watched the old craftsman at work fashioning cords, which were eagerly sought after, but of course had never seen him making a strangling cord. They did not even know about it.

But recently Red Kangaroo had learnt of its existence and discovered the secret of its making by spying upon the old cord-maker at work. And now he had made for himself a cord as good as any old Muga Tulle could make. And not a soul knew about it. No one must. What he was going to do he must do alone, and no one must know a thing about it until it was done. Thus no bad trouble could be caused to the tribe, or to anyone in the tribe, over what he was about to do. If he succeeded, then it would be all for the good of the tribe; if he failed, then it was only he who would suffer.

One night when all were asleep he crept out of his gunyah, glanced up at the dark sky—smelling. Yes, he could smell rain—it would rain before dawn, he felt certain.

He crept back into the gunyah and began thoroughly massaging refined animal and emu oil into his body to keep away rain and cold and to make his limbs slippery in the hands of an antagonist. And now his face was grim, though quiet excitement was there also.

Next morning Red Kangaroo was missing.

## CHAPTER XV

## HE TREADS ALONE IN ENEMY COUNTRY

Giluram found that Red Kangaroo's hunting weaports were in his gunyah, but his war weapons were missing. This looked ominous. The people were surprised also because a new moon was due and all were busy piling up a great heap of wood to keep fires brightly burning round the corroboree ring at the ceremonial dances to welcome in the new moon. And now Red Kangaroo's cheery laugh, his willing help, would be missed. For he could carry a large pine log that no warrior in camp could stagger under, and he loved dancing, he could dance the longest and was the most active of them all. It must be something very important that had taken him away from camp when he would miss the log-carrying. But of course he would not miss the dances!

He did miss the dances.

Seven moon days came and went and there was no sign of Red Kangaroo. The camp grew seriously alarmed. At first there had been no misgiving. The law was that a man could steal away for three nights and days and none could know his business unless he wished it. But no more than five men at any one time could thus vanish from camp. Furthermore, if a man were to be away more than three days, then on the fourth day there must be some friend in camp who could explain the reason why.

But there was no man to explain Red Kangaroo's overdue absence, not even the anxious Giluram. It was plain to see, too, that his uncle Tulumi and his friend Burradella were very worried. So was old Bungadoon, who with the warrior Boobuk was roaming all over the bush searching for trace of Red Kangaroo. After the third day many had decided to track him, only to remember that it had rained the night he disappeared. Throughout all the wide bush there came no sight, no sign, no tidings of Red Kangaroo.

After seven moon days had passed by some suggested that prowling raiders, or woman-stealers must have been spying round the camp. They had ambushed Red Kangaroo and thrown his body into the river. The rain had washed out all tracks.

Few agreed with this theory. For Red Kangaroo was too alert, too strong and quick, too deadly with his weapons; he would put up such a desperately fierce fight even if surprised that he would probably get away, even though badly wounded. At least he would kill one or more of the raiders before being killed himself, and thus signs of the fight would be left for all to see. But there was no sign of a struggle anywhere.

So now others began to murmur in secret, or in places where no one could creep up and hear. And these believed that this must be the work of the chief and the elders. They had used the strangling cord on Red Kangaroo and thrown his body into the river—through jealousy, because Jerrabri knew well that the warrior lad would one day be chosen as a warrior chief to lead the tribe in raids and war, and through hatred because he saw through the elders' abuse of the laws.

The groups huddled round the campfires at night talked in low tones now; even the children were quiet, whispering together. Silence, or glum looks, or sudden fierce frowns, were now common amongst the huntsmen during the daily hunts. As a storm gathers over the mountains, so a storm was fast gathering over the tribe.

Glowering too were the chief and the elders as they went amongst the people seeking, even demanding news, or sat frowning round their own fires. Angrily they questioned Tulumi and Burradella and the defiant Bungadoon and Boobuk and Giluram, and all the warriors and huntsmen known to be friendly to Red Kangaroo.

Fiercely the chief promised harsh punishment to Red Kangaroo when he did return for breaking the law of the tribe. But another day, another, other days continued to go by and Red Kangaroo did not return.

The whisperings now grew to almost outright accusations against Jerrabri and the elders, denied just as fiercely by their friends, until the whole camp was on the point of taking sides. Anything in a moment might start that sudden, uncontrollable rage that would set half the tribe at the throats of the other half. It was the very state of affairs that Burradella and his friends had feared Red Kangaroo might cause, and of which they had warned him. And now it had come to pass—how surprised he would have been had he known!

Burradella was as worried and

bewildered as anyone else. He did not know what had been in the young man's mind, nor did he know what had happened to him. And he saw himself on any day now suddenly taking part in a fight against the chief and the elders—the worst thing for the tribe that could happen. But he felt himself boiling with rage at the thought of what might have befallen Red Kangaroo. If only he knew whether the lad had really been put out of the way by the elders!

But Red Kangaroo had not been assassinated. When he had crept out from the sleeping camp he walked steadily west through the remainder of that night, laughing to himself when steady rain began to fall before dawn. That rain would wash out all tracks. Not a soul now could even guess that Red Kangaroo had travelled west towards Rocky Glen, bound for the Warrumbungle Ranges and the lands of their powerful Coonabarabran enemies. He simply would have vanished. He smiled to himself at the surprise, the questions, the puzzlement and doubt when day after day would pass and he did not return. He pressed on as the dark bush slowly lightened to a dull grey of rain-drenched trees and grasses and sodden earth. This cold, drenching rain would keep both friends and enemies under shelter while he travelled fast and far.

When he crossed the boundary of his tribal lands weapons and body were ready for instant use, a grim, pleased alertness to his face as he strode effortlessly on. He now trod the land of his enemies. To be seen would mean a fight for life, and should his tracks be picked up he would be hunted like a wild animal.

As he entered the foothills of the Warrumbungles he sought broken country. Not only is it easier for a man to "lose" his tracks in rough country; there also will be fewer enemies roaming there to spy them. For the aboriginal values his wonderful feet and does not hunt on rough country should game be plentiful elsewhere. Red Kangaroo was wary as he walked, for a badly cut or staked foot must slow him down and lead to his death if pursued. With the dawn of each morning he sought a cave in which to hide and sleep—"with one eye open", waking every now and then to cautiously spy out over the land. There are caves throughout the Warrumbungles for those who have the bush sense to seek and find.

The foothills soon brought him right up into the big old Warrumbungles, from the heights of which again and again he spied away out over the low country the rolling smoke of hunting fires or the lazy wisps from cooking fires of numerous small, well-scattered camps of the Coonabarabran tribe. It gave him a thrill every time he gazed out over the bush to see such smoke and easily guess what his enemies away out there were doing—hunting or lazing along on walkabout, or "bush cooking" a mid-sun meal, or smoking out game, or gathered together in a large, favourite camp. He wondered at how numerous these Coonabarabran people must be. As he travelled farther along the range he observed that the large camps were many miles apart, with small hunting camps in between, while every here and there strolled a small or a family party who hunted by day and by night camped almost within the foothills.

Yes, he slept with one eye open by day, and at night he had eyes in the back of his head. And ears and every sense were alert for the dreaded sound or sign of tribesmen dogging his tracks—tracks he made so difficult to follow. On the third day he grew grimly confident. He was far up in the mountains, gazing down to where smooth, lightly timbered slopes led away down to the low country. And he saw that in this part of the range, at least in daylight, he would see a man coming up the clear mountain slopes long before he could reach him.

He gazed back over the way he had come, towards the misty landmarks of his own beloved country. And he knew that now, should his presence be discerned, he could make back swiftly and straight as the crow could fly for his own tribal sanctuary. He grew almost confident that, even though the enemy might be all around him he would slip through and be away, even though they came loping along his tracks. That was, if he were not burdened—with the burden he sought. Ah, then discovery would mean peril indeed!

Thus he carried on, alert against enemies—swift, too, in the hunt. For he must eat, and sleep by day to keep endurance and strength. The cooking was simple; he could hide the smoke of a fire within a cave. He learnt that here and there within the belly of these big old mountains was a cave, the size of which both frightened and amazed him. Within the yawning mouth of one such, as he stared back into its mysterious darkness, he wondered if it might not be large enough to shelter every man, woman, and child of the Gunn-e-darr tribe—even more.

At sundown he would begin to come down a mountain spur, walking swiftly as evening darkness set in. When his friend the young moon rose to shed its soft light over the bush he would be well out in the low country, cautiously scouting round one of the camps he had noticed by day. While the moon lasted he would spy upon the sleeping camp, taking care to leave no tracks, taking particular care to keep well aside from patches of country where the women would be likely to hunt—he dared not leave the faintest of tracks there.

Thus throughout the ghostly moonlight nights he spied upon camp after camp, calculating the family numbers by the few bark or grass gunyahs, or by the suggestion of sleeping forms round the dull embers of the fires. Before daylight he would be swiftly climbing back up a spur of the range to seek yet another hide-out from which to locate yet another camp, alert for wallaroo or carpet snake or possum for food—after which he would be ready for sleep.

He had not found what he sought. He became anxious, for he knew that with the passing of each day the danger of discovery rapidly increased. So when the moon grew bigger and gave better and longer light he left the high mountains and came right down into the forest lands that here and there were dotted with areas of heavy scrub.

Day by day, in such a patch of scrub, he would hide, eat, and sleep, to emerge with the owls and moon at night.

# CHAPTER XVI
## THE MENACE

Thus daily from one sheltering scrub after another he watched enemy warriors stroll away for the hunt, then parties of women and children dawdle away with their dilly-bags and digging sticks to the wide spaces of the bush. The people in the main camps here were much more numerous than in the family-group hunting camps back towards the foothills. He tingled every time he watched the heavy-browed, black-bearded warriors pick up their weapons and lovingly balance them a moment before casually striding away to their day's hunting. He chuckled at the thought of how their careless attitude would change if they could suddenly know what big game was spying on them from this tangled scrub close by. What amazement! Then what an exultant howl of the pack! How they would come at him! With what savage exultation they would hunt him and hurl those long, cruelly barbed spears deep within his body, how they would race to the kill to club him to death—if they could.

If they could! He shivered. For almost every man fears death. If discovered now his case would be hopeless, for he was well away from the mountains that offered shelter to a hunted man. Here in the open bush country a few cooees and smoke signals would immediately arouse the tribesmen near and far from all around him. Even if he were not quickly killed he would at last be run to death like an exhausted dingo.

Yes, if he were discovered now he would never see his beloved tribal lands again, never again his uncle Tulumi, nor Burradella, nor old Bungadoon, nor Giluram, nor old Mullionkale the playmaker, nor any of the tribe—not even the chief, Jerrabri, and the elders.

Grimly, choosing the ground on which he would leave the faintest of tracks, if any, he carried on his search, only to find the women's parties well guarded, the older women alert. Peering from cover he would see girls and young women starting out with the children, the older women scattered among them, all carrying their fish-traps and dilly-bags and digging sticks, the old women now and then scolding them well together. He would grin impishly at thought of the panic he would cause if they only knew what was watching them. Then would come frowning remembrance of how at times he had spoken hotly against the laxity of the women and guards of his own tribe. He now grudgingly realized that the system was much more efficient than he had believed. He saw now that an enemy woman-stealer who thought that all he had to do to steal a woman from the Gunn-e-darr tribe was to sneak into its territory, hide by a camp, pounce out upon his woman and hurry her away, had another think coming. It might, and occasionally did, happen that way, but that would be the woman-stealer's lucky day.

The days slowly passed and with all his prowling he had not yet succeeded in his task. His presence somewhere in this enemy's territory simply *must* be discovered, even by chance, at any time now.

One night he was creeping down river in the dark, for the moon would not rise now until very late. He was keen to spy upon a new camp that by day he had located from the hills, and, above all, to find a place in which to hide throughout the next day. The night was chilly and eerily still, the solemn croak of a mopoke came hoarsely from a river gum. Presently the dense tall reeds of a large creek that emptied into the river barred his way. He stood there black as the night, his eyes staring appreciatively at the darkness of the heavily foliaged creek where it merged back into the bush. He waded down into the creek and up along it some little distance, delighted at the thickness and height of the reeds, for they stood his own height, six feet and over. This would be an ideal hiding-place. No chance of his being seen within this forest of reeds. And as he had waded he had left no tracks that a hunting party might cut by chance. He decided to wade down river farther now in the hope of hearing song or corroboree from some distant camp.

He turned back towards the creek

mouth and a whir of nesting ducks rose at his knees, dashing him with spray and swishing reeds. He stepped out of the reeds and stood staring. Barely a quarter of a mile down river gleamed the fires of a large camp. And now there came sweetly drifting along river the click of kylies, the drumming of the women, the chanting lilt of a hunting song.

In delight he began to wade down river. He would spy their numbers by the light of the corroboree fires, then return to the reedy creek before daylight, leaving no betraying tracks. From the creek he could spy all movement of this camp in daylight. The moon was rising now, by its growing light he saw that this reedy creek indeed was an ideal hiding-place and that its reeds and bulrushes extended far back into the bush. He began wading down river, a shadow in moonlight, drifting ever nearer those gleaming fires that now plainly illumined the figures of dancing men. Presently he could see the women as they squatted there, drumming their thighs while chanting the song, could hear and see numerous children.

Next morning after daylight he watched from the reeds as the first smokes began lazily coiling up from the camp. But it was full daylight before the camp was really astir. He judged it to be a temporary camp recently formed, for the gunyahs were thrown up carelessly, while the fires showed only small heaps of ashes. Presently eight warriors in pairs picked up their hunting weapons and waded across the river, bound for a day's kangaroo hunt. He could also see two able-bodied warriors who were apparently remaining as camp guard, but—and this made him rather uneasy—could see no older men. The lubras were yabbering some tasty gossip, but presently a shrill-voiced old woman spurred them into action. The young women picked up their dilly-bags and laughingly came riverwards, raced there by whooping children. Some women remained in camp, but about thirty, with numerous children, came wading through the shallows upstream. Red Kangaroo watched gleefully until suddenly he thought, "What if they are making for this reedy creek? It is alive with nesting ducks!"

The girls dallied in the river, laughing and shouting, splashing in the shallows until the older women took charge and scolded them on to work, to netting the pot-holes and spearing fish in the shallows. Slowly they came on, wading up river, gradually drawing closer. Now Red Kangaroo's heart began to beat fast indeed.

Bringing up the rear of the merry party were two girls barely developed into young womanhood, and these two gradually seemed to be falling just a little bit behind. Then his heart began to thump; he grew certain those two impish girls were deliberately edging across towards the reedy side of the river bank, *his* side, just a little way down the river bank towards where the reeds of *his* creek spilled out on to the river!

Breathing deeply, with an unholy gleam in his eyes, he crouched there watching, as many and many a primitive man has waited and watched and hoped since the dawn of time. Yes! Their swiftly disguised glances towards their friends wading ever farther ahead, their chuckling asides to one another while they pretended to be so busily seeking mussels—yes, stealthily now they were edging aside towards the reeds! Each carried a bark-plaited bag slung across her shoulders and into this now and then she would throw a mussel dug from the river. They were deliberately dawdling behind the party, which was now spread out across the shallows barely fifty yards below the mouth of the reedy creek. "Will the old women take the party straight on up the river," wondered Red Kangaroo anxiously, "or will they shepherd them into the mouth of this creek? More likely they will divide the party—some may turn off and come egg-gathering up this creek while the others will carry on hunting up river."

Then his heart bounded as the two girls, with one quick glance upstream leapt aside towards the reeds and vanished. They were hiding now, blissfully unaware of the menace lurking in the reeds.

They were within yards of him—his muscles grew taut—ah, what hard luck! It seemed that the old women were about to turn the party aside into the reedy creek. Then, at an excited shout, they all glanced upstream where a boy with a well-aimed spear had transfixed a big fish in a rock-hole. The yelling boys and girls began to jump in splashing leaps up to him to view the catch; other boys eager to spear an even bigger fish splashed on farther ahead; the women followed shouting encouragement with the old lubras hurrying behind, shrilly shouting to all to keep place in the line and not let so many fish escape back past them. And thus they all passed by the creek mouth and continued toiling on up river. And Red Kangaroo was crouching there with the light of the hunter glaring from his eyes, teeth gleaming in a hungry grin, his big body crouching like a panther tensely eager to spring.

# CHAPTER XVII
## WOMAN AND THE CLUB

Cautiously he peered out over the reeds down river towards the camp. A few old women were moving about, the two warriors were now sprawled under a shady tree. No sign of any of the hunters. Obviously these people did not dream of danger.

He crouched low as with a gentle splashing of feet and a rustle of reed tops the two girls waded past, an impish smile on each fresh young face. They kept wading on up the creek; he followed noiselessly, in a trembling delight. Presently he frowned, for not once did they stop to tread the bottom in search of mussel shells.

"This looks as if they are going to meet someone waiting for them in the reeds—two young men?" he thought to himself. His sinewy hand gripped his war wommera. There would be sudden, sharp trouble for two young men should his suspicion prove correct.

The girls hurried on up the creek without a word, then waded to a bank and climbed up, peering out among the tree-trunks. Then came peals of laughter and an exultant cry.

"They haven't even missed us yet! There they go, waddling up river like old tortoises! What a yabber there'll be when they find we've gone!"

"Old Waterhen will screech her teeth out," said the other girl, laughing, "and we'll hear that old crane Bobadilla cackling miles away."

Red Kangaroo, standing in the reeds with his head almost on a level with their heels, grinned up at the two shapely young bodies so tantalizingly close, their velvety, chocolate-brown skin so cool-looking in the shade of the creek. One had a mop of wavy hair, the other's was straight. He could barely resist the temptation to thrust up his arms, grip those smooth ankles, and jerk both girls into the water at his feet.

He dared not. Should he miss, should one snatch at a branch just long enough for her to scream, it would bring the whole pack down upon him. The creek just here must be close to a bend in the river, for the girls could obviously see the women and children still wading up river, and a scream would be heard. If there had been only one he would have snatched her down with delight. But two agile young bodies, slippery as eels—- !

"Don't the old waterhens look funny when they bend?" giggled the girl with the wavy hair.

"Just look at old Wulla," said the other, "groping down for that mussel! She looks like a skinny old crane burying its head in the mud with all its tail feathers fallen out."

"Look at old Nundal grabbing for a yabby!" said her friend. "She's ribbed like a poor goanna in drought time."

Red Kangaroo, staring up, could barely hold his laughter. Certainly the well-formed ribs and plump flesh of the two innocents just above his hungry eyes left nothing to be desired.

"What if we go up to the big rock where we caught so many fish last time we slipped away?" suggested one.

"Let's!" agreed her mate. "Won't our

mothers be angry with us when the crowd of them run cackling back to camp with news that we've gone astray again! But there'll be only the usual grumbles when they see all the fish and duck-eggs we'll bring home."

"Yes, and the guzzling men are not going to snatch the pick of them, either," said her mate determinedly.

"Not this time, the guzzling crows! Aren't men just the last things left in the bush? They think they are mighty as mountains, but all they are good for is skiting and guzzling and snoring. Come on, let's go up to the big rock and forget them."

They almost jumped on the deflated Red Kangaroo when they turned and leapt down the bank. With a second to spare he ducked down beside the bank as they leapt over him amongst the reeds.

Laughing and joking, they now took their time wading up the creek, and as the reeds began to thin out Red Kangaroo, cautiously following, grew hotly eager to lay his hands upon these two attractive girls, as desirable as any he had ever seen.

And soon they would be at his mercy. It was obvious now they were *not* going to meet anyone else. He grinned maliciously. He would teach them something more about men. They were wading in just the direction he would have chosen. Stealthily he followed, seeking a chance to pounce.

It did not come for quite a time, and he was growing savage when the big rock loomed up amongst the timber ahead. He grinned with wicked delight, for he recognized that high rock jutting across the creek beside the dense patch of scrub growing right down to the creek bank here. For only two mornings ago he had drunk water there, and enjoyed a meal of duck-eggs from a nest amongst the reeds. He knew that scrub, for he had hidden there, and he knew more, that in the depths of that scrub there was a handy little cave. He had found it when chasing a carpet snake for a meal; the snake had led him right to the cave.

Now he realized that the river must take a great bend. Two days ago when he had been drinking by the rock he did not know that this reedy creek ran down to the river only a mile away—and he had not dreamed that a large camp was so close by. But now he knew that the dense scrub ahead of him pointed the way to the foothills. And the Warrumbungles—and home!

Those girls were now at his mercy—if he could only control himself a while longer. Searchers would take a long time to trace them here, and longer yet to trace them through that gloomy scrub. If only his good fortune would hold but a very few days, even hours longer, he would get clear away!

With tigerish eyes he crouched amongst the reeds, wishing these two joking, irritating girls would separate, if only for a moment.

Near the big rock they expertly set a fish-net in a rock hole clear as crystal. Then, chattering gaily, they slipped back into the reeds again in search of duck-eggs.

"We'll roast the first nest and eat them ourselves," laughed the straight-haired one.

"Yes, we'll fill our own bellies first, for

when we get back to camp they might be mean enough to take all the eggs as punishment for us slipping away."

For quite a time they searched almost side by side, then edged a little apart, peering amongst the reeds for nests, happily ignorant of the gleaming eyes following their every movement. Had one turned abruptly she must have spied that hungry face glaring from the reeds, but they never dreamt of the stealthy hunter so close behind.

One bent down and cried, "Oh, I've found such a lovely nest! Come quick and see!"

"So have I!" called her mate. "It's just full of fresh eggs. Come and see mine!"

He waited only a moment longer as the girls bent low in the reeds, now separated from one another, each calling to the other as she began putting the eggs one by one into her dilly-bag. Gripping his nulla, he stepped towards the nearer girl and gazed down at the lithe form reaching into the nest for the eggs. Lifting his club, he brought it smartly down with just the right force upon that thick mop of hair. She flopped down with her face in the nest, the cracked yellow of an egg welling from under her mouth. Instantly he took a wooden gag from his hair, pulled back her head, gripped it betwen her knees as he forced open the mouth, and slipped in the gag so as not to cut her tongue, swiftly knotting the cords of the gag round her neck. Bending, he whipped a thong from his belt and lashed her wrists behind her, dumping her then so that her head could not fall back into the water. It was done in a few moments and in almost complete silence. He stood up, peered out for the other girl, and stepped tigerishly forward.

"Where are you, Nareen?" she called as she stood up, having put the last egg in her bag. She turned round to look for her friend. He pulled the reeds well round him and waited. But she called, "Oh, here is the best nest of all!" and again dropped to her knees.

The reeds around her parted as Red Kangaroo towered over her with upraised club. A low, dull thud, and she fell forward into the water. With the same speed and deftness he gagged her and bound her wrists and ankles, then carried her out to the big rock. He returned for the second girl, who lay where she had dropped in an uncomfortable attitude, showing no sign of regaining consciousness yet. Swiftly he bound her ankles, then slung her over his shoulder, snatched his weapons, climbed up the big rock, which would leave no tracks, and vanished into the scrub. Wriggling like an eel with his burden so that no vine or bush would be displaced to betray his passing, he carried her deep into the gloomy scrub to the cave, then laid her carefully down. Her eyelids flickered; she stared up into his wolfish eyes. He grinned with a flash of teeth, made sure the thongs were secure, then hurried back for the other girl. She lay quietly in the mud where he had left her and, slinging her up on his shoulder, he carried her back to the cave.

It was plain that the first girl had now recovered, for she had rolled herself right out of the cave. She stared up from terrified eyes as he paused astride her a moment with her helpless friend draped over his shoulder. He gave her a fiendish grin as he stepped over her and carried the second girl deep into the cave. Stretching her out, he made sure all the thongs were secure, then returned to the first girl, chuckling as he saw she had rolled several feet farther into the scrub at the cave mouth. Grabbing a handful of her hair he jerked her head up and glared down at her as he snarled softly, "So, Nareen!"

He brought the flat of his hand with a smack across her ear that must have felt like a thunderbolt, then dropped her head to the ground. Panting wildly, she tried to spit at him. He lifted her head again and smacked her other ear. Her toes twitched, but still she tried to spit. Well pleased, he carried her back into the cave and threw her roughly down beside her still unconscious mate. With a grin that plainly said, "You won't roll far!" he stepped from the cave and swiftly through the scrub back to the creek. Very carefully he secured the girls' dilly-bags with the duck-eggs and other small possessions and took the fish-net up from the rock-hole, grinning when he saw that the net now contained four quite decent-sized fish. He placed everything on the big rock, then waded back in the creep to wipe out all possible traces of all three of them amongst the reeds. It was easy enough. All that needed to be done was to hide the robbed nests securely under water and straighten the few resilient reeds forced aside where the girls fell. They had almost straightened up of their own accord. Taking a careful glance round, he wiped out the last few traces about the big rock, then stepped back into the scrub.

At the cave he found that both girls, fully conscious, had rolled out of the cave mouth and even tried to wriggle into the vine-entangled scrub. Nareen stared up in defiant fear, but the other glared up with flashing eyes. He grinned, put his big foot straight across her forehead, nose, and chin. He pressed, and as her nose flattened he laughed down at the hate in her eyes. Her chest began to heave urgently for breath. He felt the twitching lips, could hear the gurgling, could feel what those sharp, strong teeth would do even to his tough foot were it not for that hateful hardwood gag. When she was choking for breath he removed his foot, grinned down at her, then casually gave Nareen a kick in the ribs.

Squatting down, he unrolled his possum-skin rug, took out his reserve of cooked meat, and divided it into three portions, one to eat now, one for his mid-sun meal, the rest to carry him on. For he must move swiftly and far now. And he must move soon. But he still must keep himself under control, must act only at the right times, then surely and definitely. For if he made a false step now his sullenly obstructing women would certainly bring disaster upon him.

And vengeance would come dogging his footsteps soon enough.

# CHAPTER XVIII
## THE MASTER

Tightly he wrapped up the remainder of the cooked food, fastened it neatly with a thong, and placed it beside Nareen's dilly-bag loaded with its duck-eggs. Beside that again he placed her fellow-captive's dilly-bag the net and fish, and his mid-sun supply of cooked meat. Then, laying one of his boomerangs on the dilly-bag, he sat down and proceeded to eat, steadily and enjoyably, now and then grinning at the girls sprawled at his feet. They glared up from spiteful eyes. Bits of dried grass were dribbling from the corner of Nareen's mouth, wedged in there as she had rolled over and over from out of the cave. She could not spit the rubbish out because of the gag. He reached over with his big toe and brushed the ends of the grass, chuckling as she tried to bite through the gag to fasten on his toe at this added irritation. He finished his meal, licked his lips, then took a long drink from his skin water-bag. He offered it to the distended lips of each girl in turn. They glared like tiger-cats.

"Very well." He grinned. "You will not drink with me. But you will at sundown. I can promise you a thirst by then!" He reached down and, with each hand seizing a mop of hair, jerked the girls to a sitting position.

"Now!" he growled. "You are to be my wives. As you see by my cicatrizes I am a warrior of the Gunn-e-darr, and a good warrior, too! I do more than skite and guzzle and snore! Learn that I am a good warrior, as you are going to be two good wives! You will run in front of me all the way to our main camp of Gunn-e-darr. Now, Nareen, what is your friend's name?"

Nareen scowled viciously. Meat-ants were beginning to bite her; the nipping little pests had been attracted by scent of the cooked meat.

"Very well!" grunted Red Kangaroo, and reached a hand to his hair.

When he brought out the cord, though it was neatly wound into a tiny roll, their eyes widened in instant apprehension. So this savage thief really meant to steal them from the very heart of their country and from their people if he could! Their own camp was so very near, but to their ears came no friendly sound, only the whisperings of this gloomy scrub. They watched his grim preparations, his every expression—how their pounding hearts would have welcomed the chiding voices of those "old waterhens" now!

And now his big hands were placing the loop of the cord round Nareen's slim young neck. He sat before her, stretched one arm over her shoulder, the handle of the cord in his clenched fist. As he stretched his arm out the cord instantly fastened round her neck, biting in. Her eyes began to bulge; she tried to bunch the muscles of her neck and hold neck and head down to ease the strangling, but the grim face before her did not change as steadily he held the cord. Her breasts were heaving; she leant back, but his big hand grasped her hair and held her immovably upright before him. Saliva was gurgling round the gag stuck between her jaws as at last her tortured eyes admitted surrender.

He loosed the cord, and undid the gag from her mouth, careful of his fingers against her bite. Her mouth opened wide, she panted in deep, quavering breaths.

"What name?" he demanded, and pointed to her friend.

"Naroo!" she gasped, and her eyes filled with hate.

"Naroo!" He scowled down at the girl. "Nareen and Naroo —those names please me. And now, Naroo, see that you obey me, too!" Lightly he tapped Nareen on the head with his club. "I have taken out your gag now," he snarled, "and you can scream—if you want to. And I will stretch you a bundle of dead meat on the ground!" And she read death in his savage eyes.

He undid the cords from her ankles.

"Stand up!" he ordered.

She sat there, still breathing deeply, her twisted face working back into a stubborn scowl. Again he sat across her legs to hold her unmoving, placed the cord round her neck, tightened it, and slowly increased the pressure, calmly staring into her bulging eyes, gazing down her open, choking throat with detached interest.

When she seemed near her last gasp he allowed the cord to slacken, waited while agonizedly she struggled for breath, then, when her lungs were partly filled, slowly he drew tight the cord again. Not until her tongue had swollen and her eyes were bulging from their sockets did he read final surrender. When he loosened the cord he had to hold her by the hair to prevent her falling back while she moaned for breath—a painful, convulsive struggle. At last, with streaming eyes, she came despairingly to her knees, struggled weakly up, and stood there trembling, panting. Only then did he take the cord from her neck.

"Stand up, Naroo!" he ordered the other.

But she lay there glaring up at him, gritting her sharp white teeth, primitive fury in her eyes. He sat down across her legs, jerked her up by the hair, placed the cord round her neck, slowly tightened it.

She stood it even longer than Nareen had. He allowed her to struggle back to nearly her full breath, then gave her the cord again. He worked slowly and noiselessly, almost gently, as if he had all the time in the world, sitting here in the stillness and gloom of the scrub, just as if no one cared whether the sun ever went down or came up again. Naroo fought against it with all her strength, then with all her cunning. Desperately she tried to defy the cord, the cord that the strongest man cannot beat. She was almost done when he allowed her breathing space again.

She did not know he was admiring the hate in her streaming eyes as she lay panting there, making no attempt to struggle to her knees. Casually he gave her the cord again, while her distorted features fought back at him with the despairing fury of a trapped wildcat.

He gave her the cord yet again, his face expressionless but his heart exulting. "Two good girls! And what a mother of warriors this one will be!"

He gave Naroo the cord five times before she was beaten. Then he had to lift her to her feet and hold her limply to him while slowly, painfully, she panted for breath to stand. Just the silence, chirp of a little bird somewhere deep within the gloom, and Naroo's long, shuddering gasps.

Then he placed her dilly-bag securely across her shoulders, and Nareen's across hers. Next he took a long, flexible hide thong from his belt, rapidly made one end into a running noose, and fitted the noose loosely round Nareen's neck so that the end hung down her back. Should Nareen attempt to run away or tread on a dry stick to make a noise, or kick one stone against another to attract the attention of passing enemies, then one savage, downward jerk of the cord would bring her half paralysed to her knees. He left the strangling cord hanging from Naroo's neck. But it was very unlikely, now that both girls had accepted their master's load to carry, that they would attempt to run away. It would be so hopeless, anyway—unless there came some chance hope of a rescue.

Red Kangaroo pointed steadily ahead of Naroo with his wommera. She took the direction with her eyes.

"Hurry on ahead of me!" he ordered.

Falteringly both girls turned round,

gazing back through the gloomy scrub in the direction of their camp. He let them be for a moment as slowly the tears welled and streamed from their eyes. This was farewell. They knew that if this devil proved as good a man as he had so far then they would never see their beloved tribal lands again.

Slowly Nareen turned, started off in the direction of the wommera. Naroo followed her. They glided like phantoms among the vines, even though their arms were tied behind them. Every now and then Red Kangaroo urged them on with a growl. Too well he knew that presently the best trackers of their tribe would be seeking them, the women, who since babyhood had been trained to the faintest tracks, the almost invisible signs that betray the presence of even the very small things of the air, earth, bush, and water. Those trackers of various insects, of beetles and frogs, of birds, of all manner of reptiles, of anything that can crawl wriggle, hop, or walk in bushland or waterland—these would be the first set to find the tracks.

He urged the girls on. Yes, sooner or later the women would find signs in the reedy creek. And then—Death would be stalking at his heels, with outraged warriors mad to run him to earth, to hack out his kidney-fat and wolf it before his glazing eyes.

They broke through the scrub into glorious daylight, to the "Cark! Cark!" of crows, the screech of parrots dining on honeyed tree blossoms, the whispering of a breeze among the forest branches, the scent of grasses luxuriating in the fresh earth. Spread out before them were the open bushlands to the foothills, and behind these the towering mass of the Warrumbungles.

And here Red Kangaroo insisted upon fastening the gags back into his captives' sullen mouths. Well he knew that, ungagged and with their ankles freed, the girls, if he had the bad luck to run upon some hunting party in this open bushland, would scream the alarm and leap aside and run for it. In such case he would have no time to do anything but fight for his life.

"The faster you travel," he promised grimly, "the sooner then I shall be able to take the gags out for good. Now—trot!"

For a moment they hesitated. He stepped up behind Nareen and lightly jabbed her in the buttock with the cruel point of his war spear. She hissed back at him like a snake. He drew back his arm for a thrust, but with a sob she turned and started to jog-trot. He glared at Naroo, the spear at the ready. She spat at him as she leapt forward and ran behind Nareen. With tears of rage welling from her eyes she ground her teeth into the gag, wishing it were his throat.

Through open, clear forest country they covered a surprising distance with that steady, almost tireless jog-trot of the wild aboriginal. Once Red Kangaroo's ears tingled to a distant cooee. The running girls were listening also, but their spirits dropped as presently answering calls came from yet farther away. That hunting party were moving away from them. Red Kangaroo breathed in heartfelt relief.

Near sundown they were among the foothills, making for a steep little hill, the summit of which stood as a black sentinel of almost perpendicular rock. There was a cave away up there from which, several days before, Red Kangaroo had spied out over a wide area of open bushland. He undid Nareen's arms and helped her up the steep rock-face and into the cave. Then he tied her wrists and ankles again and returned for Naroo. With freed limbs she climbed up like a monkey of her own accord, though attempting to dislodge a stone to fall on his head. He grinned as he dodged and jabbed upward with his spear point. She gave a choking gurgle as she sprang upward, in a blazing fury at his hearty laughter.

When he had them hidden within the cave he gazed out over the country from the entrance. It looked lovely, bathed in late afternoon sunlight. He had completed his job as the hunter; he had snared his prey, but would he be the hunted one now? Carefully he gazed near and far and all around. No sign of pursuit as yet—just a distant hunting call away at the left near where rising smokes showed life in a camp he had spied upon some days before.

He returned into the cave and, taking the gag from Nareen's mouth, said, "I am going to eat and drink. Will you eat and drink if I free your arms? You can light a fire in there and cook the duck-eggs. You will need them soon, for we are going to travel swiftly all through the night. Where we shall rest and eat again I cannot say. If your friends come too swiftly on our tracks I promise you that we shall neither rest nor eat again until we have crossed over into my own tribal lands—and that is far from here. Now, will you eat?"

Sullenly Nareen nodded. He undid the gag, frowning questioningly.

She rolled her eyes, eased her tongue and jaws, swallowed distastefully a few times, then muttered sullenly, "Yes, I'll eat. I'm thirsty, too. I could eat some eggs. I won't scream or call out here if you leave the gag out."

"I'll bash your brains out if you do!" he promised grimly. Then he ungagged Naroo. With a vicious nod she agreed to eat and drink.

He saw to it that they did not waste time. Then he bound their wrists together again, not tightly behind the small of the back this time, but in front, comfortably, though not so loosely that they could suddenly thrust up their hands and jerk the gag from their mouths and yell should they come within screeching distance of some wandering hunting party. The gags, too, he fixed a little more comfortably, not so far back in the jaws that it was difficult to breathe, let alone bite hard. But he fixed each gag expertly, so that as they walked along a girl could not gradually work the stick across her mouth with jaws and teeth so she could bite through the thong should opportunity for escape occur.

They sat there in furious silence as his long, strong fingers put the hardwood gag back over Nareen's tongue into the mouth, fitted it to his satisfaction, lashed the thong round her neck, then pulled the stick this way and that, then a little farther back until he felt the firm grip of the teeth on the stick to his satisfaction. She glared sullenly back into his grim, boyish face as he worked. Naroo glared with the devil-cat in her eyes. Sitting back with a half-smile, the cicatrizes of warriorhood standing out across his big chest, his hands clasped loosely across his knees, he surveyed the finished job with satisfaction. A fat green fly came importantly buzzing into the cave.

"You find it hard to keep your mouths shut?" He grinned. "But you'll have plenty of time to talk—later on, when you are my wives, my two good wives who will hunt and work for me, and bring me sweet honeycomb and cool water when I am lying thirsty in the shade. Yes, the seasons will come and go and come again in our happy lands of the Gunn-e-darr. Yes, you'll both have plenty of time to talk. But when that long time comes, then see you do not talk *too* much!"

Nareen stared. Naroo glared.

# CHAPTER XIX

# RUNAWAYS IN THE NIGIIT

Red Kangaroo fitted the dilly-bags round the girls' shoulders and picked up his weapons. A lizard scuttled away in alarm.

"We keep moving," he growled. "Follow me and climb down."

He undid the thongs on their ankles, keeping a wary eye lest they loose a stone upon his head as they climbed down the steep rock-face. But their attention was fully taken up in saving themselves from a fall, for their wrists were still bound, though loosely.

They set out along the foothills parallel with the big old range, Red Kangaroo's heart singing as he pointed with his wommera away out towards his own country.

"Home!" he growled. "And hasten!"

Travelling swiftly, they had less chance to leave a heavy imprint on softer ground, snap a dead twig, or kick over a pebble here and there.

"You will only stub your toes," he snarled at Naroo as swiftly she tried to overturn a stone in passing, "and if you break your toe I shall thrash you and hurry you all the more. Try that trick just once again and I'll clout you across the head with this nulla—you can make yourself sore all over if you want to!" Savagely then he jabbed Nareen in the buttock with his spear point. She leapt ahead with arched back and a startled gurgle. He laughed maliciously.

"A jab like that for every leaf you drop from that bush you're hiding in your hands. I'll jab your tail so full of holes you won't be able to sit down for a full moon!"

Nareen, her teeth clenching into the gag, dropped the bush and stepped out like a cat on hot bricks. In spite of her tied hands she had surreptitiously snapped off the top of a densely leafed bush, hoping to pinch off the tiny leaves and drop them one by one, leaving a trail that eagle-eyed pursuers could follow almost at the run.

Long shadows from the mountains brought the coolness of evening. Red Kangaroo urged them on until the darkness slowed them down. This rough country was intersected by scrubby creeks and steep gullies, and there was danger now that the girls, handicapped by tied hands, might stumble over a fallen log or slip down a rocky slope and break a leg. This possibility terrified the girls, for each knew that with a broken leg she would be abandoned to the bush and the night. From away up on the range floated the blood-curdling howl of a dingo.

"Watch your step," warned Red Kangaroo, "but if you want to break a leg or stake yourself, then do so. After all, one girl would do me, and remember, I can travel faster and more easily and safely with one than with two. No dawdling! Ah!"

They turned at his exclamation, anxious eyes gleaming.

From far behind them, but away out on the low country, rose a quivering pencil of fire above the tree-tops, climbing swiftly, a crimson finger apparently piercing the sky.

"So your friends have only just found our tracks," he said grimly, "your old waterhens at the big rock away back in the reedy creek—where you two naughty girls slipped away from the old women to find your duck-eggs and—me." He grinned. "I was quite jealous as I followed you up, for I thought you were hurrying to meet young men. But it was only I whom you met, and now your friends wish to meet me, too—your fathers and uncles and brothers and all the young warriors so anxious to cut out my kidney-fat to prove what great warriors they are." Grimly he watched the hope shining in their eyes, limpid black eyes, deep with life. "You would like to see them," he said softly, "bash me to the earth, rip out my kidneys with those sharp stone knives of theirs, snarl over the rich red kidneys and wolf them and rub the fat into their bodies to imbibe my strength and cunning. How brave they will be then—when they have eaten *my* bravery!"

They gazed up at his smiling face, but his eyes were not smiling.

"You must be patient a little while longer," he went on, "for they must await sunrise—plain daylight—before they can read our tracks, if any, within that dark scrub."

They just stared.

"Ah! You see now! I was really cunning after all. Never mind, you will learn a lot more before they catch me. We shall see what a chase we can lead them before you have the pleasure of watching them rip out my kidney-fat. Let us see now," he mused. "That signal fire is calling the warriors to gather now at the big rock. Soon they will be thirsting for my blood, shaking their spears, boasting that they will run me to earth like a hunted dingo!"

They gazed up at him, quiet as little ebony statues in the silence of the night.

"They must camp at the big rock tonight. In the morning the scrub will hold them up for a while; even the women will track us, but very slowly through there. When they come out into the open bushland they will dog our footsteps much faster, and won't need the women any more. Then the foothills will steady them up again. They are rough, these foothills, and since you've felt my spear point a few times you've been quite careful not to leave obvious tracks." He paused, grinning. "Ah well, at daylight the pack will be in pursuit. Of course, we could travel a lot faster down on the low country. But we are *not* going down on the low country."

Their faces fell as this sank in.

"Surely you did not think that I would walk down into the low country into the arms of others of your friends camped to left and ahead of us! We have a fair start," he went on grimly. "By dawn we shall have a long start. But—we have a long way to go. Should they catch up with us then it means the end of me; you may watch them fight over my kidney-fat. But remember this! If you two, my wives, do not travel as fast as you possibly can while I still live, if you do anything to help those coming behind, then it will mean the end of you, too. For I will still take you both with me. You have obeyed me, you are my wives by law as you know, once we have crossed my tribal boundary. I promise you this, if they catch me fairly then you can watch them kill me. But if you do anything to delay me, if you do anything to help them follow more easily or to catch me, then I will kill you both before I turn to fight."

Gazing into that face, they gradually abandoned hope. They would either be his wives truly now, or they would die with him. He drew a deep breath, relaxed, pointed with his wommera into the darkness ahead.

"Travel on!" he growled.

They set out swiftly, silently, the cool breath of the night bathing their bodies, the sighings of the bush a sad lullaby of farewell. Far away out in the darkness to their left quivered up another pencil of light. A big camp out there had received and was answering the fire signal from those back at the reedy creek. Presently still another pencil of light shot up far ahead of them, but again away out in the lowlands.

As they hastened cautiously on they knew that tribesmen and women and children away to their left many miles ahead would now be excitedly grouped round the fires awaiting daylight to spread out and cut them off. Those tribesmen would expect them to be running across the open, level bushlands where the going was much the easiest. They would comb the country for many miles right to the foothills, those ahead spreading out in a long, well-spaced line, then confidently watching and waiting to cut them off. Those now nearest them would seek to cut their tracks in case they had passed by in the night, while those coming from the rocky creek would stick doggedly to their tracks, no matter where they might lead.

He pushed on in secret delight that the two girls were now doing their best, even though only driven by despair. He had liked these two little wild-cats from the first; already he felt himself becoming fiercely fond of them. What wives they would make if only he could get them back to his beloved tribal lands! Oh, and what a triumph when he should reach camp with these two—

A snort, heave, and rush, and they jumped back as an old-man wallaroo bounded agitatedly away to a clatter of stones and breaking sticks.

Red Kangaroo, who had nearly fallen over backwards from shock, laughed boyishly. Nareen and Naroo, after their first gasp of surprise, gurgled with amusement behind the wooden gags. In that moment he would have liked to relieve them of the gags, but up here in this night silence one piercing yell would carry far away over the low bushland, perhaps to expectant ears. They pushed on again, and somehow the tension of distrust on his part, and of hatred and fear on theirs, seemed to have eased.

After midnight, under diamond stars, the earth became silent and cold in the mountains, bitterly cold in the small hours. He knew that if it were not for the gags the girls' teeth would be chattering. They had pushed speedily on since morning now, and they would be growing tired, but it was their feet on these steep, rocky hillsides that he worried about. Neither had been staked or badly cut yet, but he knew that if one should wear her feet too tender she would sooner or later lie down, huddle up, and sullenly suffer death rather than stand up again. That stage was a long way off as yet, but with every mile they hurried on he wished less and less to lose either girl.

Within two hours of daylight he guided them up to a black mass outlined by starlight into castellated rock. He led them to a sapling, put warning fingers to his lips, slipped a long thong over the thongs at their wrists, and lashed them face to face to the sapling. Then he picked up his weapons and vanished among the boulders. Silently he climbed up to the very mouth of a cave and listened. There came no sound of a breath drawn in sleep. With spear in right hand and tomahawk in left he crept noiseless and invisible as a black snake into the pitch-dark cave. Cautiously he probed with the long spear to right and left and ahead, then crawled on again to probe. But there was neither man nor animal in the cave.

In relief he climbed down for the girls and brought them up to the cave. They sat down in the cold blackness with choked sighs of relief. He went out, swiftly pulled a big armful of grass from the long, coarse tufts growing thickly amongst the rocks and spread this out on the cave floor. He undid his possum rug and brought out a long cord. With this he tied Naroo's right foot and Nareen's left together, then whispered to them to lie down on the grass and spread his possum rug over them. They were asleep within a few minutes.

He awoke to the call of the birds. Startled, he was at the cave mouth on the instant. Sunlight of a rosy dawn was flooding the mountain tops, though the plain country below was still veiled in shadows and mists. Hurriedly filling his water-bag from a near by spring, he congratulated himself that he had spied out this route in daylight and brilliant moonlight, seeking his surest way of escape as well as seeking his prey. So far his foresight was aiding his good fortune wonderfully. Snatching up kindling wood, he hurried back into the cave and woke the sleeping girls—a difficult task, for they simply did not seem able to open their heavy-lidded eyes.

"Nareen! Naroo!" He shook them urgently. "Awake! Cook and eat and drink! We have a long, long way to go!"

As he undid each gag, slowly they worked their numbed jaws in relief. As he freed their hands he said, "Cook all the duck-eggs, no one can see a little fire away back in this cave. We'll eat the last of the cooked meat, too. Eat well, for again we must travel far and fast!"

Vigorously with his firesticks he started a fire, throwing on broken pieces of bark. Soon, the bark would be warm ashes in which the eggs would quickly cook. Shivering, the girls spread their arms round the little blaze. He went to the cave mouth to watch the sun eating up the mists as if to show him the fair bushlands spreading far away, seemingly going on and on for ever.

No sign of enemies. Then, even as he looked he saw the smoke of cooking fires arising near a dense line of creek trees some five miles away. And he knew that such an early breakfast meant that the folk there had seen last night's fire signals and were but awaiting full daylight to seek sign of the runaways.

He did not fear them much; he was nearly sure they would keep to the low country—until too late, anyway. But he knew that far away behind him those waiting by the big rock in the reedy creek would soon be on his tracks.

## CHAPTER XX

## THE FIGHT

They ate ravenously. Grimly Red Kangaroo prepared to move on; tiredly the girls clung to the warmth of the fire. He rolled his few belongings in the possum rug; he could carry weapons only, ready for instant action. He rolled up their now empty dilly-bags and divided all into two light bundles, adding the filled water-bag. He fastened a bundle on each girl's shoulders, untied their feet and tied their wrists, then picked up the gags. Nareen made as if to protest, but determinedly he shook his head and held the gag to her mouth. Reluctantly she opened it. He gagged Naroo, smiling into her sulky eyes. Picking up his weapons, he nodded towards the cave entrance. Reluctantly they crawled up and stepped outside into sunlight and birdland, with the Warrumbungles towering beside them, mists rising from bushlands and forest, from dark lines of creek timbers and open, grassy plains, with the sweet smell of early morning fresh from the bosom of the earth.

Red Kangaroo stood, a picture of the wild, his wommera outstretched towards distant mountains.

"Gunn-e-darr!" he said proudly, lovingly.

They started out, breaking into a jog-trot. No dawdling now. The time for rebellion, for guile, for pretence and sulks was past. They must obey to the limit or he would react with swift ferocity. As they trotted along, down and up gully banks, across grassy, steep hill-slopes, he was alert for game, for he dared not delay to hunt for food and this would be his main chance, before sundown, of surprising game as it emerged hungry for its early-morning meal. And his chance came as they were trotting round a rocky hilltop. A black-faced, thickset old wallaroo sat back in surprise, his whitish chest a target as he bent forward, then bounded aside, stretching convulsively in mid air as the spear caught him through the ribs. Red Kangaroo leapt forward and clubbed the writhing, clawing, hissing thing. The nuggetty, strong-pawed wallaroo can put up a good fight for life.

With tomahawk and stone knife he quickly severed the thick, heavy tail and the meat from the hindquarters. With a satisfied grin he divided the meat upon the loads of Nareen and Naroo.

"Now we shall eat at midday after all," he said with pleased relief, "and of rich red meat. We'll eat tonight, too. So hurry along, knowing that when you're tired we'll fill our bellies with the meat that helps make warriors."

Nareen shot him a twisted smile; she would have said something impudent but for the gag. Obediently the girls started off at the jog-trot again, their bare feet noiseless over the grass, the rocks, the gravel of a creek-bed. Sure as the wallaby, graceful as the Spirit of the Wild, leaping lightly on to a big old log and barely touching the ground on the other side, gliding between close-growing saplings, they carried on for mile after mile.

The grass stalks were stretching up straighter and straighter to the warmth of the life-giving sun; the birds, their first early-morning hunger satisfied, were chattering, gossiping, scolding, and whistling to one another from gully and tree. An eagle floated apparently motionless high above a crag of the Warrumbungles.

From a height they paused a moment to glance behind. Far away back over the hilltops a thin column of black smoke was rising towards the clear blue sky.

"They have worked their way through the scrub and have tracked us now to the edge of the foothills," said Red Kangaroo grimly, "but we have got a long start. See that we keep it."

The girls turned and ran on as an answering smoke signal rose from the lower bushland far to their left, noted by Red Kangaroo's watchful eyes.

"Signalling those down in that direction," he thought. "They'll get busy, but they'll think we must have come down to cross the low country under cover of night; they'll be certain we shan't have kept to these foothills, which must slow us down so much."

As they ran on another smoke signal rose ten miles ahead of them in answer to the second, but again down in the lowlands. On and on they jogged. Red Kangaroo noticed the sweat beginning to form in beads, then dribble down the lithe bodies of the two clean-skinned girls running before him. Anxiously he hoped he had fitted the gags comfortably and to allow easy breathing.

At high noon the bush breathed silent and still, heat shimmering from rocky hill-slopes. They came running down a grassy spur into a valley from which a dark belt of pines stretched upward into the mountains. When deep within those pines Red Kangaroo grunted, and the girls dropped down, gently panting. He undid the gags and their hands and gave them the water-bag. They drank long and deeply, sighing quietly as the water slowly satisfied their tired, thirsty bodies. Within moments he had a fire alight, slashed off three hunks of meat, and threw them on the fire. It was restfully quiet and cool here, deep within the shadowy recesses of this sweetly smelling pine forest. And the cool friendly feeling of Mother Earth to tiring bodies—the girls felt they could close their eyes and lie there … and lie there …

They awoke to his big, urgent hand as he gave each a hunk of appetizingly smelling meat. They wolfed it, feeling strength warmly gathering within them. A big meal, all too quickly it was eaten. He reached for the gags again. Nareen's limpid eyes became large and dreamy.

"Won't you leave the gags off now?" she pleaded. "We have come a long, long way from our camp. And our friends are too far away to hear even if we did scream—which we won't, and with the gags off we could breathe deeper and last longer."

"Not until we come into the lands of my own tribe," he answered firmly.

She saw that he meant it. "Well then," she asked, "can't you leave our arms unbound now? We could brush aside the bushes then; our hands would save us from a fall; we could travel faster."

"And snatch out the gag and scream," he replied, "if there was a chance of rescue—or hit me on the head with a rock and run for your lives. Come on now—open!"

Reluctantly she obeyed.

"Nareen," said Naroo, grimacing, "what do you think of your man now? Won't trust us far as he can see us!"—and opened her mouth as he turned to her. Thus he again gagged them, bound their wrists, and loaded them.

"We'll push on now," he said, "and must fill the water-bag at the first chance. It will be hot and we must climb again when we get out past these pine-trees. We shall soon be thirsty."

It was several hours later when they came to a shady creek, a joy with its cool water. Thirstily they knelt to drink, and Red Kangaroo filled the water-bag. The girls stood up ready to go as he tied it to Nareen's back. And his heart missed a beat.

Out of a patch of scrub across the creek

two tribesmen came walking, the bearded elder carrying a kangaroo across his shoulders. They stopped dead and stared. Red Kangaroo was standing immediately behind the girls, his hand fitting spear to wommera.

"Nareen! Naroo!" called out the grizzled warrior. "I thought you were back in camp! When did you come here? Where have they moved camp to now?" He peered a moment longer and called, "Who is the warrior with you?"

His young companion shouted, "Look out! They seem bound and gagged—he must be an enemy!" and leapt aside hurriedly, fitting spear to wommera. He swept back his arm to throw, but Red Kangaroo's spear was already hurtling through the air. It caught the young warrior fair in the chest and threw him back to the earth, where he writhed with talons tearing up the grass.

"Throw yourselves to the ground, girls!" shouted the grizzled warrior, heaving the kangaroo off his shoulders. But Nareen and Naroo stood as if carved in wood. The warrior jumped from side to side with his spear ready, believing that the girls must be held there at spear-point, since the head of the unknown enemy was peering from directly behind them. Then, at a swift crouching run, he darted up along the creek timber, seeking a clearer throw.

Red Kangaroo leapt back and as the spear came hissing parried it with his shield. It skidded aside amongst the timber—to his disappointment, for he urgently needed that spear, not knowing if these two obvious hunters were alone, or if at any moment a whole pack might come yelling upon him. Keeping an eye on the crouching warrior, he edged back into the timber, seeking the weapon. The warrior, thinking he was running away, yelled contemptuously, and leapt down into the creek, and came plunging across. As he reached the bank Red Kangaroo threw his war boomerang, but the warrior sprang aside with a lightning twist of his shield that sent the boomerang thudding amongst the trees. He came on, leaping from side to side, then suddenly hurled his boomerang. Red Kangaroo parried it, watching this ceaselessly moving foeman. They drew closer in short, crouching leaps, seeking for an opening, each now armed only with nulla and shield, though each believed he had a tomahawk at his belt. Suddenly the foeman rushed and Red Kangaroo caught his nulla on his shield as both sprang aside. Again they closed in, to hissing grunts and sounds that made Red Kangaroo frantic, for he knew that the sharp, rapid, echoing blows of club against shield could be heard a mile and more away through the bush.

They were apart again, circling one another, when the grizzled warrior made his mistake—like lightning he threw his nulla at his opponent's knee. Red Kangaroo had leapt high and the nulla struck the ground under him and skidded away behind him. Then he hurled his nulla at the belly of his enemy, who with marvellous quickness knocked it aside with his shield. Red Kangaroo snatched for his tomahawk and knew an instant of cold terror. His last weapon was missing! Then his enemy was upon him; their shields smashed together; they clutched at each other's face with gouging fingers. Suddenly Red Kangaroo's shield jerked down in a slashing sweep, and he grunted as the heavy body of his opponent fell away and he stumbled over it, glaring down at those protruding eyeballs.

The fallen warrior writhed there, gulping out his life, his throat severed from ear to ear right to the neckbone. Red Kangaroo had instinctively used the shield blow as the lightning chance occurred. How thankful he was now that he had persevered to make his shield end into that secret weapon he had dreamt of so long!

But for the panting of the victor, the gurgling from the bloody throat of the dying, there was a hushed silence throughout all the bush.

# CHAPTER XXI
# RED KANGAROO RETURNS HOME

Red Kangaroo stood there shivering at the memory of that second's panic when he had snatched for his tomahawk and felt it missing. Mechanically his hand now groped back to his belt and felt the empty thong. In a flash he realised that the tomahawk must have slipped out when he had knelt down to drink at the creek. But why had his enemy not seized the advantage and used his own tomahawk? He turned the dying man over. Yes, his tomahawk carrier was empty, too! He, too, had known that icy chill of fear. What a strange fate, that each man in dire extremity should find his last weapon missing! But for Red Kangaroo, not quite the last. He gazed with grim triumph at the sharp, gory end of his shield.

He ran down to the creek. Yes, there lay his tomahawk, just where it had fallen from his belt as he knelt to drink. He thrust it deep back into its hide carrier; this would be a lesson to him. Always he would make certain that his weapons and those of his warriors were secure. He splashed across the creek and ran to the young warrior, lying dead under a wattle-tree. A golden blossom had softly fallen and now was slowly turning crimson on his chest. Red Kangaroo pressed his big foot on the chest and pulled and tugged and twisted his spear from the body—a tough job, done with urgent swiftness, but skilfully. Earnestly he glanced at the awful thing, saw that the barbs were unbroken, and breathed a deep sigh of relief. He snatched up the young warrior's boomerang and tomahawk and possum rug, then the older man's rug. He opened it, and there was the missing tomahawk! He recovered the boomerangs, handling the weapons in feverish delight. He was armed again.

He gazed round, listening. Neither sound nor sign of enemy. With growing confidence, but in anxious haste, he ran back and crossed the creek. Nareen and Naroo were still there, standing exactly where he had left them. He stared a moment and they gazed back at him. Slowly a smile lightened his grim, anxious face. Nareen smiled from dark eyes shining from excitement, Naroo pointed into the timber where the elder warrior's spear had gone, then to the nulla under an ironwood-tree. Swiftly then he found his own wommera.

What a brave pile all these weapons made! What a fight he could now put up! Smiling at the girls, he listened tensely. There came no sound but the chortling of magpies, the lilting tingle of water rippling over stones, a sighing from the creek oaks. Back in the mountains long shadows were climbing down gorge and gully. Hurriedly he rearranged the girls' bundles with the captured rugs, gave them spare weapons to carry, then smiled.

"We push on fast now—we travel all night again. It looks as if these were but two hunters returning to some near by camp. They will be missed at nightfall; tomorrow morning their friends will come looking for them. When they find them—!" He stared grimly at the girls then pointed with his wommera. "At a fast jog-trot!"

They bore away from the creek towards ranges that led to the Mullaley Plains. Red Kangaroo breathed deeply of the cool, fresh air—if only he could cross those plains. He *must* cross them. Once across those plains and the boundary of his own tribal lands would be welcoming his feet. He must urge the girls on—no, they were doing their best. He trotted behind them, anxiously gazing back now and then. He breathed more freely when they came under the long shadows of the ranges. At nightfall he called a halt deep in a boulder-lined gully. With a sigh they sat down. Quickly he lit a sheltered fire, threw on the last of the wallaroo meat, and took off the gags. The girls thankfully loosened their jaws and drank deeply from the water-bag. Their dark eyes glistened in the sheltered fire-glow, but he saw that those eyes were tired.

"We eat," he said, "and rest here until full starlight. See that you eat well, drink well, rest well. For when we are on the move again we do not stop until we reach my own country, and it is still a long way away."

They said nothing, just sat there resting

with their backs against the rocks, gazing silently at him.

"Tell me," he said, as he turned the meat upon the fire, "why you girls did not throw yourselves on the ground when your warrior tribesman called to you to do so? Had you obeyed he would have had me a close target for his spear."

They remained silent, until Nareen said softly, "You had not a spear then."

"I know," he replied, "and that made the advantage all on his side. Why did you both not throw yourselves to the ground?"

At last Naroo said quietly, "We did not give him his target because—we are your wives now!"

In the silence he gazed from one to the other. A star shone brilliantly far, far up. His heart was singing as he turned to the fire to take off the cooked meat. How good this meat would taste! They ate hungrily, ate all that remained of the strength-giving, rich red meat. With a satisfied sigh, the girls lay back to rest.

"That middle-aged warrior was a good man," said Red Kangaroo reflectively. "Who was he?"

For a moment the girls gazed at him from half-closed eyes.

Then Nareen murmured in her soft voice. "Yes, he was a good man, but you proved yourself a better. Perhaps it is just as well you did not know whom you were fighting, for he was Kulki, the best and bravest warrior of our Coonabarabran tribe. He is—was—the leader of all our tribal war parties, the most fearless man of all. He was the brother of our chief. Our warriors wanted him to be chief, but always he refused, answering that his brother was the best chief, for he could use his head for the good of the tribe, whereas Kulki was only good for fighting. His brother could plan for the tribe, but he could only fight for it. And now our tribe has lost its fighting leader."

Like a dirge for a native son rose the long-drawn, mournful howl of a dingo from the hills. Far out over the low country floated that howl, rising quaveringly again like the despairing cry of a lost soul. The girls shivered, huddling fearfully together. Red Kangaroo knew then from their eyes that the slain warrior had been of the Dingo totem. And now the Dingo had taken back its own.

Stars came to make lovely the sky in clusters of golden light. A stone, dislodged by some prowling animal away up some distant hillside, came clattering down a rocky face like the tinkling of a silver bell. Abruptly, the night silence seeemed listening. It came again farther away, dying out over the hills, that lone, mournful howl.

He rested them for three hours, then they hurried on under starlight. No question now but that the girls were doing their best. In anxious exultation he led them along the range, very eager to hurry down to the Mullaley Plains where they could run on all through the remainder of the night and through the dawn until they should reach his beloved tribal lands.

Next day, away across the Mullaley Plains in the lands of Gunn-e-darr, all the tribe in the main camp were squatting sullenly round the campfires or by their gunyahs, in broad daylight. Even the "Cark! Cark!" of the camp crows seemed but occasional and dispirited.

It had been so for the last three days. No one had gone out hunting. So hunger had added fuel to their perplexity and growing anger, the anger of half the tribe against the chief and elders and their supporters, the perplexity and rage of the chief against the fast-increasing animosity of the many friends of Red Kangaroo. For of Red Kangaroo there still was neither sign nor trace. And chief and elders knew positively they had not killed him, which made their anger the greater the more the people murmured their suspicions. And now warriors every here and there were fingering their weapons while the chief himself watched the camp, awaiting the first open sign of hostility that would send him in berserk rage against the hostile one.

All knew that at any moment men of the tribe might be at one another's throats. And all knew, too, that this day would not pass without something happening.

Through the ominous silence, came the long-drawn note of a distant "Coo-ee-eee!"

The camp froze; men, women, and children stared wonderingly. Then here and there a man sprang erect—listening.

After a time, closer now came—yes, there was no questioning it!—that powerful, ringing cooee of—Red Kangaroo!

On the instant every man was upon his feet, the camp broke into a hundred smiles, hysterical laughter, then shrill chattering of women, screams of youngsters.

Red Kangaroo! Red Kangaroo was coming home! Warriors put hands to their mouth, the whole camp sent out a wild, hysterical, "Coo-ee-eee!" And back came an answer, full-throated, confident. Men seized weapons and started running; women and children excitedly followed. Only Jerrabri and elders remained, frowning doubtfully.

And thus Red Kangaroo returned to camp. The people streaming out, cooeeing to meet him seemed struck dumb as his tall, smiling figure appeared with two fine young women, dead tired but defiant, marching obediently ahead of him carrying his possum-skin rugs and weapons, staring everyone in the eye as they marched into camp, the cords of captivity round their throats, the ends of the cords held in his left hand, his wommera in his right.

Those who had remained in camp stood and watched, those who had run out to meet him followed behind quietly, to stand also and watch in an amazed silence as proudly he marched his captive wives to his own gunyah. There he took the captivity cords from their necks in front of all, and ordered them to take off their bundles and lay them within the gunyah. Silently they obeyed. He ordered them to collect firewood. They turned to the bush to do so, returning with an armful of kindling. When they had prepared a fire his uncle Tulumi came from his own campfire with a blazing firestick in his hand, quietly walking to Red Kangaroo. For this was the custom, that if a warrior brought to camp a captive woman it was his father's right to bring the brand that would light the marriage fire. Since Red Kangaroo's father was dead the right passed to his uncle.

Red Kangaroo bowed his head to his uncle, took the brand, and held it towards the girls. Only when each gripped it did he let it go. Both girls, holding the blazing firestick, bent to the wood-pile and thrust it in. The kindling crackled, smoke appeared, and the fire blazed up. The warrior Burradella, friend of Red Kangaroo, then came with the hind leg of a newly killed kangaroo. Gravely he offered it to Red Kangaroo, who as gravely accepted the gift, handed it to his wives, and said, "Cook me meat!"

They bent to the fire to obey. Slowly then the people drifted away to their own gunyahs to talk excitedly in little groups, leaving Red Kangaroo and his wives, his obviously very tired wives, to themselves. For such was the custom.

Thus Red Kangaroo returned home.

# CHAPTER XXII
# THE CHALLENGE

Next morning a messenger of the seven elders came gravely to the gunyah of Red Kangaroo. He was summoned at high sun to appear on the corroboree ground before the chief and the elders to explain why he had been absent from his tribe for a whole moon—without permission of the elders, to explain where he had gone, and why, and what he had done during that time—and how he had become possessed of two wives. For a young warrior of but one summer and winter was entitled to one wife only. He must bring his wives to the meeting, for all women, too, must be there.

And Red Kangaroo knew that the crisis had come.

At high sun the tribe in a hushed circle waited upon the corroboree ground, Jerrabri and the seven elders of the council in the centre. Excitement sparkled in all those eyes as Red Kangaroo came boldly walking into the circle, his two young wives following, heads held high. Red

Kangaroo carried his war weapons, the two girls the possum-rug bundles slung round their shoulders. But there were no cords of captivity round their necks now. Upright as the straightest of the slender reeds of the river, defiantly they awaited their acceptance into this, their new tribe. Red Kangaroo strode straight to the council and threw his spear at the feet of Jerrabri, in token of respect to the chief. "Speak!" Jerrabri commanded him.

In a strong, ringing voice Red Kangaroo began, "The tribe demands that I explain why I have been absent from the tribe for a whole moon. This is why—because I went to get myself a wife! If I had not caught one, then I should have remained away for another moon, and yet another, until I succeeded, or was killed.

"We all know that there are no marriageable young lubras left in our tribe for the newly made warriors, a whole summer and winter and more after we pass through the Bora ceremonies! The chief and the elders and their friends are to blame. They have taken three, or no less than two wives each in the last two years, while for long past only after a hard trade bargain has any one of them handed over his eldest wife to a Bora warrior. In the midst of our enemies our tribe has been weakened by this unjust tampering with the laws. For you see around you not half the number of warriors we should have to defend our tribe and lands, you see not half the number of children that should be growing up to take our places. While all around us our many enemies are growing stronger and stronger summer after summer, with their hungry eyes upon our rich tribal lands."

In the quiet midday all the bush seemed to be listening, not a piccaninny whimpered. Red Kangaroo glanced round and felt all those eyes upon him and his own eyes flashed as he turned again to Jerrabri and the grim-faced elders.

"While so many young warriors remain unmarried," his strong voice resumed, "no warrior should be allowed to take more than one wife from our tribeswomen. If he wants more, then let him and his friends form a strong raiding party and raid some enemy tribe for their young women. This was always done by the chiefs and warriors of our tribe from long, long ago, nearly to the time of our present chief and elders. But long since our chief and elders, with the support of the tribal councils, have tampered with the laws to suit themselves, against the well-being of the tribe. Never have they called a council of all the tribe to discuss these new laws they were making on the rights of chief and elders and their friends to take *all* the young marriageable women! I question not the right of all elder warriors to take those girls who are theirs at birth by right of law. But they have laid claim to *all* girls, whereas by law since the Dream Time there have always been a certain number of young tribal women who must be kept for the young Bora warriors alone.

"Yet by agreement amongst themselves the chief, the council of the elders, and most of the elder warriors, have long since, for their own selfish benefit, altered the laws that go back even to the Dream Time. That main law said that no man of the tribe—chief, elder, medicine man, or warrior—can take more than one wife from the tribal women if there are not sufficient women to go round. This can be done only at such times when there are more marriageable women than men in the tribe. And while there are unmarried warriors a man whose wife has died cannot claim another wife from the tribal women.

"But our new tribal law says that he can, and all other warriors must form raiding parties at the risk of their lives and carry off young women from enemy tribesmen if they are to have wives. These raids are lawful under the old, true law; I have but obeyed the law, whereas the chief and his elders have disobeyed it by wrongfully dividing all the young women amongst themselves.

"And now, yet again, the chief and the elders say they can claim one of these my captive women, who are now my wives in the sight of all the tribe, as a wife for one of themselves! Now the law has always stated there is no limit to the number of wives a warrior may own, providing he steals them from another tribe. So that these two young women whom I captured from the Coonabarabran tribe are now my wives.

"And now you know why I have been away from the tribe so long. I rightfully went out to steal wives, because a wife from my own tribal women was denied me by the bad laws of the chief and the elders. I claim I have done no wrong. And now I have got my wives. And what I have I hold!"

The frowns on the brows of the elders had grown angrier, then more and more uneasy, as Red Kangaroo addressed the tribe. But now Jerrabri leapt up in blazing anger and, motioning to the oldest of his wives, strode across to Red Kangaroo.

"I am giving you a tribeswoman for a wife!" he shouted hoarsely. "Since you have complained there were no marriageable women in the tribe when you were made a new warrior, here is your wife. Take her!" And he pushed his eldest wife forwards.

But Red Kangaroo motioned her away and angrily faced the chief.

"You can't give me what I haven't asked you to give!" he shouted. "When I needed a woman of our tribe as wife by just right you and the elders saw that there was *none* forthcoming. So I went out and got my own. And now neither you nor any other man can force your unwanted wife upon me!"

"So say you—cub warrior of barely two summers!" snarled the chief. "And now I tell you *this!* It is the order of the elders and my right as chief that I take one of these Coonabarabran women as my wife in exchange for the wife I have just given you! I take *this* one!" and he reached out and grabbed Nareen's hair and jerked her towards him.

She snapped at his wrist as she snatched the nulla from his girdle and clubbed him straight upon his big, broad face. With a startled "Whough!" he fell upon his back, blood spurting from his nostrils to dye crimson his jet-black beard as he glared up at her while she hissed, "Handle your own wives as you will, but I am Red Kangaroo's wife and I'll kill any man who dares lay a hand upon *me!*"

The chief snatched a boomerang from his belt and leapt up in mad fury, but Red Kangaroo sprang against him and savagely wrenched the weapon from his hand.

"Ah! Chief Jerrabri, the woman-killer! Not of *my* wives though!" he snarled. "If you're a man, Jerrabri, then you fight *me*, not my woman! Here's your boomerang, but—it needs a man to throw it in fight against a man!" And he threw the weapon hard at the chief's feet.

Not a whisper broke the silence as the two glared face to face, hands clenching and unclenching, the elder man's teeth gritting in rage, eyes blazing hate for hate. On any other occasion they would have been straight at one another's throats, but Jerrabri instantly realized that this hated stripling had caught him in a trap from which there was no escape except for the victor in an arranged duel to the death. That boomerang, thus contemptuously tossed at his feet, was the tribal challenge. And this accursed Red Kangaroo had the right to make it before all the tribe.

For the chief had just broken two tribal laws before them all. No man may take, or attempt to take, by force a wife from a tribesman who has stolen her from a hostile tribe. And no man has the right to throw a war or hunting weapon, or hold one in his hand to strike the wife of a fellow tribesman. The husband alone possesses that right over his wives.

Standing there in shivering rage, Jerrabri knew that if he leapt upon this hated challenger to throttle him to death he would again break a law, and by breaking it deprive himself of his chieftainship, even if the tribe did not rush in and tear them apart. No, there was only one thing to do—accept the challenge and fight the duel in strict accordance to tribal etiquette. After which—his big chest drew a deep, shuddering breath, and slowly he bent to pick up his war boomerang, turning the heavy weapon round and round in his gnarled hands. After he had killed this dingo mongrel, Red Kangaroo, then—he glared at Nareen, but she stood there fearlessly returning glare for glare—ah, this slip of a captive girl who had reddened his pride and made him a laughing-stock—he would bash her with his nulla till she could only lie there and moan! He would teach her—again and again, and *yet* again!

For it is the law that he who loses his

life in a duel also loses his property to the victor. Red Kangaroo's property consisted of his war weapons, his hunting weapons and traps and fish snares and cooking utensils, his possum rugs, and now—these two young wives.

Licking his bleeding lips, slowly Jerrabri walked away towards the silent elders. Immediately his friends came hurrying to him, while to Red Kangaroo the warrior Burradella, with Tulumi, Bungadoon, Giluram, Boobuk, Kibiri, and many other friends came crowding. The bush breathed again with the patter of hurrying feet, the shouts, the excited yabbering of women, the squealing of piccaninnies. The birds, too, had been roused to excitement; cockatoos on tree-tops raised their yellow crests and shrieked excitedly, magpies warbled in carefree abandon, and a flock of parrots dived low in a flash of crimson and green over the scampering tribe.

# CHAPTER XXIII

## THE DUEL

On the seventh day the duel was to be fought on the Breeza Plains upon clear, level ground. Solemnly those in charge began preparing the duelling ground, even to burning off every blade of grass. The contestants at the start would face one another, standing at long spear-throw— one hundred yards apart by white man's reckoning. Carefully those in charge measured out the exact distance beforehand, marking where each man would stand so that everything would be perfectly equal, and neither would have any advantage of distance, ground, position, light, or weapons against the other. The duel would take place exactly at high sun, so that the light shining down upon each man would be equal.

Red Kangaroo, who had eaten this week as never before, not only of the food prepared by his own wives but of the very best that old Bungadoon's wife Pumbul and Boobuk's Kapota could tempt him with, rested the day before the duel on the advice of his uncle Tulumi, while Burradella, with Boobuk happily suggesting advice, went carefully over his weapons. He must sleep well that night, so the warriors gravely advised, for he was in for the fight of his life.

At early morning time Tulumi, Burradella and Boobuk were anointing Red Kangaroo's limbs and body with emu oil, massaging it well in to help suppleness of joints, muscles, and sinews. Then they painted him in war-paint of red ochre with bars of yellow and white, lastly adding bunches of brilliantly hued feathers to his hair and limbs. They would make sure that Red Kangaroo looked what he was, a fighting man, when he took his stand on the duelling ground before all the tribe. Yes, he would look his best on this day, whether he was fated to see the sun set or not.

There was no question as to whom the women and children and the younger warriors at least would wish to see the sun set.

Soon after sunrise the particular men

appointed for this duty came to each contestant, and with due etiquette claimed his weapons. Carefully each weapon was examined and counted. Two war spears to each fighter, two war boomerangs, his favourite tomahawk, favourite nulla, and shield. Gravely these men, three on behalf of the chief, three on behalf of Red Kangaroo, carried the weapons from each man's gunyah to the duelling ground, and laid them neatly out at each man's position. Then they returned to camp, except for one from each group, the guardians of the weapons. One stood silently by the weapons of the chief, Jerrabri. The other stood watching over the weapons of Red Kangaroo.

The sun beat down more strongly upon the cleared duelling ground. A crow, from away back on the timber line, carked inquiringly. Time droned on. The two guardians of the weapons, silently standing one hundred yards apart, the weapons neatly arranged at their feet, were like statues in ebony.

A little before high sun the contestants, in full war-paint, appeared walking some distance apart, each with his little group of weapon men following. While away behind came the whole tribe down to the youngest piccaninny, the oldest old man and woman hobbling along after.

The contestants took their places, facing one another. Their weapon men retired. But each guardian of the weapons still remained on guard at his place on the duelling ground. In deadly seriousness each contestant fitted and balanced his spears in turn in his wommera, chose which weapon he would throw first, and thrust the other to stand upright in the ground. Then stood, facing his antagonist, waiting.

The council of the elders took their place, then the people streamed round all, squatting down in a wide-eyed, silent circle. Each guardian then strode to the weapons and placed them neatly in order at the feet of his man. Then with serious care he placed the two boomerangs and the nulla into the holding thongs attached to his man's belt, securing each weapon in its correct place, handy to hands and feet of the duellist. The onlookers waited in complete silence while this important duty was being done to everyone's satisfaction.

Then, at a nod from Jerrabri, his man wheeled round, facing Red Kangaroo's man, who had already turned round, waiting. Both guardians then strode with measured paces towards one another. They met exactly in the centre of the duelling ground. Each stood a moment, then stepped backward twenty paces, then each turned, one stepped twenty paces to the right, the other twenty paces to the left. Each turned again. Immediately their faces turned towards one another each wheeled round and shouted down towards his man.

Instantly Jerrabri was bounding forward and his spear was sighing through the air. Red Kangaroo, with split-second agility, just managed to parry it and threw, but the chief was leaping back for his second spear, intent on dazzling his opponent with speed. Both threw viciously, and Jerrabri's shield edge barely warded off the long spear, which left a thin red weal across his hip. Red Kangaroo snatched out a boomerang and threw for the legs, but Jerrabri leapt high in time. He feinted to throw, but Red Kangaroo was not to be drawn into throwing his last boomerang, so Jerrabri, with legs wide-spread, now came slowly, crouching behind his shield, then swiftly bent forward and threw. The boomerang thudded to earth to the left and behind Red Kangaroo, who instantly fell flat as the unpredictable weapon came whirling straight back and up at him; it would have broken his back had he not acted like lightning. He had barely sprung up and aside, thrusting out his shield, as the second boomerang smashed against it with shattering force, knocking him off balance. He threw as Jerrabri came leaping, but the chief expertly turned the weapon aside.

Both men now faced one another, seeking the opening to throw or to spring in and strike. Both feinted, then instantly each threw at the other's tomahawk hand, dodged like lightning, and whipped out his nulla. They were panting now; Red Kangaroo sprang back, and his sweating face showed fear as Jerrabri, with a triumphant yell, lifted his shield and leapt in for the kill. Instantly Red Kangaroo threw low and the nulla smashed Jerrabri's knee cap. As the chief was thrown backward to the ground Red Kangaroo was upon him. He snatched the nulla from his opponent's hand and smashed it against his temple, thrusting down and sideways the sharp edge of his shield, which slashed the chief's throat almost from ear to ear. Red Kangaroo stood panting, glaring down as Jerrabri writhed out his life. He did not hear the low murmur, then the roar of excited people as they jumped up and came rushing in, while from behind them arose the mournful death wail of the wives of Chief Jerrabri.

That afternoon at sundown, back in camp, Red Kangaroo claimed the victor's rights. So the elders brought to him the three wives of the dead chief, his war weapons, hunting weapons, possum rug and cloak, his fish-traps, nets, and lines, implements and cooking utensils that were within his gunyah, and all things that had been his. The people crowded round, curious to see what Red Kangaroo would do. Nareen and Naroo sat there, hostile of eye as they glared at the late chief's two young wives waiting with bowed heads. Then Naroo glanced at Nareen with a mischievous smile, quickly hidden. An answering light gleamed in Nareen's eye—both suddenly felt perkily confident of their own charms.

Red Kangaroo stood up and called together the Kubara, all those young warriors who had gone through the Bora initiation with him—except for Giluram, to whom Red Kangaroo had whispered and smiled. But Giluram, after one swift glance towards Weetah, had resolutely shaken his head.

"There are seven of you," said Red Kangaroo to the young fellows, "and none has a wife as yet. Here is a chance for two of you." He held his clenched fist towards them. In it they saw the quill tips of seven emu feathers, all evenly spaced. He nodded towards Jerrabri's younger wives.

"He who draws the longest feather of these seven," he said, "will have first choice of these two young women as wife. He who draws the shortest feather will take the other. Now, who will have first draw?"

The seven young warriors stared at the quills, each reluctant to be the first to put his fortune to the test. All the men smiled broadly; the women began to giggle, then delightedly urged the young fellows on.

"Look at them," said mother Vamai, "standing there like wet shags on a rock! They've been moaning for ages because they haven't got wives, and now not one dare take his chance!"

"Look at Kulgoa," shrilled a vixen, "gaping at those feathers as if they'd bite him! Howling for a wife these two summers past, and now he looks silly as a mopoke in a thunderstorm!"

"What warriors they are," cried another, "afraid of two little women! Why not let the women draw the feathers? *They* wouldn't be so slow!"

At last Barrum took the plunge, and there was a sudden hush as he picked a feather. Alas, it was a miss. Breathlessly the people watched as another feather was drawn—another miss. Then a delighted "Ah!" to the third feather, an extra long one. Then a howl of laughter at the next— a very short one. Thus they drew for the two younger widows to the bashful content of the winners and the disappointment of the losers.

The middle-aged wife of Jerrabri Red Kangaroo gave to a warrior whose wife had died not long before, leaving two young children. Jerrabri had no children. Red Kangaroo divided all Jerrabri's household goods amongst the three new wives. He kept Jerrabri's war weapons, but gave the hunting weapons to Jerrabri's old father.

Three days later a big tribal council of all the older warriors was held. Gravely they debated, and the upshot was that nine picked warriors came from the council to ask Red Kangaroo to become the war chief of the Gunn-e-darr tribe.

He had been prepared for this and his reply was already thought out. Since he had learnt the value of thinking before he spoke, or acted, he was very different now to the impulsive lad of two summers ago.

He stood before the messengers and replied impressively, "The offer of the council is a great honour to me. No man could rise higher than to be the war chief of a fighting tribe. But I am not really a man, though in fair fight I have already killed five grown warriors. But my head is still that of a boy, whereas the tribe needs middle-aged heads to think and plan against enemies, to be quick-witted in a tight place where the enemy are many and we but few. The tribe needs experienced heads that also can think out the best ways to build up our tribe and hold our good country against the enemies that I now know are all around us. In two more years, if I am alive and in health and strength, then if the tribe still want me to be their war chief I shall accept. Meanwhile, give me leadership of a warrior party under your new chief."

The warriors nodded gravely, and returned with his answer to the council.

The council finally chose Tulumi as war chief for two years, with Burradella as second chief and chief adviser, and Red Kangaroo as leader of a warrior party.

Throughout all the excitement the life of the tribe went on, for nomads must hunt to live, and must often be on the move. Even in a well-watered country of rich lands the seasons vary as they come and go, the game comes and goes and often must be followed as it moves. Moreover, it must not be wiped out in any one locality lest it should not come again. Plant life varies, too, with localities and seasons, while the fish vary with the rivers and billabongs and the waters and foods that flow in and out of them. And no waterhole must be fished right out because then fish will be slow to breed again. Thus a tribe must be constantly on the move within the limits of its tribal lands. Also, the digging of foodstuffs takes time and work, as does the replacement of traps and nets, carrying utensils, weapons, stone or bone or shell knives, awls, and sewing needles, and other necessary things. And all the time vigilance must be maintained, feud and raid both guarded against and carried out, and without fail the important ceremonial life of the tribe must be kept up. The life of the wild Australian aboriginal is much more complicated than it appears.

But all things seemed easier now somehow to the Gunn-e-darr tribe of the

Kamilaroi. There was now no distrust, no gloom; there was much more laughter in the camps since Red Kangaroo's duel with Jerrabri. Old Bungadoon's voice could be heard rolling round the camp, joking more than ever. Even the warrior Boobuk had been noticed absent-mindedly doing little things for his wife, Kapota. But this, of course, was too good to last.

Red Kangaroo's lone raid on the Coonabarabran tribe to steal his wives, and his duel with Jerrabri, were worked up into a great corroboree by old Mullionkale the play-maker. Red Kangaroo was especially pleased that his deadly shield blow, against both the Coonabarabran warrior, Kulki, and Jerrabri, was acted in special detail, for nothing could better convince the warriors of the worth of this blow, which he believed in his heart could mean such a lot to the protection of the tribe. And he had the satisfaction of seeing the warriors sharpening the ends of their shields and eagerly practising the blow. He was certain this would prove a surprise to any enemy; he had already proved it three times himself.

Tulumi and Burradella led the tribe with care and caution. Red Kangaroo was content to make suggestions, silent if his uncle or Burradella or the council of the elders, after consideration, decided against his suggestions. But some were acted upon, such as that the boys—and the older warriors—must practice the shield blow until they thoroughly understood it. They were with him, too, in encouraging the warriors to go on wife– and boy-stealing raids to build up the strength of the tribe again as quickly as possible. But only after each proposed raid had been carefully talked over and planned by the elders was it to be carried out, lest vengeance bring a real war that might overwhelm them.

For quite a time they expected an attack in force by the powerful Coonabarabran tribe to avenge Red Kangaroo's successful raid upon them. It did not come, to their relief, perhaps partly because he had killed their warrior leader, Kulki, whose reputation was known far and wide—a lucky killing that had added to the already formidable reputation of the Gunn-e-darr fighting men. Their strength in numbers, also, was believed to be great by their enemies, otherwise they would surely not have sent woman-stealers so impudently into the lands of such a powerful tribe as the Coonabarabran.

So time went on, while the new chief and the council watched carefully over the tribe, cautiously attempting to build up its strength—far too slowly, it seemed to Red Kangaroo.

And Giluram still waited for Weetah, both now hoping against hope, for the time was fast coming when old Tulduna would claim her. But here Red Kangaroo was able to help his friend, through his uncle the chief and the warrior Burradella. A bargain was made quietly. Red Kangaroo would give a possum-skin cape and a kangaroo-skin rug, a good spear, a nulla, and two boomerangs that he had taken in his fights, if Tulduna would waive his claim to the girl Weetah for but twelve moons more.

Tulduna eagerly accepted. A good bargain this, almost something for nothing. He must, of course, lose the girl's services for a year. But the compensating payment was high. And he could easily wait for those twelve moons.

Red Kangaroo grinned to himself. He knew what he intended to do towards the end of that twelve months. But he kept the secret to himself. As for Weetah and Giluram, they lived in hope again, thinking the world had grown suddenly wonderful. That night they hardly heard the stories round the campfire, they were trying so hard not to look at one another.

A beautiful night, such as might smile in heaven. In a dome of deepest blue the twinkle of many stars, while below on earth the cool, sweet breath of the bush was a joy to breathe. And all so still and silent—just a sigh now and then amongst the leaves, as a babe might sigh in sleep.

All the children in camp, and many of the older folk, were sitting tightly crowded round old Mullionkale the storyteller, the children the closest, the youngest daring to touch his bony knees as they clustered round him like bees. And so unusually quiet. All those young eyes gazing up at his kindly gnarled old face of a hundred wrinkles, eyes kissed a second by starlight should they move, ears so wide open, striving to catch every word of the gentle old voice that carried so far and easily in this listening silence.

This night old Mullionkale was telling them about Baia-me, but only so much as it was good for such little people to know.

"As you all know," spoke the old voice reverently, "Baia-me is the Great Builder, He Who Made All Things—the stars and the sky, the bush and the waters, the birds and animals, the snakes and the lizards, the fishes, the trees, and the wee insects. He even made you and me! When your father and your mother build a gunyah, a canoe, anything—we say "baia"—to make or build. And Baia-me, the Great Spirit of All Things, is He Who Built All Things.

"Having made the skies and the earth and all upon it, Baia-me came to earth. And thus was born the Dream Time. He then made man, in the pleasant country of our Namoi, Barwon, Calalal[1] and Narran rivers. Having rested awhile he flew back to the skies. And there, deep within the

1 *The Peel River.*

Milky Way, he built the Pleasant Lands, the lands where we all go up to when we pass through the Land of Shades. For know this, we are not only built of skin and bone and flesh, but of what is *inside us,* and which we cannot see even if we cut a man open. And it is 'this inside us', which we call Tohi, that when we die flies up to the Pleasant Lands that Baia-me has prepared for us. It is only the skin and flesh and bones that go back to the earth. But of these things you will learn more as you grow older. Be good girls and boys and pass through the ceremonies. And after a long time those among you who are judged worthy to learn the Sacred Language will in great secrecy be told of the Deep Things.

"Now, although Baia-me has never come back to earth since he returned to his home in the skies, still he sees all things, hears all things, knows all things. And to us here on earth he sends the 'One Between'—Turramulan. And of Turramulan, who watches over us here on earth for Baia-me, you will also learn more as you grow older.

"And now the pelican sleeps, his wise old head tucked up under his wing. It is only the hoary old mopoke and the fiery-eyed owl who listen and watch and wonder why you boys and girls are not snug and asleep under your mothers' possum rugs. And hark! Just out dancing in the moonlight sings the willy wagtail, that carrier of tales. A sharp-eared little busybody is he! Hurry away to your gunyahs now, lest he slip away to your mothers and twitter that you are here with me, listening to the Teller of Tales. For I know that you would not like to get poor old Mullionkale into trouble. Away now, for another night will come. The stars will always shine. And there will always be a Teller of Tales."

# CHAPTER XXIV
# THE WALLABY TRAP

Following the game in their nomadic life the tribe congregated, calling in the scattered family groups then leisurely hunting their way through bush to the Mullibah Lagoon camp just below the Bindea[1] or Porcupine Ridges, adjoining the range upon which towered the look-out post Carrowreer. These ridges were covered in many parts with coarse, needle-tipped porcupine grass and prickly and thorny bushes. Other large areas of these ridges were clothed in the dense, dull green of hoop-vine scrub, a tangled mass of almost impenetrable undergrowth binding the scrub trees together. The hoop-bush itself, growing only to six feet, with a maze of roots, was entangled by looping cable and maze of cane and vine, creeper and fern. Within the very heart of the largest area of scrub was the Secret Camp. This

*1 Bindea means "the place where the spinifex and shrubs with thorns like porcupine quills grow".*

gloomy hideout had been a sanctuary of the Gunn-e-darr tribe on occasions of dire peril from time immemorial, especially for the women and children. When once the helpless ones were safe within the Secret Camp the warriors could defy their enemies from the outskirts of the scrub, creeping forth from its shelter to attack when opportunity occurred, flying back to its sheltering labyrinths when hard pressed. Thus the Mullibah Lagoon camp, overlooked by the Porcupine Ridges with their dense scrubs and Secret Camp, overlooked again by the bold outpost of Carrowreer was a favourite and easily the safest camp of the Gunn-e-darr Tribe.

From Porcupine Hill[2] and Carrowreer the look-outs had a wonderful view of the course of their River Namoi with the pretty Mooki winding through the Breeza Plains to its junction with the Namoi near Porcupine Ridge. Far away out over the Breeza Plains the look-outs could see while watching for possible enemies, the daily progress of their own hunting parties

2 *Porcupine Hill overlooks the present day town of Gunnedah.*

by the smokes they sent up. A favourite hunting ground of the tribe was the rich Breeza Plains, abounding in the red and grey kangaroos and in emus, wallabies, kangaroo-rats, pademelons, bandicoots, brolgas, and the fat plain turkeys, with waterfowl in abundance in the waterways.

Though the Mullibah Lagoon camp was a favourite camp it was in pleasant anticipation that all looked forward to the full-moon seasonal wallaby hunt. This particular hunt only took place on Porcupine Ridge above the Mullibah camp. And this particular full-moon night was given up to the "Wallaby Trap", a natural trap in the edge of the big scrub up on Porcupine Ridge towards the north-westerly side of the Black Hill.[3] Just there, a natural U-shaped space ran straight back deep into the edge of the scrub, exactly as if it had been cut back into the scrub edge by the modern axe. This open

> 3 Not Black Jack look-out. The Black Hill, a small rise on Porcupine Ridge, was a handy look-out over the country immediately round the Mullibah Lagoon camp.

space penetrated into the scrub some one hundred and thirty yards, and was about forty yards wide. No trees, not even shrubs grew within this deep, narrow space, but only short grass and bracken fern. Along each straight side of this narrow *cul-de-sac* was a dense green wall of trees, hoop-vine, and tangled undergrowth. The end of this natural laneway was a wall of scrub.

And this had always been the tribal Wallaby Trap. Fronting it, as one stood out from the scrub edge and gazed downhill and away over Mullibah Lagoon, was a mile-long narrow strip of perfectly open country with only short grass growing upon it. Beyond this long strip of open grassland were the forest trees of the ordinary bush, sloping down to Mullibah Lagoon camp. The grassland ran like a green road for a mile between the dense wall of scrub and the lightly timbered bushland. It was midway along this strip that the Wallaby Trap ran back into the scrub.

At sunset scrub wallabies in droves came cautiously out from the scrub edge, peered round to see or sniff any possible danger, then, if all was clear, they would hop out on the green grass and commence to feed. For all along this laneway between dense scrub and forest land the grass was shorter and sweeter than for miles around. Also at threat of danger the wallabies could hop back into their sheltering scrub. When eventide came this laneway of sweet grass would be alive with scrub wallabies. And they would continue to eat and browse and play all through the night. At dawn, full-bellied and heavy with sleep, they would hop back into the scrub to find their dark lairs and sleep away the daylight hours.

At times of the full moon the moonlight shone brilliantly down along this open laneway of grass, and partly into that natural space going deep back into the scrub edge. Within this Wallaby Trap space all was clear moonlight, but along its sides and at its end the walls of scrub threw black shadows.

On "Wallaby Trap nights" half the warriors and half the elder boys in late afternoon would arrive at the Trap and line its sides and end, a fair distance apart. Thus a line of hunters with their backs to the scrub edge would be facing another, evenly spaced, with the open grass and fern between them, while away down at the end of the Trap would be another line, much shorter, of hunters facing up towards the distant mouth. Anything that came within that Trap would risk spears, boomerangs, and throwing sticks raining towards it from both sides. Then, if it ran to escape down to the end of the Trap it would run into hunting weapons thrown at it from there. If it had still escaped, which would be very unlikely indeed, then it could only double back and flee straight up along the Trap to the mouth. And during this frantic attempt to escape it would again run the gauntlet of weapons thrown at it from all along both sides.

Having lined both sides and end of the Trap, the hunters would sit down with the wall of scrub at their backs, quietly waiting for full moonlight and the springing of the Trap. Towards sundown all the remainder of the tribe, except the very old people or sick, armed with all the hunting weapons they could carry but especially with boomerangs, nullas, and throwing sticks, would leisurely leave camp and stroll up towards the scrub edge where the Wallaby Trap was.

When fairly near they would spread well out to right and left along the line of forest trees—men and boys, women, girls and children, in unusual quietness eagerly stealing through the bush to hide and wait. A mile-long line of them, now facing that strip of open grassland, the darkening wall of scrub behind it. A few would remain back in the forest edge right opposite the mouth of the Trap, but most would be away to right and left, and particularly down at both ends of the open strip. From here a few of the men and boys, widely spaced, would creep right to the scrub edge, then some little distance along it towards the distant mouth of the Trap, and then wait, invisible just within the scrub edge. And the day sounds of the bush would gradually cease as shadows merged with shadows as the sun went down, the last noisy birds went to sleep.

In silence the hidden people would wait for the rising of the full moon, while now from all along that black wall of scrub the hungrier wallabies were coming peeping out, to hop on to that grassy laneway and begin to feed. From the forest trees also bush wallabies began venturing out on the sweet grass. By the time the full moon rose in its silvery glory that long, grassy laneway separating scrub from forest seemed alive with the dainty creatures, bathed in the bright, soft light of the silvery moon. Some were sitting back on their tails to wash their fur with tongue and little paws, or energetically scratch themselves where annoyed by a scrub tick. Others were busily eating, or merely tempting appetite by leisurely sliding along by rump and forepaws to nibble at some more succulent morsel, while here and again were a couple of bucks vying for the attentions of an apparently not-much-interested lady friend. These amorous ones would stand back upon haunches and tail and spar up to one another in threatening grunts and hisses, angrily clawing one at the other. Here and there, too, there would be some young doe, genuinely intent upon her own business, being annoyed by a lovesick swain. Sooner or later, with an exasperated hiss, she would wheel upon him and soundly box his ear and nose. Yet others, the early ones with their bellies comfortable in the first eating, would commence playing. All among them were young wallabies very busily eating or enjoying themselves to their hearts' content.

Presently some of the wallabies scattered over the grass away along at each end of the grass strip became aware of definite black shadows that seemed to be advancing silently towards them, but as they looked became motionless as a burnt tree-stump. Those wallabies that saw would stand back on their tails, ears twitching, seeking sound, eyes gleaming for sign of movement, dainty nose sniffing for smell, and especially smell of that most terribly feared of all enemies—man. But there was no sound. And no smell.

How could the innocent little wallabies know that every man, woman and child that were these black stumps had bathed in the lagoon to wash away body taints, and the smell of ceremonial oils and greases, then lightly plastered themselves with mud or with dust to further deaden any lingering taint?

Presently the shadows took another step, a definite step or two towards them. Those wide-awake wallabies that had noticed had never seen fire-blackened stumps move upon them like this in the moonlight before. To ask others if *they* saw what they saw they tapped a little warning upon the ground, a soft, inquiring "Thud! Thud!" with the end of their tails. Heads rose inquiringly as some sat back upon their tails, glancing round curiously, sniffing. Soon, here and there; again a black stump stepped towards them, to stop as a wallaby uneasily hopped a few paces away, sat back again and watched, then confidently resumed his feeding.

  Presently they were each in turn hopping a few yards away more frequently from these strange black stumps that so silently moved, only to stand motionless, only to move towards them again. Those wallabies away down at the right-hand end of the grass strip were hopping a few hops along towards the left, parallel with the black wall of scrub, those away down to the left hopping a few yards along to the right. Presently their numbers began to increase towards the centre as their uneasy hoppings took them further in that direction and they began to mix with more and more feeding mates. Some noticed, too, that while they moved *along* the grassy strip the black tree-stumps did not bother them, only to keep them gently, every now and then, moving yet further along. Their number began rapidly to increase.

Here and there a forest wallaby among them became alarmed and began to hop back uncertainly towards the bush trees, generally sitting back, when near safety, to glance uncertainly back at his cousins, those scrub wallabies congregating in such an unusual manner on the open grass. Should he decide that discretion was the better part of valour and bend to hop slowly back into the bush, then the whiz of a boomerang came at him from nowhere. It either broke his legs and left him writhing or launched him upon a frantic bound back into the bush.

But there was no other movement or noise. Then a black tree-stump here and there would step on again. With an uneasy slithering those wallabies fronting it hopped a little further along among their fellows.

And now the more experienced or more uneasy among the scrub wallabies began one by one to hop slowly back towards the blackness of their sheltering scrub. But as sure as any did so a black stump would step out of the scrub shadows and halt him. He would sit back uncertainly on his tail. The stump would definitely move threateningly—it was an out-thrust arm holding a bush that warned the stray back—and the wallaby would uncertainly hop back again to his friends, friends fast increasing in numbers and uneasiness now. This was happening from both ends of that mile-long, narrow strip of grassland. From both ends the wallabies along it were being slowly but surely driven together along this grassy lane between scrub and forest, and were now nearing the mouth of the Trap, the entrance to the little *cul-de-sac* that ran straight back into the black scrub.

The wallabies were now in two mobs, those queer black stumps cleverly urging them together. And now an occasional wallaby would make a frantic dive back to the scrub. Something would jump towards him and threaten him back or, if he persisted, throw a boomerang at him. If not killed, he would crash into the scrub. All the others, now frightened, were commencing to hurry along in the only way it seemed safe for them to go.

When the two mobs met opposite the entrance to the Trap they became mixed in a spreading alarm, causing more and more frantic break-aways to the black scrub. And now at last all seemed clear before them, just that wide gap leading into the black scrub they knew so well and now so much desired.

But for some strange reason the milling mob now hesitated to make the dash to safety, only a few here and there bounding forward to make a break for it. It seemed that the now thoroughly alarmed animals were about to race away in all directions, when from right behind them rose a hundred unearthly yells as women and children, clattering their throwing sticks, together rushed straight upon them from behind.

With one forward bound the entire mob was into the mouth of the Trap and heading straight down it. Spears and boomerangs came whizzing amongst them from both sides as many crashed head over heels over the falling bodies of the crippled ones, while fierce yells from close behind and now from both sides kept them in frantic terror leaping straight down towards the end of the Trap. But from here there suddenly sprang out a line of yelling figures as boomerangs and spears and throwing sticks whizzed straight at them. Numbers fell, while others, frantic with terror, bounded blindly on to thump violently against legs or chest of the spear-throwers or crash against the scrub wall to reel back and be killed by club. The main mob, swarming upon one another in panic, disentangled themselves to flounder back against one another and the writhing cripples, then bound back up along the Trap, again kept clear of the scrub sides by the yelling huntsmen. As this terrified mob surged back up along the Trap they were met by the tight-packed, yelling women and children, striking madly with digging and throwing sticks, often striking one another in the confusion as frantic wallabies bowled over children and even brought women—"Oough!"—to the ground with a terrified bound against their stomachs

On this particular night was the greatest slaughter of wallabies ever known in the Trap. It had been arranged by Red Kangaroo. From boyhood no one had been so keen, so cunning in suggesting timing and vantage places for the hunters, no one so crafty and patient at suggesting yet more sure ways of droving the greatest number of victims to and within the Trap. And for the night he had been given full charge.

Those particular full-moon nights were eagerly looked forward to by the whole tribe. There was only one hunt every three months, which gave those scrub wallabies a chance to build up their numbers again. For, although game was generally plentiful, centuries of experience had taught the tribe not to waste it nor to harry it from its haunts too much.

Neither was one single wallaby wasted in the subsequent feast, even though this "Night of Red Kangaroo", as old Mullionkale sang in the resulting corroboree, had seen the greatest slaughter of wallabies ever known in the Wallaby Trap.

# CHAPTER XXV

## THE SPEECH OF THE RED CHIEF

The chief, Tulumi, closely advised by the warrior Burradella, continued to work wisely for the good of the tribe. Planning carefully while acting cautiously, in two years he had helped strengthen the tribe a little by preventing wasteful killings, insisting upon greater caution among the wandering family groups and the tribe in general, by keeping as much a check as possible upon feuds and raids, and when such could not be prevented insisting upon more careful organization and care in planning the get-away.

The troubles in the tribe had gradually simmered down and confidence returned. The majority became satisfied to wait for the hoped-for changes they felt sure Red Kangaroo would introduce when he became chief. The remainder, becoming reconciled to what they knew now must come, were confident that at least the chief to be would not interfere with the actual immemorial laws of the tribe.

Thus two summers and winters drifted by bringing the time for the people finally to decide whether the warrior Red Kangaroo would become chief of the Gunn-e-darr tribe.

The answer was overwhelmingly yes.

To a shout of, "The Red Chief! The Red Chief!" as every warrior threw his spear to the ground in token salute before Red Kangaroo every shield was held to the chest while every nulla swung to the shield with a "Clash! Clash! Clash!" as their feet in unison began stamping to a roar of war song joined in by the wild chant of the women. Upon the sunlit corroboree ground the tribe with immemorial ceremony made him their warrior chief. As he faced them his red-ochred body seemed afire under the sun, his heart beating wildly, his face glowing as his ears rang to that stamp of feet, clash of shields, roar of, "Red Chief! Red Chief!"

Enough to set a much older man on fire, that wild enthusiasm of his very own warriors bedecked in brilliant feathers, each wearing his skin cape, each ochred in the coloured bars of warriorhood as he danced and sang his allegiance to the tribe and the new chief—the Red Chief. And thus the one-time warrior lad, Red Kangaroo, became the Red Chief, warrior chief of the Gunn-e-darr tribe of the Kamilaroi.

The council appointed Burradella as second chief, Tulumi gravely retired to become one of the seven, the council of the elders.

The Red Chief next day called a council of the elders and all the warriors. In his ringing voice he addressed them on the corroboree ground in front of all the people.

"Now that you have made me war chief, and I am a grown man in body and thought, I will act—for the good of the tribe, not as Chief Jerrabri and his elders, who acted but for themselves. They neglected the good of the tribe, and tampered with some of the tribal laws to their own selfish advantage. I am going to settle this question now for good and all, otherwise it will always cause trouble in the tribe, and finally would destroy us. So now! All elders and elderly warriors who have more than one wife of our tribe may keep one tribeswoman wife but must hand the others over to the younger warriors, and to warriors who have no wives. And they must do so this day! For it is bad for a tribe that old warriors should own two, three, four and more young wives while younger men have but one old wife, and the young warriors none at all.

"And you all know that the law is that so soon as a lad passes through the final initiation of the Bora ceremonies and is granted his right by the council to wear the Bor, Belt of Manhood, then he is also entitled to a wife. The wearing of the Bor gives the new warrior the lawful right to call upon his tribe for a wife. Otherwise they must take for him a wife from an enemy tribe. And it must be so!"

He allowed this to sink in, but there was no need, the eyes of all the tribe, their ears were all for him. No sound of the bush were they conscious of, of nothing but the words, the flashing eyes, the calm though impassioned tones of this wonderful new chief.

"One more law has been tampered with," he cried, "and this again must be put right this very day! And that law is—that a girl baby, unless given at birth by right of our marriage and totemic laws to a grown warrior, cannot be sold to a grown warrior without the full consent of the whole tribe. By law she may be claimed, when she is a woman, as wife by a warrior—always providing his and her totem and moiety[1] allow it."

Giluram's fists gripped his wommera, he was staring as if awakening from a dream. Weetah leant forward, hardly daring to breathe. Here and there a young warrior stared hard; here and there the eyes of a girl grew big and bright, her lips parted, hardly breathing.

"Any old warrior," went on the new

---

[1] *An aboriginal tribe was divided into two moieties or classes, which inter-married, but marriage within each moiety was forbidden. In the Kamilaroi and other tribes these classes were further divided into sub-classes, which complicated the marriage laws.*

chief, "who has thus, years ago, bought a baby girl without right of the marriage laws, must here and now give her back to the tribe!"

Giluram sat back as if exhausted after a long, long run. Weetah sighed deeply. Was she about to laugh, or cry? For she no longer belonged to old Tulduna! She knew that the marriage laws were good for Giluram and her—his group and her group could marry. If only he would claim her now! She glanced towards him again. He was sitting up very straight now, staring towards her, his eyes gleaming. She smiled. They hardly heard what the big new chief was saying next.

Many other girls were staring with shining eyes towards the young warriors. But those thick-heads did not seem to understand; they were all ears and eyes for the new chief.

"And listen yet again!" shouted the chief. "There are some who have sold a wife to a warrior at a great price—the price of a lifetime of work—thus not only acting unfairly to the buyer, but to the tribe. For a warrior forced to buy a wife at such price cannot do his duty by the tribe. All his time is taken up in providing for his family and for the seller, too. Thus the tribe loses the services of a warrior, a hunter, or a weapon-maker through the greed of one old man. And such wrong things must cease. Know then, that from this day for every wife thus unfairly sold, the price is now fully paid!"

Bilar the spear-maker was staring like a fool, mouth sagging open, as he gaped across towards the Red Chief. Gille the Moon, Bilar's wife, started to laugh, then to cry. Old Kuluman's bleary eyes glinted in anger. But then, what could he do about it?

"And from now," shouted the Red Chief, "we shall make more raids on other tribes to steal young girls for wives, and boys that they may grow up with us and become warriors of the Gunn-e-darr tribe, to help quickly strengthen us. For our tribe must die out if we have not enough wives for all our warriors, for then there will be fewer and fewer children to take the place of warriors killed in fight, in the hunt, or who just die.

"We are no longer the tribe our fathers'

fathers knew—nothing near so strong a tribe as our enemies fortunately believe us to be. We can muster barely fifty able-bodied fighting men. And you know that at the next Bora only six young warriors will be made. We know there are tribes around us who can muster one hundred spears, not counting elderly warriors, and that distantly there are tribes that can muster one hundred and fifty! And those distant warriors have long been looking towards our own fair lands. We cannot hold our wonderful lands if we have not many more spears. So let us get them! Meanwhile, while seeking to avoid powerful enemies we shall fight fiercely, but craftily, all warrior bands that come against us.

"At the same time let us offer life and protection to all who might care to come in and join with our tribe—those who are harried by powerful enemies, or who are frightened and think they are weaker than we. They can bring their wives and children to help build up our strength. And—we shall attack and absorb, one after the other, the weakest first, the four smallest tribes near our boundaries. For long we have lost a fighting man or two to them from our small hunting parties, and in small, badly planned raids. But now we shall attack the weakest tribe suddenly, and in strength. To those not killed we shall offer the protection of our tribe, their men, women, and children will become one with us, the Gunn-e-darr tribe. Then, later on, watching for our well-planned chance, we shall attack the next weakest tribe, and absorb them, too. Then the next, then the next, growing stronger each time. By the time we have absorbed these four small tribes we shall have become much stronger. From then on we shall really begin to build up our strength, until in a few years we shall be strong enough to resist any strong tribe that comes against us, or to attack in force any tribe we learn is planning to attack us. Only by quickly acting thus can we hope to become strong enough to hold our wide lands against those distant but very strong tribes that sooner or later must come against us—who would have come long ago, had they only known how weak we are."

The Red Chief paused a moment, then added impressively, "We must begin to carry out our tribal plan quickly, and continuously. Even now we may barely have time. Think of this! Should two enemy tribes, say of one hundred and fifty spears each, combine against this our Gunn-e-darr tribe, what chance would we have?" Upon their intent faces he read his answer.

"We should have *no* chance!" he shouted. "We should be wiped out to the last man, our women and children and lands taken. So we shall start immediately to strengthen our tribe in the hope that we still may have time to build up a power that can resist the combined attack of any two large tribes."

And this the young Red Chief, the council of the elders, the warriors, and the whole tribe, enthusiastically agreed to.

# CHAPTER XXVI
# MAKING MEN STRONG

The ceremonies, the dancing and feasting celebrating the initiation of the Red Chief, were over. Old Mullionkale the playmaker was planning a corroboree to commemorate these stirring events, for no such popular happening was recorded in the legends of the tribe. And so many happy things had happend with it. Giluram had claimed Weetah as wife, Kerran claimed Burunda,[1] Gurie claimed Millimumul,[2] Kubado claimed Karella,[3] Duri claimed Bhan,[4] and Keri claimed Yulowirri.[5]

Young men claimed a score of young girls who, against strict law, had been bought by old men. Bilar the spearmaker was smiling all over his patient face. He was going on his first prolonged hunting

1 *"Swan girl."*
2 *"Swan."*
3 *"South wind."*
4 *"Sweet-scented mistletoe."*
5 *"Rainbow."*

trip for a long, long time—hunting for his family, and the tribe.

Strangely enough, it was Boobuk the warrior who gave a bit of a grumble.

"Just as well this Red Chief allows us to keep at least *one* wife," he growled, "otherwise I might have lost Kupota."

"But I thought you wished so much to get rid of her!" chuckled Bungadoon. "How many times have you come here swearing and bellowing and wishing Red Kangaroo and his cubs would take her?"

"Oh, I couldn't let half-grown pups like those have her," explained Boobuk. "And no warrior would have been game enough to try!" he added grimly. "Anyway, I don't hear that you're in any hurry to lose Pumbul."

"So long as she behaves herself and hunts well," answered Bungadoon grandly, "I'll keep her."

"H'm," mused Boobuk doubtfully. "Oh well, I suppose they're handy to have around the place."

The children, listening in as usual, giggled—more, when Pumbul solemnly shook her head at them.

Yes, this new Red Chief certainly had stirred up the tribe. Cleverly, too. Yet shrewdly again he had called before the council all those who had been forced to give up what they did not rightfully own, and there with friendly smile and soft words complimented them in the name of the tribe until their gloomy looks turned to smiles and they left the council with lighter step, feeling they were good men who had made a sacrifice for the benefit of the tribe.

The Red Chief was happy and wanted everyone else to be happy, too, for his lively young wives Nareen and Naroo had presented him with a baby boy apiece.

Just to make the people feel that the world was all their own old Nundoba the witchdoctor solemnly prophesied, before all the tribe, that from now on the seasons would be good for many a summer and winter, the game and the roots and bulbs of the bush would be plentiful, the birds and the fishes multiply and fatten, and that the Gunn-e-darr tribe of the Kamilaroi under the Red Chief would grow and increase and prosper with the seasons as it had never done since the Dream Time. The moon and the stars and the night and the whisperings of the Spirits of the Bush had told him so.

And time was to prove that Nundoba the witchdoctor prophesied truly.

So with all behind him the young Red Chief had a wonderful start in his lifelong work of building up his beloved tribe. Though, as he had foreseen, it was going to take a long time to achieve the strength he desired, within his first two years he built up the tribe to sixty-five fighting warriors. Fifteen of these were near 60 years of age, twenty were from 35 to 40 years old, while thirty were young warriors from 17 to 26 years. In woman-stealing raids they had brought back to the tribe twenty-seven young women, with the loss of but five warriors killed, and causing much heavier losses to the raided tribes. During that time four different tribes had raided them in turn, but the Red Chief's cunningly prepared ambushes had caused particularly heavy loss to the enemy, and only six Gunn-e-darr warriors had been killed, and two crippled for life. No women had been stolen. So the tribe was much stronger and better prepared, and alert, confident, and contented—and adoring their young Red Chief.

The season eventually came for the "strengthening of the warriors". This particular season was propitious, and Nundoba the witchdoctor had verified the fact. The people believed that at this particular time the meat and fat of the emu contained exceptional strengthening, and medicinal properties—particularly for the younger warriors, from those of the Kubara to four-year warriors.

So now big emu hunts were to be organized so that the older warriors could be rejuvenated through feasting on the rich meat, and the younger grow strong in body and heart against their enemies. They also sought the fat, which, mixed with fine ashes of acacia wood, they would rub thoroughly into their bodies to help keep them supple, to keep out the cold and rain, and also keep out the sickness that sometimes rises up out of the earth.

For although these Stone Age men believed that a fatal illness is usually caused by an enemy working through the machinations of a witchdoctor, or in lesser degree by an evil, earth-bound spirit that still has the "earth-power" to do them harm, they realized that sickness can sometimes "enter the body" by damp contact with "bad places" in the earth. So that emu fat, in a particular season and properly treated with acacia ash by the medicine man, was greatly valued in "keeping out" sickness.

All was bustle about the camp, excitement amongst the children squabbling as to who should help carry the family goods, scoldings and laughter and gossip amongst the women busy at collecting all things from the gunyahs, and packing up. Most of the women, too, were anxious not to forget the hiding-place of some valued little article. For the Red Chief had given orders that the camp was to be shifted from the Burrell Lagoon to the Mullibah Flat Lagoon, where a possible surprise attack by enemies in the height of the ceremonies could be much more easily guarded against.

On the western and southern side of the Mullibah Flat Lagoon myall, wilga, and box grew thickly. On the eastern side, on the open flat country, big red gum-trees and mullibah (yellow-jacket) thrived plentifully. But close round the camp was no dense scrub, and no undergrowth of any sort to give cover to a lurking enemy. The big tree-trunks were all he could hide behind, and between them the earth was carpeted with short green grass. So there was no protective cover for a creeping enemy to stage a surprise attack. But near by there was perfect cover for the tribe, for only three-quarters of a mile away loomed the Porcupine Ridges, the dense patches of hoop-vine scrub sheltering the Secret Camp, into which almost impenetrable sanctuary the women and children could swiftly disappear in case of dire emergency.

And yet, where all seemed so well planned and safe, the Red Chief was soon to be put to the test of his life. It was to prove a long, successful life, afterwards sung in the legends of his people for as long as one solitary member remained. But this emergency, when he was but two years a chief, was to prove to be the severest test of all.

The loaded tribe, happily making their way among the big old box-trees and yellow-jackets, yodelling their way past clumps of myall and wilga, came out on to the pleasant greenery and sunlit waters of the Mullibah Flat Lagoon. All hands were busy then at building the gunyahs, gathering wood and setting this favourite camp and corroboree ground in order.

The Red Chief selected the look-out men, the leaders of the hunting parties, and the camp guards for the women and children. The warrior Burradella, second chief under the Red Chief, with twenty-four young warriors was to remain in charge of the camp and look-outs, guarding the women and children and old people. He was responsible, too, for guarding the country immediately round the camp and watching for possible smoke signals from Carrowreer and Ydire look-outs, while boys for practice and utility could also watch for and relay signals to Burradella from Black Hill. The remainder were divided into three hunting parties, according to their totem, the most envied at this season being those who were entitled to hunt the emu. At least a week of solid hunting was ahead for all three parties.

No simple task for the Red Chief, that of allotting for every single man and boy his duties. For the lives of these Stone Age men and women were strictly governed, day by day, season by season, year by year, from birth to death, by strict laws governed by a culture deep, intricate, and clever, developed through we know not what great ages of time.[6]

So, in this series of hunts the Red Chief did not choose the hunters by favour nor yet because of their skill alone. For, in somewhat the same way as the intricate cross system of marriage laws was so cleverly designed to keep each tribal strain pure and virile, the totemic laws as

> 6 *The widely held belief that Stone Age men had little more brains than were necessary to hunt for their living and roughly chip a tomahawk head from a lump of stone is quite erroneous. Very probably the same mistake has been made about Stone Age men in other lands than our own.*

applied to hunting were designed according to spiritual beliefs, also as a safeguard in the preservation of game.

The tribe strongly believed in reincarnation, not only in the form of man, but of animal, bird, and reptile also. Thus a warrior of the Emu totem would not hunt the emu, for who could know, if he killed an emu he might kill his own brother who had returned from the Land of Shades in the form of an emu, his totem bird. And so with all things. For no one harms any living thing within the family of his totem, even to the trees, or the grasses, or the foods that give totem creatures shelter and upon which they are temporarily living, except in time of fearful drought. Only then, to save the life of his wife and child, will a man sorrowfully take the risk of killing that animal or bird or reptile in which may now be the soul of his own brother.

So the Red Chief carefully chose the hunters so that in each band there would be men of various totems, which meant that any game meat could fall to the spears of some. Those who could not eat of the flesh of their totem kangaroo or emu, for instance, could eat of wallaby, fish, or waterfowl. Thus none would go hungry, while the hunters of the greatly desired emu, and also of the kangaroo, could give their individual attention to this particular game, which they were entitled to kill.

At last all the plans were laid to the Red Chief's satisfaction— but not to that of the young warriors. Hurt, then angry, they received in selfish disappointment the order to remain in camp. They were now much more outspoken than when they had gone in dread of Jerrabri and his council. That night mutterings of discontent broke out around the young fellows' campfires.

"Why aren't the *old* warriors detailed to guard the women and children?" murmured one. "It has always been their job!"

"It's all they're good for," answered another. "They cannot stand up to the long, hot day's chase as we can. Anyway, why cannot those fifteen elderly warriors remain in camp, while we draw lots among us to make up the other nine? That would give fifteen of us a chance, anyway."

"We should *all* go to the hunt," growled another, "not only fifteen of us. Those old fifteen, and the elder warriors, have enjoyed many, many huntings of the emu, many a feast on the rich meat that makes a young warrior grow strong."

"Yes," agreed another eagerly, "they have had their day and now it is their turn to guard the women and children. It's all they're fit for, anyway."

"Better not let them hear you say that," chuckled his mate, "or you might find yourself out on the duelling ground. There are some quick-tempered tough old boys among them."

"Bah! They couldn't hit a kangaroo if it sat back on its tail and looked at them," broke in a young buck who fancied himself, "let alone stand up against a fighting warrior! Look how the Red Chief himself stood up against the best in the tribe when he was but a Kubara!"

"Ah," replied one quietly, " but there is only one Red Chief! And whether but Kubara or grown man, *he* could stand up against the best of any tribe!"

They were uneasily silent at this, but presently mutterings broke out again.

A few of the fathers and uncles,

sympathizing with the disappointed men, talked together and next day agreed they would stay behind and help mind camp. After all, they agreed among themselves, they had enjoyed many an emu hunt. They did not really mind whether they went on this particular hunt or not. They would stay behind and help guard camp, while a younger warrior could go on the hunt in place of each of them. This delighted the young fellows, who now won some of the women's sympathy also.

To the Red Chief came the warrior Burradella to report the camp gossip of the women at the younger warriors' grumblings. The Red Chief frowned angrily, then lapsed into thought. Presently he asked for bearers, and sent them with a message stick to every warrior of the tribe commanding all to a high-sun council of the warriors that very day.

Before high sun every warrior was on the council ground, curious to know what this unexpected council had been called for. As each arrived he laid his spear before the chief, then quietly took his place in a semicircle sitting before the Red

Chief, beside whom sat the second chief, Burradella.

At high sun Burradella stood up. Immediately then every warrior struck hard the ground before him with his nulla, once. Every nulla striking as one, a sharp ringing blow.

"This council is called," said Burradella clearly, "because there are bad murmurings of discontent amongst the younger warriors of our tribe. And where there is discontent, the talk flies to the women's ears. And they talk that discontent back to the warrior or warriors of their own gunyah. And each woman takes her side with her warrior against the woman and warrior of the other gunyah. The women then continue to talk against other women and other women's warriors. The warriors hear it. There are black looks. Then the warriors begin to quarrel, one against the other. Quickly sides are taken, the trouble spreads. Finally the warriors spring up and fight, and a man or more may be killed. This our tribe cannot afford to lose one single warrior killed in that way. Those whose loose talk and discontent would cause such killings are enemies to our tribe.

"The Red Chief talks to you now. I order you all, listen to him with both ears, for it will do much good to all, and to the tribe."

As the Red Chief stood up, every warrior struck his shield sharply with his nulla, the ringing blow sweeping out over the bushland. The Red Chief, a towering figure now of polished bronze from the sun streaming upon his red-ochred body, slowly turned completely round, gazing upon all. Stern his face, grim-set his jaw, but he spoke not in anger, yet with an authority that no warrior there, nor any dozen combined dared question. His deep, strong voice rolled out over them.

"You one-, two-, three- and four-year warriors have thoughts only for yourselves—grumbling because you must remain in camp to guard the women and children, without whom there would be *no* young warriors at all! Your only wish is to boast of your kills, with the added pleasure of the emu hunt and your gorging on its meat for the next seven suns. You would leave the oldest warriors to guard this camp.

Are not our wives and piccaninnies, your sisters and your friends' sisters and all the near-marriageable girls worth fighting for? Would you rather gorge on emu meat out in the bush than stay here and protect your mother, your sister, and your friend's sister?

"Ah! Yes, yes, you mutter *now!* But you are ready to leave them to a feeble guard of old men at the mercy of any picked party of enemy warriors who may attack the camp while our strong, fighting warriors would all be away. These seasoned old warriors have done many years of guard work and fighting to protect the women and children of our tribe before you and I were born. Many is the time they have fed us and fought to protect us while we were helpless children, looked after us throughout all the seasons until we became Bora warriors ourselves. And yet you want these few old warriors to remain and guard a camp that holds many more women and children than either you or I ever knew before! What chance would these few old warriors have against a strong party of young enemy warriors sent against them? They would fight to the last. We should return to find their eyes picked out by the crows, find the bodies of all the elderly women, find the young women and children stolen away. And what use would your bellies stuffed full of emu meat be to you then?" He glared towards them, but they could not meet his flashing eyes.

Then he roared, "There are ninety wives in our tribe! Twenty are old women, but sixty can still be mothers of children. And there are twenty young lubras who very soon will be of marriageable age. And there are one hundred and thirty boy and girl children. All these mean much more to the tribe than *you* twenty-four warrior cubs. The tribe could do without *you!* But the tribe could *not* do without the women and children!" He paused a moment, his big chest drew a deep breath as scornfully he gazed down upon the now bowed heads of the young warriors.

"And now," he asked quietly, "do you still want to fill your guts with emu meat? Or are you content to remain behind and guard the women and children?"

"No, no, Red Chief!" they all seemed to murmur at once. "We stay behind and guard the women and children of our tribe. Say no more, for your words burn us like firesticks."

Next day the Red Chief, with thirty-nine warriors, strode out for Breeza Plains, followed by the ringing cooees of encouragement and wishes of good luck from Burradella's guards and the women and children. A beautiful day, with the trunks of the big old yellow-jackets reflecting the warm sunlight, faint hum of insects, booming call of a swamp pheasant. The forty warriors strode along in the wake of the Red Chief, gossiping cheerily in anticipation of the seven days' hunt, the sun shining warmly upon the strong bodies of these primitive children of the wild.

For seven glorious suns they hunted the emu and feasted on the strength-giving meat away out over the Breeza Plains. At dawn of the eighth sun the Red Chief ordered the final drive, back towards camp, to secure a good quantity of the best meat to carry back to the hungry guards. He, with nine picked warriors, would hunt his way back to camp this day. Meanwhile he placed Boobuk, the seasoned warrior in charge of the remaining twenty-nine men. Their job was to hunt kangaroos diligently and return to camp loaded with the best meat by sunset the following day. To a waving of hunting weapons, a rousing chorus of cooees, the two parties went their separate ways.

Thus in a rosy dawn the Red Chief and his nine men moved leisurely back towards camp.

## CHAPTER XXVII
### THE LOST DILLY-BAG

On that morning of the eighth sun the warrior Burradella, with the guards, escorted the people from the camp for the day's hunting. The women and children were eagerly chatting of the warriors' impending return as they strolled along under the ironwoods and box with their dilly-bags and fishing nets and traps, their yam-sticks and grain containers. They knew the warriors had enjoyed great hunting, for the Black Hill look-out had been told so by smoke signals. Enthusiastically they debated their champions' chances of having secured the most game. The Red Chief would be first, of course, but who after him?

Hungrily they looked forward to the warriors' returning loaded with the rich red meats on which all whose totem, ceremonial, and mourning laws allowed it could feast as a change from fish and birds, small game and plant foods. And after the feastings would come the seven exciting days of the dance and totem ceremonies.

There was no dawdling, no young girl straying from her party or falling behind, no mischievous children running ahead to hide and not answer when called—all were too scared to play such tricks. For the warrior Burradella was painfully strict. His orders to the young warrior guards were that should a woman stray from her party the guard was to rap her on the head with his nulla hard enough to give her a ding-dong headache, while any child who played up was to receive a switching that would tan his hide so that he would not sit comfortably for seven suns. Should any guard prove lax in vigilance Burradella would attend to that man himself. Thus daily Burradella made certain that no woman or child would be stolen by prowlers while he had charge of the camp.

So on the morning of this eighth sun there was no lagging. When they came to the Namoi at a favoured spot[1] most of the crowd spread out along the river bank cheerfully to set their nets and traps and lines. A small party had been ordered by Burradella to proceed upstream and wade across river by the shallows to a small lagoon.[2] Near mid-shadow time (towards three o'clock) they were to cross back again and hurry to rejoin the main party when all would return to Mullibah Lagoon.

This little party waded through the shallows and hastened to the lagoon in lively spirits. They spread out across the shallows, energetically stirring up the mud with their feet, chattering and laughing in joke and gossip while continually picking

*1 Where the bridge spans the river now.*
*2 On the left side of the road that now runs to Gunnible.*

up with hand or toes the fat mussel shells their feet were digging for. Soon their bark and rush-plaited game bags were filled with the mussels. Meanwhile, as the muddied water became thicker, here and there the head of a fish poked gasping to the surface, smothering with mud-clogged gills. Vain for him to sink when they splashed towards him, for he must come up or choke to death on the bottom. The piccaninnies gleefully snatched up the woebegone yabbies and turtle that went crawling out to the lagoon bank sickened by the mud. At mid-sun they cooked and ate a hearty meal of this good food, for it was so plentiful today that they would still fill their food containers to overflowing before returning to the main body.

Towards mid-afternoon the guards mustered them, urging haste, to wade back across river and rejoin Burradella's main party. They had not gone far[3] when Weetah stopped with a little cry of dismay. She had lost her dilly-bag; she

3 *They had reached the place where the Osric Street drain now empties out on to Mullibah Flat.*

remembered now she had left it on a log at the river crossing while she paused a moment to attend the baby, the proud Giluram's masterpiece. That bag contained many things useful to a young married woman—varying needles painstakingly fashioned from splinters of kangaroo and emu bone, finer needles from fishbone, awls from the long tooth of the kangaroo, sewing threads laboriously spun from bark fibres and hair of humans and animals and prepared from sinews of animals. Her tying cords of animal hide, flint and shell knives, tinder to dust on her fire-making sticks when rubbing them together to make a fire on a wet day, balls of dried clays and kaolins that when wetted are used to put over a wound with acacia-leaf ash from a particular tree, fish-hooks of bone and shell, with other indispensable family things, were treasured in that dilly-bag.

There was a "something" else, a little something she prized ever so much more highly than anything else in all the great big world, excepting Giluram and the baby. But—those medicines! She might need those medicines any time; she dreaded a day when Giluram might be brought home wounded, and she carried these medicines securely wrapped in a neat, secure, waterproof little bag from a particular part of the skin of a kangaroo. It was within that comfy little bag that she carried the "something" she prized so much. No one else had ever seen it, except once when shyly she had shown it to Giluram. But she had found it long before her happiness when Giluram had been able to claim her; she had found it when she thought she could never have him; she had found it and wished over it—oh, so many, many times! It was her lucky charm—a little, rounded, pearly stone.

She had found it in the head of a big old river jewfish some years before, when she was a very young girl. All alone she had found the big fish stranded in a shallow waterhole on a day when *she* had strayed from the women's party, when for some unexplainable reason she had felt rebellious and miserable. The sight of that great big, helplessly stranded fish had been a thrill.

She had stared at him with a smile; from great eyes he had gazed back; she had felt him to be her very own. She had sat there and watched him a long time, she hated to pull him from the water. At last, of course, she had to.

Knowing now her escapade would be forgiven when she came staggering back to camp with such a mighty fish, she still felt rebellious, felt she wanted to do something she ought not to do. So, all alone by her little bush fire, she had roasted and eaten part of the enormous head. She could not eat the great big eyes. She had taken them across to a deep waterhole in the Namoi and let them sink back into the river. Thus the spirit of the mighty fish would swim for ever in that great big awful river.[4]

It was when she had returned to dine upon the head that she had found her lucky charm—a small, pearly pebble growing in

---

[4] *The tribe called the Namoi their "River of Life", and also referred to it as the "Great, Big, Awful River", probably in fearful memory of vast floods when in ages past the river was far mightier than now.*

the "backbone-neck" of the fish, right behind the huge head.[5] She had told no one, but had slept with it, in the little bag, under her head ever since. She was certain that her lucky charm had helped her get Giluram. And now the baby.

And she was certain that as sure as Walcha the sun arose every morning, so would the lucky charm be putting great power for good into her healing powders. No matter how badly Giluram might one day be wounded, those powders would save him. And now the lucky charm, and the powders, and the dilly-bag were away back where she had left them by the log at the river crossing.

She called Giluram, who was acting as a guard, and explained softly, "I *must* bring back my dilly-bag! You take baby and carry on with the women and children. I'll take little brother Tuki with me and run

---

*5 Just occasionally thus is found the "pearl" of the jewfish. It is not a pearl, of course; it is a bony growth the size of a small marble, in some cases with a pearly tinge.*

back and get the bag. You tell Burradella that Tuki and I will run fast there and back and will quickly catch him up.

"All right," said Giluram as he took the baby. "But remember that Burradella will have no mercy on me if you do not soon both catch us up. Run all the way and return back along the lagoon creek.[6] The going is rougher that way, but much shorter."

Weetah and Tuki ran back along the low bank of the creek until dense variegated thistles growing seven and eight feet high along both banks of the creek barred their way. They slipped down into the dry creek-bed and continued running until they were within a hundred yards of the river. Here the creek mouth was heavily snagged by logs, a matted barricade of dead, mud-encrusted timber, and they slowed down, to step or scramble over log after log. They did not talk, saving their breath for the long run back. Within twenty yards of the river crossing they froze in their tracks as a

---

[6] *That creek is still the natural water-run from Mullibah Lagoon to the river.*

man's guttural voice said, "Come here! Look at this!" and another grunted in reply.

Weetah put her hand over Tuki's mouth as she looked warningly into his startled eyes.

"Hss!" she whispered. "Enemies!" She pointed up at the wall of thistles growing away out from the bank. "Be a snake! Follow me! And keep your nose to my heels!"

They crept up the creek bank and noiselessly in amongst the thistle leaves, the giant stalks now high above them. In that smothering weed jungle of broad, mottled green leaves they vanished. Two little black bodies writhing straight in amongst the prickle-edged leaves and tough butts of the giant stalks with no more noise than the rustle of the snake they were so perfectly imitating. In their nostrils was the smell of heavy earth bearing prolific growth, acrid tang from the forest of thistles. When a good way in they came to a rich patch of moist black loam where Mother Earth not only reared her luxuriant thistles eight feet high but proudly bore, too, a prolific growth of brilliantly green clover rioting down there amongst the denseness of the stalks. Here Weetah halted Tuki by holding her foot to his face. She squirmed round like a possum, her eyes staring into his big round ones.

"Tuki!" she whispered, and stretched her arm through the leaves back towards the camp. "Crawl right through—that way—until you come out into the open bush. But before you leave the thistles, be very, very careful! See everything! Hear everything! Be not seen, nor heard! If any sign of an enemy, try to guess how many are there. Then you must creep back into the thistles, and work your way out another way. For you must hurry back to camp and warn Burradella. You *must* do this thing! But remember! If you are seen, or heard, then they will kill you!"

While talking she had been groping in amongst the thistle stalks and quietly pulling at the long, strong clover vines massed with their little green leaves. Then she was twisting the vines into cords and these with their leaves she twisted round Tuki's head until his head, his thick black hair was a mass of green. She stood up, reaching up for some of the smaller thistle leaves. She squatted down again beside Tuki and firmly stuck these white and green mottled leaves in among the emerald-green clover covering his head.

"Ah!" She smiled warmly. "Now, when little Tuki peers from the thistle edge no eye of man or animal or bird can possibly see him in his quietness. For remember, Tuki, it is only your eyes that must first peer out on the open bushland. And then you can move your ears that they may hear. And your nostrils that they may smell should there be tang of rancid fat upon the painted bodies of enemies. And now, Tuki, hear me well again. I do not think you will meet any enemies on the other side, on our camp side of these thistles. I think the men whose voices we heard were but scouts who had only just crossed the river shallows and had found our tracks. They will send back word, then wait until their main party comes up. So, if you see and hear no sign of the enemy when you reach the thistle edge, then quickly make down into the creek. Be sure to choose low ground for the best cover. Once you are into the creek its banks will hide you. Run for your life back along the creek to camp. The people will have arrived back by then. Tell Burradella that we heard voices of enemies talking on this side of the river at our crossing place. But of what tribe, or how many others there are, we don't know. Tell him that Weetah will stop here and try to spy on them and learn who they are and how many there are. Then I shall come back as quickly as I can by the creek way. Now, do you understand all?"

Tuki nodded, his eyes big and shining, his gaze had never left his sister's face. She smiled softly, reached her hands to his head, gently pressed his cheeks to hers.

"Little brother," she whispered, "the elders will soon take you from the women to start your early training for the first Bora warriorhood. But if you can only safely warn the warrior Burradella of these enemies now creeping down upon the camp then old Mullionkale the play-maker himself will make the story. Your deed will be sung in corroboree long before you are made a warrior. Now go!"

With one last, long look at Weetah Tuki

turned and crawled away. Weetah gazed at the dense leaves, her heart hurting as she listened to the faint rustle which in a moment died into silence.

## CHAPTER XXVIII

## ABANDON CAMP

Weetah crept back towards the river almost to the bank, where the thistles died away before the big river trees. As she peered out from the thistles her heart leapt at sight of two painted warriors sitting on a log by the crossing bank, her log, the log on which she had sat with the baby and left her dilly-bag. It was not only that they were enemies, it was that they were the most feared enemies of all. There was no mistaking those vivid circles of white ochre emphasising the fierce, deep-set eyes, the queer dash across the forehead, the strange splash down the cheeks that caused the shaggy faces to stand out like living skulls. Cassilis warriors!

Leaning across the log were their long, cruelly barbed spears, wommera and shield to hand, war boomerangs, nulla, fighting axe and bone dagger looped by thong to their belts. Such weapons told Weetah at a glance that these men were not just hit-and-run raiders. She listened for sound of others coming. They had spread out the contents of her dilly-bag between them on the log, were examining the little treasures with interest and an occasional guttural joke.

Then one held up the little bag—the precious little bag—they laughed as at a great joke. He tipped the contents out on to the log and Weetah's heart missed a beat as he held up the little charm. They examined it curiously, then contemptuously he flipped it out towards the river. Weetah watched the flight of that little pebble as never before she had followed the flight of a wild bee to its nest. She was with it at its tiny splash and her heart leapt with joy as she knew it was in the shallows—she knew she would *never* forget that exact spot. The charm was of the river and had gone back to the river, but Weetah knew the charm was of her, too, and the river would give it back to her, because she had given back to the river the spirit of the big old jewfish through its eyes. And in a flash she knew she need never fear the river, their tribal river, the "great big awful river" of the Gunn-e-darr. No matter what else befell, neither she, nor Giluram, nor the baby would ever drown.

Then up from the river bank stepped two more warriors, coming casually towards the log. Despite her fear Weetah felt a momentary admiration for these solidly built men, striding forward as arrogantly as if they owned the country their big feet trod upon. These were picked warriors and must be of a large party, for they had braved their way through other tribes' lands.

Weetah trembled. How many were there? If they were in large numbers, then they might steal down upon her tribal camp this very night. And the Red Chief with the hunter warriors was still away!

And now here was a long-feared enemy by the greatest of bad luck coming by the river crossing where he had walked right upon the women's hunting tracks of this very day. But he would wait until after dark to follow them, not knowing the warriors were away.

Oh, had little Tuki got through? He, she, *must* find Burradella so he could warn the Red Chief. She *must* get back to warn the camp!

The two newcomers, each standing easily balanced upon one leg, hand resting upon upright spears, were questioning the two scouts sprawling on the log. One of the log men stood up, faced towards Weetah's hiding-place, and pointed with an upthrust of the chin. She knew he was explaining that these fresh tracks they had found were apparently returning towards the Mullibah Lagoon. From somewhere down river a crow urgently called, "Cark! Cark!" The scouts listened, the crow called again, and three scouts immediately turned and started to run—in the direction of the distant Burrell Lagoon. The fourth man swept the things back into the dilly-bag, then he, too, seized his weapons and ran on after his mates.

"Most of them must be making for the old Burrell Lagoon camp," thought Weetah. "They think to find us there. But these scouts will tell them of all these tracks leading towards the Mullibah Lagoon! They could all be back on these tracks before sunset!"

She peered up and down river, listening. Stood on tiptoe, searching, listening. No faintest sign of an enemy now. She took a desperate risk, but did not hesitate, stepped out of the thistles, raced to the river bank, peered, then swiftly began to wade, her ears alert for any sound anywhere, but her eyes only for one spot. She began to swim, then dived, but she knew she would find it—it would be waiting for her—exultantly she saw the little pearly sheen blinking up at her from the crystal clear bottom. Lovingly she picked it up, slipped it between her lips while still under water—and under water she swam back to the bank. As she climbed out she knew they would never get the charm, if chased she would swallow it and dive back into the river. But she felt now that everything would be all right. Little Tuki would get through; she would get through. Giluram and the baby and the tribe would be quite all right.

She stepped up the bank, raced across the clear bank back towards the thistles and, skirting them, vanished down into the dry creek-bed like a startled bandicoot. With her heart in her mouth she raced back towards the camp. Had the fleetest enemy scout been there to see it is doubtful indeed if he could have caught her.

Little Tuki won through. Suddenly he appeared, racing through the camp as if all evil were at his heels. He stumbled to his knees gasping, "Burradella! Burradella! Enemy! Enemy!"

Burradella was standing gravely there before the boy could talk. Tuki's heart felt like bursting, but he gasped out then the message from Weetah, word for word.

And the warrior Burradella acted swiftly, and definitely.

"Bunnadunne!"[1] he said. "Race to the Black Hill. Tell the look-out to

*1 "A swift runner."*

smoke-signal Carrowreer look-out, and the Red Chief away out on Breeza Plains, 'Enemy been heard talking on river crossing between Burrell Lagoon and Mullibah Flat Lagoon camp. Women and children being rushed to the Secret Camp under guard.' " And the swiftest runner of the young warriors was speeding away towards the look-outs.

"Giluram!" ordered Burradella. "Take Kubado and Burowa. Run up the creek. Find Weetah. Carry on swiftly and spy on the enemy. Count tracks. Rush to me some idea of numbers, and who they are, and where camped, if they *are* camping. If you can't send me any news, say, not later than three hours after sunset, then don't send here, for I may be gone. Send a runner straight to the Black Hill and fire-signal me and the Red Chief."

Handing over the baby to his mother, Giluram seized his weapons and with a grunt to Kubado and Burowa was running up along the creek in anxious haste for Weetah, his prized young wife.

"Quick!" shouted Burradella. "The youngest woman and oldest children make this camp look as if we've left it hours ago, just taken our time to walkabout to another camp. We must gain time, make them believe we do not suspect there are any enemies at all anywhere near. Now fix those fires so that they look hours old—when the enemy scouts come there must be no embers left, only warm ashes. Hurry! All other women and children make ready to start for the Secret Camp! Bundle up food and water. Fifteen warriors collect all weapons to accompany the women as guard. Be quick!"

Young women and children ran to the fires, snatching the burning and charred sticks and running out into the lagoon to thrust them deep into the mud, then splashing back to the fires to scrape the live embers on to pieces of bark and hurry these, too, out into the lagoon. Very soon the fires were out, leaving only hot earth and ashes looking as natural as if they had been abandoned hours ago and slowly burnt down to ashes.

The older women and children were collecting their precious belongings and bundling them up for the get-away. Babies wound chubby legs round their mothers' necks, clinging to their hair while hastily they collected the precious belongings of themselves and their absent husbands—what a howl there'd be if a wife left behind any precious trinket of *his!* Children were scrambling for the bundles they should carry, everyone fearful of overlooking some family treasure—old Mulliwah nearly in hysterical tears because she could not find the dried eagle's claw that kept her from harm. The guards were hurrying to collect all weapons left in camp, sorting out all they could carry and fight with, quickly burying the remainder and all camp gear that could not be carried. Then all hands swiftly set to disguise tracks and give the camp every appearance of having been leisurely abandoned for the time being.

Soon the women and children, loaded with everything they could possibly carry, came streaming out from camp, hurried by their fifteen guards. The warrior Burradella stopped them and ordered the oldest twenty women to stand fast. Then he called the guards, as he pointed away from the Porcupine ridges out towards the open country.

"Take the women and children as if you were only making for the Mooki River to form a camp there. Your tracks leading away from this camp will be plain to see, going right away in the opposite direction to our Secret Camp. But when you get well out in the long thick grass spread out, then turn south back towards the Black Hill. And so on up to the Porcupine Ridges and big scrubs and the Secret Camp. That will puzzle their scouts in sunset time, and delay them for a time at least. And remember—we need *all* the time we can gain. Now go!"

As they moved off he turned to those women silently waiting. None of these twenty were under sixty years of age, several were eighty.

"It is best you women do not travel with the others," he said kindly. "The way is long and rough. For you can be sure there will be a lot of twisting and turning to deceive our enemies. And those impatient young guards will hurry the women and children along. In the dark hours you might never reach the

Secret Camp. So easy also to snap an ankle, to stake a foot, to drop exhausted in urgent flight at night. The enemy would hunt you down in daylight, when my few scattered guards will be fighting elsewhere, and will not be there to protect you. Have no fear, though. We shall get you to safety by a slower, but a sure way."

He smiled at their lined, anxious faces. They were ready to just sit there and wait what might befall them should he order it, and for a moment they had thought he meant to. For it is a law of every tribe that, if hard pressed, the weak ones must not hinder the safety of the tribe. When a man or woman becomes too weak to keep up with the tribe then his or hers is the choice—to meet swift death at the hands of the tribe or to wait there and perish by thirst or slow starvation and weakness in drought time, or by the rough clubs of a pursuing enemy in war time.

Yes, these old twenty were ready—it was the law. But life, unless one is suffering too much, is sweet almost to the very last—when we may welcome it, or just don't care, or just don't know.

And hope dawned again in the hearts of these weak old ones who had toiled all their lives for the tribe, came surely as their eyes that had seen so much gazed up into the warrior Burradella's face.

"Now all take your time," he said earnestly. "Stick together, one help the other. And I know that you can all travel in the night, so long as you go slowly, and keep together. Have no fear, for the enemy may not come before dawn—may not come then. Even if he did he would not hurry aside on the tracks of a few old women; he will be most anxious to find the tracks of our fighting men. But long before he comes you will have lost *your* tracks. And by then," he added grimly, "some of us at least will be ready to keep that enemy busy. So don't hasten and weary yourselves, but do carefully what I say. Make straight for the Porcupine Ridges but turning off to climb up to the edge of the hoop-vine scrub by the big tree of the eaglehawk's nest. There a wallaby pad wanders deep into the scrub—you know it quite well. Once on that pad in the scrub, and your tracks are lost. It may be dark when you get there, but I know that, one behind the other, you can slowly feel your way and crawl through the scrub, with the wallaby pad to guide you. Crawl right through that first scrub, you then come out under starlight upon the porcupine grass at the foot of Big Porcupine Hill. Climb up the little way to where the black scrub starts again. Enter carefully just there. Crawl on into the blackness just a little way. You will be weary for a rest then, so sit quietly and eat. No talking above a whisper. And, of course, no fire. When you have eaten, lie down and rest, sleep if you can. And then, just as Djurrabl the evening star is gliding down to sleep over the tree-tops of Porcupine Ridge, I shall send a warrior messenger running to you to tell you further what to do. And now, farewell. And have no fear."

And the twenty smiles, with the murmur of respect due to the second chief, warmed Burradella's heart as the twenty old ones stepped away towards the shadowing hills as if they were young girls again.

Burradella would save these old women if he could. He knew that few enemies bothered to kill old women, considering them useless to either side, though they did kill the old men at times, for generally they were the weapon-makers for the tribe, and thus valuable to their enemy.

But—if an enemy just missed out on a prize then his rage would be ungovernable. He would club every man, woman, child, baby, he could lay his hands upon. And—Burradella smiled grimly—there would be vindictive hearts and raging heads among the enemy in the morning. For if this reported enemy really did prove to be a strong war party then they would rush a large—but abandoned camp—with the dawn. With daylight the tracks would shout up at them that they had had a large camp at their mercy. They had missed out. They would go crazy, seeking revenge on anything they could reach with spear and club.

# CHAPTER XXIX

## DANGER COMES FAST

Burradella turned back to the ominously silent camp, anxious indeed for news, hoping he had done the right thing, while wishing that the enemy voices Weetah and Tuki had overheard might prove to belong only to scouts of a raiding party. He could guard the women and children against raiders, but a war party would be a different thing altogether. He must swiftly get in touch with these enemies and harass them if possible until the Red Chief could collect the warriors together. He drew a deep breath of anxiety—his twenty-four young guards were now almost as scattered as the tribal warriors. He glanced towards Black Hill, from which several hours ago a smoke column had told him the Red Chief had answered his signal. He breathed more easily, remembering how swiftly the chief could act when need demanded.

He strode towards the six young warrior guards remaining to him here, and the twenty boys standing silently by them, boys of from twelve to fifteen years of age. Invaluable in an emergency as runners, slippery as eels in scouting, too. And now, nearly jumping out of their skins to do something. Grasping their small but vicious spears, little boomerangs, nullas, wommeras, and shields, every pair of eyes imploring the warrior Burradella to order *him* to do something against the enemy. Burradella smiled. It was good to see the tribal boys keen like this, boys he had helped to train himself.

"Warriors of the Bora, and warriors to be," said Burradella, "we shall hold a council of war. We do not know if it is war yet, for our news is only that an enemy has been heard close to camp—but that enemy is of the Cassilis! If it should prove to be war, then we are prepared, for we have sent the women and children to safety. Our job now is to learn all we can about the enemy, to puzzle him and hold him away from the women and children and give time for the Red Chief to gather the warriors to our help. We shall wait here for Weetah; she should be here now with news. If not, we wait for Giluram. If their news means war, then we prepare an ambush up on Porcupine Ridge. For in the morning the enemy will track the women and children up to the edge of the big hoop-vine scrub where they have entered it on their way to the Secret Camp. We shall spread out and fight from the shelter of the scrub edge. As you know one man fighting from the scrub is worth six fighting out in the open. And, for a time, our enemies will not guess how few we are. But we *must* act swiftly. You boys will be ready to run like the wind to the lookout posts, and to the women hiding in the Secret Camp, and to wherever my young warriors may be, and take their places so that what warriors I have can gather around me. The elder boys among you will take their places with us and fight. And now—rest until we hear news."

All struck their shields with their nullas, then sat down in silence until Burradella jumped up as Weetah came running into camp, gasping for breath. In swift sentences she told her news.

Immediately she spoke of the four Cassilis warriors in war-paint Burradella knew relief that he had acted rightly, though his anxiety was greatly increased. Weetah had met Giluram with Kubado and Burowa running up the creek. She had told them the enemy seemed to have gone in the direction of the Burrell Lagoon. Giluram and his two mates had then turned off and run straight through bush for the lagoon while she had come on here to camp.

The warrior Burradella gravely thanked her for what she and little Tuki had done for the tribe this day, advised her to eat, wrap up her things, then make her way quietly to the Secret Camp.

"Kuppa! Burrai!" Burradella said sharply to two of the elder boys. "You both have been trained in smoke and fire signalling. Now run to the Black Hill look-out, tell the three men there to send smoke signals—fire if it is too late—to the Red Chief saying 'Cassilis enemies. Four seen on river. Looks like war party camped close.' Do you understand?"

The boys nodded.

"When they have signalled," resumed

Burradella, "tell them to signal the two look-out men away on Carrowreer to repeat that signal. After which the two men on Carrowreer are to make their way to me here. Understand?"

The boys nodded again.

"Right. Then tell the men on Black Hill to run down and join me at the edge of the hoop-vine scrub where the women enter on the way to the Secret Camp. You two stay on look-out duty, in case the Red Chief signals. If he does, one of you hurry with the message to me. Now run!"

And the boys sped away.

"Kaleboi![1] Kuliya![2] Mullion![3] Dhina-wan![4]" said Burradella. "You four boys make your way swiftly to Carrowreer, climb the mountain, and do look-out duty when the dawn comes. Be cautious, for you may run into some enemy party. Be very careful when you are climbing the mountain, for the enemy may send, or may already have sent, a party to ambush our look-outs there. So be very wary. But," he added kindly, "I know

1 "Brown snake."  3 "Eagle."
2 "Gliding possum." 4 "Emu."

you can make it, even though you must travel through the night. The spirits of the night are on our side, for this night our tribe is in grave danger and the spirits of our departed warriors will gather all around you, guarding you from harm." The warrior Burradella let this sink in, knowing so well how full-grown warriors feared the spirits of the night.

"Yes, I am sure you will make it," resumed Burradella. "You have only a few miles to go, and soon the cloak of night will shield you from enemies. You are as slithery as the snake, secretive as the squirrel mouse. And with the dawn your eyes will be those of the eagle to see our enemies' movements, you will be swifter than the emu to bring me news. Now go!"

And with one clash of the nulla to their little shields the boys were swiftly away.

"Guru," said Burradella to a young warrior, "you with Keri and Duri take these fourteen lads quickly to the hoop-vine scrub on the tracks of the women. At the edge of the scrub face the lads, two together, seven spear-lengths apart, lining the edge of the scrub. You,

Bigur, take the centre, just where the women enter the scrub on their way to the Secret Camp. Watch—and wait for me there."

Swiftly they departed, leaving only Burradella and one young warrior in camp. It was the hour before sunset and now Giluram and his two mates came running into camp, saluting the second chief.

"It is a very strong war party," reported Giluram between deep breaths. "From the warriors we have seen, and the tracks we crossed both coming and going, there are more enemy warriors than all the warriors of our tribe put together!"

He paused, breathing deeply while this startling news sank in. "They are camped at our old Burrell Lagoon camp," he resumed. "We crept as close as we dared—they were eating, gorging on *our* game. From good cover we watched ten scouts being sent out at the run to follow the women's hunting tracks of this morning and locate our camp—they'd got the news from the four who had found our tracks at the crossing—the four that

Weetah saw. Those ten scouts will be here very soon—we ran on ahead of them!"

Burradella turned to the warrior lad beside him and ordered, "Run up to the Black Hill and tell them to signal this news out to the Red Chief. Then run down to the hoop-vine scrub and await me there. Giluram," he said, "you and Kubado find a hiding place and spy on those ten scouts when they come into this camp. Find out all you can. The rest of us will go and wait by the edge of the big scrub. You know where to join us."

Burradella and Burowa hurried back towards the scrub, but on rising ground overlooking the camp climbed up into forked trees with bushes in their hands. From behind these bushes they peered, and soon saw the first scout spies come creeping into the camp. One soon appeared at the crouching run, to duck behind a tree and peer towards the camp. Burradella signalled Burowa and they slid down from their trees.

"Those scouts will send back word to those following behind that all is clear," he said. "They'll all be in camp very soon now. But it will be too late for them to move further tonight. We climb up now to the hoop-vine scrub and join our boys. We have much to do tonight."

The warrior Burradella had already done a very great deal during the last few hours. And he was soon to be sure of what he already dreaded—that the very existence of the tribe was at stake.

Softly fell the shades of sunset, a curlew called mournfully from away down on the flat. The long dark lines of the hoop-vine scrub already looked black and forbidding, but its tangled depths were a sanctuary to those now in desperate need.

Down in the abandoned camp Giluram and Kubado watched the scouts warily appearing among the timber. They stopped, while two crept on in a wide semicircle to crawl into the silent camp from opposite sides. Seeing and hearing no sign of life, they suddenly leapt up and ran through the camp towards one another. No spear, no cry of alarm greeted them from this apparently abandoned camp. One held back his head and trumpeted like a brolga. Their eight friends leapt up and came racing into camp from scattered points. They sped among the gunyahs, peering in with spears poised. Several found tracks of the women and children and guards leading from camp and around these they yabbered excitedly. Three ran the tracks for a short distance out into the open country until convinced the tracks were leading towards the Mooki. As they were in danger of being seen out in the open they raced back to the empty camp and reported. Five of them then set off in a fast run back towards Burrell Lagoon, while their five friends scattered and hid in the myall thickets on the west and south sides of the camp.

Silence fell but for the quiet bush sounds of advancing sunset. In hiding almost within the camp, Giluram and Kubado waited.

The sun was setting behind the ridges to the west when sixty Cassilis warriors came jog-trotting into camp, the five scouts jumping out from the myall thickets to join them in eager talk. The chief held out his arm with an upthrust of the chin and three scouts dashed away on the women's tracks while the warriors divided into three separate groups to squat down amongst the gunyahs. They lit no fires. Should any Gunn-e-darr men come strolling into the camp now they would walk into spear and club. In the gathering gloom Giluram squirmed close up to one group, Kubado snaked his way towards another, listening for snatches of the guttural conversation.

"Where can their new camp be?" wondered one. "Just where are all those tracks of the women and children going to?"

"Oh, they're not far away," replied a scout. "Their tracks are heading straight for the Mooki—it's barely two miles away, alive with fish. Our scouts will soon bring news that they can see their campfires."

"Ah, then our chief will take us fishing at dawn!" said a warrior, grinning. "Big fish we'll catch—two legged ones."

"I know the ones you'll try to catch," answered his mate, "and it won't be the *big* ones!"

With a guttural chuckle one said, "If the Gunn-e-darr girls can run as well as they say the men can fight, they'll take some catching!"

"Catch the men first," growled a sour old veteran, "or the only fish *you'll* catch will be what feed on your carcass."

This reminder of the sterner job on hand brought a scowl from the amorously inclined ones.

Within half an hour the scouts came running back to report no sign of campfires along the Mooki, nor gleam of fires upon the ridges to the south.

"They cannot be far away," said the chief, frowning, "but it is their warriors I'm worried about. We must get on their tracks in the morning and locate the fighting men. All these women and children roaming about with only a few warriors to guard them could mean a trap."

"They may be hiding up in those big scrubs by that Black Hill," suggested a warrior.

"Wah!" growled the chief. "We shall scout the scrub edge in the morning. And now we'll place guards all around this camp. And let no guard sleep," he growled fiercely, "lest these Gunn-e-darr men fall upon us in the night. Remember, they are no fools! And we don't know definitely just where they *are*—nor in what numbers!"

Giluram and Kubado had seen and heard enough. They crept away to report to the warrior Burradella.

Burradella now had seven young warriors with him, and with the thirteen boys were stationed in place along the scrub edge, silent as the evening. And to the anxious Burradella was coming news—they all hearkened to it—the soft, rapid footfalls of a lad running along the edge of the scrub at full speed. And he panted at Burradella.

"The look-out has received signals from the Red Chief. He is coming at the run with nine picked warriors straight for the Secret Camp. He has signalled Boobuk's party. They will follow on at the run."

"Wah! Wah!" laughed Burradella. "Good lad! We shall beat them now! They cannot follow tracks until dawn!" He turned and called softly. Two lads came swiftly.

"Hurry up to the look-out," he ordered. "You will meet the three warriors coming down—they should be here by now. Carry on and tell the boys to come back with you here. They will not be needed up there now!"

As the lads vanished in the darkness he called softly to four others.

"Make your way through the scrub to the Secret Camp!" he ordered. "You are to be message runners for the Red Chief when he arrives. When he does, tell him I wait here with seven young warriors—three more will join me at any moment—and thirteen boys of fighting age. Tell him what you have seen here, and that here I wait until he comes—or sends me a message. Understand?"

"Wah!" they whispered.

"No talking as you go—and no noise. Now remember this! Be very careful when you near the Secret Camp. Then, Birumba, you give two calls of a curlew, one following the other, you are as good as the bird itself. Then listen! An owl will hoot. Soon, another, but this one from a different direction. After the second hoot of the owl you, Birumba, will give the curlew call again. But only *once* this time, remember. Then wait silently. Presently, a voice will say 'Come to me!' Walk forward slowly, for a guard will be there with spear in wommera ready to throw—so make no false move! When you halt before the spear of the guard whisper to him that the warrior Burradella has sent you to act as guides for the Red Chief, who has signalled that he is running for the Secret Camp. Now repeat what I have said."

They did so, word for word. Burradella nodded. The boys vanished into the now pitch-black darkness of the scrub.

An eerie experience that, even for full-grown warriors, to find their way through that black night of a thousand tangled vines and canes, shrubs and creepers, ferns and undergrowth and trees, to the very heart of this dense scrub sheltering the Secret Camp. Only those who knew it from birth could have done so. Even in the gloom of daylight no stranger would find the Secret Camp unless he stumbled on it by sheerest chance. And before then, if the camp had been tenanted, an invisible guard would have transfixed him by spear or dashed out his brains with a club.

The lads obeyed their instructions to

the letter, to find themselves presently standing motionless at the very point of a spear. Even they could see nothing but a momentary glint from the guard's eyes.

They whispered their message, then stood silently. A tree-frog croaked—twice. Another invisible guard came to the croak of the tree-frog.

"Messengers from the warrior Burradella," whispered a guard's voice, "to be messengers for the Red Chief who is swiftly coming. Take them inside the camp."

Exactly thus, as I have written it, was the Secret Camp of the Gunn-e-darr tribe guarded in times of emergency years ago, according to the account given by the last of the tribe.

# CHAPTER XXX

## THE TRIBE IN DESPERATE STRAITS

On that warm day of the eighth sun, while Burradella and his people were fishing near the Namoi crossing, the Red Chief and his nine warriors had come leisurely to the meandering Mooki River, heavily loaded with emu meat. They followed the Mooki to where it shallowed into a long, narrow, reedy waterhole. Here they spied a shoal of fish jumping and flapping amongst the sun-warmed reeds. With boyish laughter they threw down their loads and splashed into the water, making merry at spearing and clubbing the fat fish so easily cornered amongst the reeds.

Very soon fish gleamed in the sunlight as they were thrown from the water to flap helplessly along the narrow bank. The hunters lit fires and roasted the fish on the coals. After a week of gorging on emu meat those fish were a tasty change and each warrior ate a strong man's meal. Lazily they discussed whether they would spear more fish to carry back to camp, only fifteen miles away from this point of the Mooki, or whether it would be too much with their already heavy loads. Suddenly Kuribri jumped to his feet and pointed away out towards the outline of Porcupine Ridge. From the look-out a long finger of black smoke was shooting up into the clear blue sky. As they watched, the smoke column changed to white. After an interval it changed to blue. The Red Chief and his warriors, all standing, watched silently as the column faded. It was duplicated swiftly from the distant ramparts of Carrowreer. Then a big ball of black smoke shot up. It died out. A small ball shot up. It faded away. Then, at intervals, arose smoke rings. Some black, some blue, some white. Presently, this smoke also faded away. There was an interval, then the black column shot straight up again. The signal was being repeated.

"Kuribri," said the Red Chief quietly, "tell me what that smoke talks to you!"

" 'Enemies!' " answered Kuribri. " 'On Namoi crossing. Come quickly. Secret camp. Burradella.' "

"Ah!" grunted the Red Chief.

He waited until the signal again was being repeated then said, "Tell me what the smoke talks to you, Yuluma."[1]

And Yuluma slowly read practically the same message.

"And it talks so to me, too," said the Red Chief definitely. "Our people are in danger, we hurry straight to the Secret Camp. Leave the meat, carry only your weapons. I shall stay here long enough to signal Boobuk and his men—luckily they will be able to see a smoke from here, flat country though it is. You nine run for the Secret Camp—I shall catch you up."

And he kicked one of the fires into a blaze and hurried to pull armfuls of grass, both dry and green. He ran to dip some into the Mooki so that it would give off denser smoke. He hurried then to pull armfuls of reeds for the different smokes they would give out. Soon his smoke signals were rising swiftly up.

He waited, then to his relief a smoke

---

*1 Yuluma means "wallaroo", and this would be Yuluma's totem animal.*

rose up miles away across the plain. Boobuk and his twenty-nine warriors had answered his signal to swiftly rejoin him. With a laugh the Red Chief picked up his weapons and commenced running after the nine. And now he gloried in his long, effortless strides, his tireless endurance. He caught up the running nine within four miles. Running beside them, he ordered them not to pause until they reached the Secret Camp. He would meet them there or, if he had to act sooner, he would leave a message for them where to follow on. Then he began to spurt ahead, his powerful legs carrying him swiftly on and on until he vanished among the timber.

But the Red Chief had been too hasty when he laughed to the answering signal of Boobuk. It was not Boobuk and his twenty-nine men at all who answered, it was Tulumi, his uncle, answering Boobuk's hunting signal.

Boobuk had divided his men, sending Tulumi with a party on a wide detour. Thus several mobs of kangaroos had gradually been driven to coverage together. When the time was ready

Boobuk had sent up a smoke to Tulumi to rejoin him quickly. And it was this signal which the Red Chief in his haste had naturally concluded was the immediate reply to his own. He had run off without attempting to verify it. Boobuk and his men, intent on the hunt and not dreaming of danger, especially now that the Red Chief was returning to Camp, had not noticed either the signals from either the distant look-outs or the Red Chief on the low plain country.

Hours later when the Red Chief waited in vain for the warrior Boobuk and his twenty-nine men his heart grew cold with a feeling of disaster, but events were to prove that it was a happy chance indeed that Boobuk had not seen that signal.

When the Red Chief came noiselessly into the Secret Camp the huddled people sighed with relief; mothers held their babies tightly and bent their cheeks to theirs. Nareen and Naroo hurried to give the adored chief food, then urged him lie down, rubbing him from neck to ankles with porcupine fat to keep the stiffness from creeping into his limbs. A guard quietly told him the news as he knew it, adding that neither Weetah, Giluram's young wife, nor twenty of the oldest women had yet come into camp, unaware that Burradella had sent the old women to shelter elsewhere.

The Red Chief called for little Tuki. In an awed whisper Tuki told all he knew. And just then a guard brought Weetah, exhausted, into camp. Silently she held out her arms to her mother-in-law for her baby.

The Red Chief's eyes gleamed sombrely as Weetah told her story. Then he said, "Weetah, you have done a warrior's work this day to find and spy alone on our enemies, and send Burradella and me such urgent news about the Cassilis men. And," he said to the guard and placed his finger over Tuki's heart, "a brave warrior is growing up fast inside here."

Little Tuki nearly fainted with pride.

Shortly afterwards his nine warriors came into camp, breathing heavily. There had been no pause throughout those fifteen hard, swift miles. The Red Chief ordered them to eat and their wives to rub them thoroughly with porcupine fat, then they were to sleep for two hours. The guard would wake five of them to help with guard duty. The other four would be awakened one hour later. When Boobuk and his warriors came in they must take over the camp guard. By then his nine men would be rested, and would come straight down to Burradella, and meet him there. And now he would take nine of the fresh camp guards to join Burradella, and learn any recent news. Meanwhile, every guard must keep alert. Sleepy guards hear things that are not there and miss those that are. The sleepy guard does not even hear the thump of a passing wallaby, whereas the wakeful guard will hear even the soft whirr of an owl's wings as he flies by in the night.

They must remember, too, that the enemies were Cassilis warriors and Burradella seemed to fear they were in large numbers, and that all the women and children were in the care of but a few warriors until all could gather together.

He then, with nine of the guards and four boys, squirmed his way back through the scrub to Burradella, stepping out of a dank, black world into the starlight of the open forest land.

Low-voiced, Burradella told the Red Chief all that he knew, adding, "We are desperately outnumbered. Giluram here and Kubado have been spying on the camp down there. There are more warriors there than we could muster, even if Boobuk's men were with us. And I feel certain there is another body of them somewhere! They have lit no fires, which could mean they believe we have not yet discovered they are in the camp. It is a trap— should we return."

"Ah!" said the Red Chief. "I was hoping to steal down and kill a few while they slept. We must weaken them somehow. But if they are prepared, then I dare not risk the loss of a single man. But we must do something—and quickly. Hold them until all our warriors can gather together. If we skulk here they will come for us tomorrow and must wear us down. Sooner or later then they will find the women."

"I don't think they'll attack tomorrow," answered Burradella. "There is another party to come yet—I feel sure of it." He turned to Giluram. "Now, Giluram, be certain as to what you saw. How many warriors did you really see?"

"*Bularui dinna,*"[2] answered Giluram and, holding up the five fingers of each hand, gazed expressively down at his feet and spread out all his toes. He closed fingers and toes, said, "*Bularui dinna*" again, and again spread out all fingers and toes. Closing them again, he repeated "*Bularui dinna*", and once more spread out all fingers and toes. And the Red Chief knew that Giluram had counted sixty Cassilis warriors.

"And I'm sure there is another party!" added Burradella.

"Then we *must* think of something," said the Red Chief urgently, frowning, "something to cripple them down to our numbers without losing too many men ourselves."

Burradella sent for four boys. "You four make your way back up to the Black Hill

2 Bularui dinna *is the number twenty. According to various writers the Australian aboriginal could not count above ten. According to old Bungaree, this was definitely not true of the Gunn-e-darr tribe of the Kamilaroi.*

look-out," he ordered. "Be very careful. The enemy will have seen this afternoon's smokes—they may have sent men up there. If not, creep up, but see you are not caught should an enemy creep up there with the dawn. If you can stay there, then when light comes spy all around, and far and wide. As soon as you have news send one boy running back here. Stay there all day if you are not hunted away—and keep sending us news."

As the eager boys hurried away Burradella asked, "What shall we do with the old women? I promised to send them word."

"Send one night-wise warrior to tell them to stay where they are," replied the Red Chief. "They are as safe there now as anywhere. The enemy may find their tracks in the morning, but they won't bother to waste time tracking old women. They'll find them whether or no if they can wipe us out."

"That's right," grunted Burradella soberly, "but I'll send young Gilwan with a message of cheer to them. He'll find them and be back by dawn."

"He'd better be!" answered the Red Chief grimly. "Every warrior, whether young or old, is worth ten to us now. Boobuk will come with the dawn—that will be another twenty-nine warriors."

But Boobuk did *not* come with the dawn. And for the first time the Red Chief felt a chill of dread.

A cold dawn brought in a fiery sun threatening a hot day. The smoke of cooking fires arose down in the Mullibah Lagoon camp, in plain view of the Red Chief watching up at the scrub edge.

Before dawn two of Burradella's young warriors and two boys, Bagor and Kyari, had crept down close to the camp from separate vantage points to spy on the enemy. The Cassilis warriors seemed in no hurry as they gossiped round their fires, occasionally pointing up towards the Black Hill and Carrowreer look-outs, then towards the edge of the long, dark line of scrub.

Burradella had been right. This war party was not collected together yet. Half of them were scouting round the Burrell Lagoon country and along the Namoi, seeking to make sure there was no large camp of the Gunn-e-darr men hidden away waiting to take them in flank or rear. They now knew the exact number that had been in the Mullibah Lagoon camp by counting the tracks. But—where were the remainder of the Gunn-e-darr warriors?

The Cassilis men decided that their second party would spend the day scouting, trying to find out. Their chief men were suspicious of entering that big scrub otherwise, believing it could be a dangerous trap concealing all the warriors of Gunn-e-darr. And they believed, as they had for long, the strength of the Gunn-e-darr tribe to be three times what it was.

Meanwhile their party here would hold the Mullibah Lagoon and watch the line of scrub on this side. These tactics at first puzzled the Red Chief, gazing down from the Porcupine Ridge by the scrub edge with Burradella and their few men. Twenty-one, twenty-three counting the Red Chief and Burradella. And fourteen others, but these were deep within the scrub guarding the Secret Camp.

Suddenly a warning yell, abrupt

movement in the camp below as warriors snatched weapons and started running, their yells coming plainly up to the edge of the scrub.

It was the boy Bagor. In his anxiety to distinguish himself he had crept right up to the enemy camp, eager to worm his way close enough to a group of warriors to overhear their talk. Out of the corner of his eye an enemy warrior had noticed the grass tops moving and the chase was on.

Young Bagor ran for his life, twisting and turning like a startled eel amongst reeds, the pursuing warriors leaping high in the effort to keep the crouching, racing little figure in sight. To piercing yells they spread out, racing to form a big circle and trap him within it.

But Bagor knew every inch of this his country, and around this camp he knew every tree, every shrub, almost every blade of grass. He got away and came gasping to the Red Chief at the edge of the scrub. Bagor could not speak for quite a time—he felt sure his heart would burst.

# CHAPTER XXXI
# THE GREAT PLAN

An hour later the Red Chief's men watched Cassilis scouts from Mullibah camp come taking their time along the tracks of the women and children. They found the old women's tracks, too, and four of them branched off to follow these up.

"Looks bad!" Burradella frowned.

"I still don't think they will bother with them yet," replied the Red Chief uneasily. "Anyway, I can't spare men to protect them. They must take their chance now."

The Red Chief was right. Those Cassilis scouts halted a safe distance from the scrub in which the twenty old women remained hidden. They decided that they could go in and get that easy game any time if the fight went their way. But they were taking no unnecessary risk of walking into a trap now. The old women could wait.

The scouts turned parallel with the line of scrub and began to walk back along it, well out of spear-throw from the scrub edge.

"They seek to cut tracks leading to, or out from the scrub!" growled the Red Chief.

"Yes," answered Burradella, "but they won't find any except those of our own party entering here, and of the old women away across there."

"They suspect there are more of us in the scrub. Look! These fellows coming towards here have stopped, too. And they turn. They are going back along the scrub—in the opposite direction."

"Yes," agreed Burradella, "and taking their time about it, too. They're making certain as to just how many of us there are in the scrub, from this side, anyway. I wonder where their other men are? This does not look like an attack today."

The Red Chief frowned uneasily, watching the enemy scouts walking away along the edge of the scrub. "If they don't attack," he muttered, "it gives us more time. But in a way it looks worse for us—they must presently learn our true numbers. If they do they'll wipe us out."

"Boobuk should arrive any time now."

"Not if the fool has not seen the

signals!" replied the Red Chief angrily. "But someone *did* answer me—or seemed to. Their eyes must have been all for their bellies. They'll be away out on the Mooki now, gorging themselves with kangaroo meat and just loafing along. That is," he added uneasily, "unless they've run into an ambush!"

"I don't think so," replied Burradella. "The enemy's other party seems to be scouting along the Namoi and the Burrell Lagoon."

"They appear to be scouting the whole country." The Red Chief frowned. "If they cut the tracks of our hunters they'll chase them to earth, party by party. We're in a bad way. We'll be finished if the complete tribe does not swiftly gather. We must do something quickly—if it is only to break their plans—before they are sure they have us cornered."

"Ah!" exclaimed Burradella. "Here comes young Kuppa from the Black Hill. And," he added, "Dhina-wan from Carrowreer running behind him!"

"I did not think the boys could get there!" declared the Red Chief. "It's a wonder the Cassilis chief did not send men up there to make a trap before the dawn."

The Cassilis warriors *had* done so, as young Dhina-wan told them with shining eyes, still panting for breath. Four had arrived there at the same time as the boys. The boys had heard them, followed up close behind them, then hidden on the hilltop almost beside the enemy warriors, who had expected Gunn-e-darr look-out men to be already there, or to come with the dawn—but never to climb up with them and hide almost beside them.

When daylight came and showed no sign of any Gunn-e-darr look-outs the four Cassilis scouts had become careless, merely watching for a sign of an enemy climbing up the hill. Then, when full daylight came, every now and then they would point away out and down at the bushland to where, towards the Burrell Lagoon, groups of their own warriors were beginning to leave camp. And these men, so the lad told, in small scattered parties, yet working close enough to run together should they be attacked were now beginning to work their way right round the back of the scrubs.

And Kuppa, who with Burrai had been chased from the Black Hill, had news of enemy scouts encircling the Black Hill scrub similarly.

"They are seeking to cut tracks on all sides of the Porcupine Ridges," said the Red Chief fiercely. "They will learn by today that there are no tracks leading in from round there! They will know then that we are the only people in this scrub. Tomorrow they will come in and get us!"

"Boobuk and the others will arrive long before then," declared Burradella.

"You boys have done very well," said the Red Chief warmly. "All the boys have. When the fight is over I shall tell old Mullionkale the play-maker to make a corroboree of the deeds of the boys alone."

The eyes of Dhina-wan and Kuppa grew big and shiny at this promise of a corroboree from the Red Chief; their feet itched to run back with the great news to their mates.

"How did you manage to sneak down

from Carrowreer without the Cassilis warriors seeing you?" asked the Red Chief of Dhina-wan.

"We didn't," answered the lad ruefully. "They saw *us*. A carpet snake slithered over the rock behind which Kaleboi was hiding. A warrior came to catch it for his breakfast. We jumped up and bounded down the hill while they stared—we were out of spear-throw before they even yelled."

"Never mind!" The Red Chief laughed. "You have done great work. Where are your mates now?"

"Away back in the scrub edge near the foot of Black Hill, watching some of the Cassilis scouts. We can see a little way round the other side of the scrub from there, but not far."

"Good," answered the Red Chief. "Hurry back and tell the boys to keep at it, and run with the news to me or the warrior Burradella as you learn fresh news. But warn your mates to be very careful or you will be squirming like an eel with a spear through your ribs before sunset."

And the boys were away with impish grins on their faces.

The Red Chief frowned down towards the Mullibah camp.

"There is but little more movement down there," he mused.

"No," answered Burradella. "All their scouts are out along this edge of the scrub. They must be waiting for their other party of scouts away behind the scrubs. My scouts are watching them down there in Mullibah camp, a runner will bring me news if there is any movement."

The Red Chief gazed round restlessly. The morning was warm; all seemed so quiet and dreamy; the "Cark! Cark!" of crows, the warbling of magpies came plainly up from the bushlands below.

The Red Chief nodded to Kerran. "I *must* think of something!" he muttered to Burradella and with the young warrior following began walking slowly along the edge of the dense wall of hoop-vine scrub towards the north-westerly side of the Black Hill.

Frowning as he walked, he was thinking as he had never thought before, seeking a plan to defeat time and overwhelming odds. He walked for some little distance, then turned and stood staring back into the scrub as if with unseeing eyes. And actually his eyes, in a way, did *not* note what they saw.

He was gazing into the Wallaby Trap. Staring into the dense scrub with its gap just there as if a giant had chewed a mouthful straight out of the wall of trees and vine. How often he had taken a delighted part, during those full moon nights, in the driving, then slaughtering of the frantic wallabies trapped deep down within those dense green walls!

Suddenly he was staring hard deep into that narrow gap in the scrub. He wheeled to Kerran and excitement transfigured his face.

"We have them!" he laughed. "Stay here, Kerran! Spy whether any enemy scouts stray along near here, but don't be seen yourself. I'll return soon." He ran swiftly back to Burradella.

"We have them tight as a dingo holds a kangaroo-rat in his jaws! Come with me." Excitedly he told his plan as they hurried back. "We'll trap them just as we have often trapped the wallabies," he explained, "as we trapped them on the night of the great slaughter not long ago. Only instead of hunting skill and rich green grass to coax *these* wallabies we'll use cunning! And for bait we'll plant a sleeping camp! Then, when they rush in to attack, they'll find spears raining into them from all sides while their escape will be cut off—just as we used to cut off the wallabies' escape. If only we are cunning enough, patient enough, then if every man, woman, and child, acts his or her best we'll cut them to pieces, few though our numbers be. We'll *slaughter* them," he added enthusiastically, "just as we did the wallabies! You remember?" He strode in between the walls of trees for about forty yards. "Here is where our camp guards will light their little fires," he went on excitedly, "a little distance in, but straight across the open mouth, from one wall of trees across to the other. While down along both sides of the Trap, and across the end, we shall place our warriors, and every boy who can throw even a little spear, at even distances apart, waiting invisible with their backs to the wall of scrub. Both lines of warriors will be facing one another, while the men at the end will be looking in between the lines up towards the mouth of the Trap. Down there at the very end we shall build our dummy camp, with the women and children busy in it.

"Now, night comes. The guards light their little fires down there towards the mouth of the Trap—safely concealed, of course, from our enemy scouts, dim within these walls of trees. But the enemy scouts will be prowling close along the scrub edge soon after sundown. As night grows blacker one scout must sooner or later be *made* to see the faint glow of a fire somewhere down here within this blackness of trees." The Red Chief paused, his eyes gleaming, a fierce, mirthless grin spreading from ear to ear as he faced his old warrior friend.

"We know, Burradella," he said grimly, "that by sundown the enemy scouts will have scouted completely round this big scrub. They will report to their chief that no tracks lead away from the scrub, and that the only tracks leading into it are those made by our women and children and by ourselves. The chief will then know that we are still hiding within the scrub. He will know more—that we have not even forty grown men to defend all these women and children!" He paused, glaring into Burradella's eyes.

"The enemy chief," snarled the Red Chief, "will be eager to find us and wipe us out before we can be joined by what he thinks are numerous absent members of our tribe. If he can only wipe us forty out, then he can turn on the others as they arrive and ambush them party by party. He will feel certain he can thus wipe us *all* out, then round up the women and children at his leisure."

Burradella nodded. "That is clear, Red Chief," he murmured.

"Of course!" The Red Chief laughed harshly. "And what a victory for him—to wipe out all the Gunn-e-darr tribe and return to his own Cassilis tribe driving our women and children before him like a mob of kangaroos!" He was grinding his teeth in a mounting rage. He pulled himself together, knowing that rage blunts the wits.

"Oh, well!" he grinned. "We give the enemy chief what he will be eager to have when sundown comes—knowledge of our camp! His scouts will see the faint reflection of a fire deep within these trees. They will creep up closer, and now, Burradella, listen well! Our guards will sprawl round the fires, occasionally strolling from one fire to the other during the early hours of night, while away down at the end where the camp is, the women will build their little fire before each gunyah. The unmarried girls will stroll from fire to fire talking with the married women. Young boys and girls from nine to ten years old will run about the camp and play until the setting of Djurrabl the evening star, when the elder women will scold them to sleep. As the camp quietens two older women will stage a quarrel. Guards will come down and quieten them. All presently, except the guards will settle down to sleep.

"But a baby will start to cry and a young mother will bring it to the fire where she will warm it and croon it to sleep. Through the cold hours, just now and then, a baby will start to cry. The mother will come out of her gunyah to the fire, stir the fire up just a little, and soothe baby until it falls asleep again. We shall act just our daily camp life. But it must be well done. The campfires will die down to nothing, and the camp be in deep sleep three hours before dawn. And then the women and children will slip into the blackness of the scrub down at the camp end there and quietly start to make their way back to the Secret Camp." He paused. Burradella nodded in grave understanding.

"By then," resumed the Red Chief earnestly, "the guards' fires down at the mouth of the Trap will nearly have died down— before the grey of dawn they will have burned down to warm coals and ashes. The dark shapes of the sleepy guards will one by one coil round them in sleep." He grinned at Burradella. "Some of the enemy scouts will have hastened away to tell their fighting chief the great news that they have found the camp. Other scouts will remain. The enemy chief will come creeping up here with all his men. His remaining scouts will be certain by then. At the first grey of dawn they will come creeping into the Trap!"

Burradella was gazing at the Red Chief with eyes big with admiration. He struck his chest twice with a loud "Wah! Wah!"

"We will slaughter the 'wallabies'!" laughed the Red Chief.

## CHAPTER XXXII

## THE TRAP IS BAITED

"And now, Burradella," said the Red Chief earnestly, "choose the guards carefully—those men who can best act their part. Then set them to work preparing the Trap. Each man must wrap his possum rug round a bundle of grass and sticks so that it will look like a warrior wrapped in his rug asleep by the dying fire. He will hide his dummy in the grass this afternoon, to arrange it in the darkness by the coals of his fire just before dawn. And by his rug, the dummy that seems to be him, he will leave a spear sticking upright in the ground as usual. He will be there, too, after the fires die down but lying flat among the grass—and very wide awake. Immediately the women and children have slipped back into the scrub the guards will crawl away to the sides of the Trap. Seventeen men to you, sixteen men to me—with every boy who can throw a weapon of some sort— the mothers will just have to put up with it! We shall have near double the number of warriors if only Boobuk will come in time—he must arrive in time! I shall take one side of the Trap, you the other, Boobuk and some of his men the end. You and your men will stand back two feet within the scrub, I shall line the opposite side.

"With the dawn, if our bait has been well set, the Cassilis warriors will creep into the mouth of the Trap, then down it to kill the guards and rush down to attack the sleeping camp at the far end. They will first have to creep forty yards in towards the glow of the coals where each dummy guard will seem to be asleep by his dying fire. They will creep up to within close spear-throw, then hurl their spears and leap into the kill with the nulla, while most will rush straight on down towards the women's camp. As they do so we step out from the scrub and, without a war-cry, hurl our first spears into their flanks—they won't know what hit them! But listen, Burradella—no man must leap out eager to club any near by warrior! Each man throws his first spear in silence, remaining standing there while swiftly he fits the second spear to wommera, for the enemy rushing on down to the gunyahs will then be another close-packed target for our second spears. Only at the throw of the second spear will every man leap forward with the war-cry and nulla. Many of the enemy will then have fallen, the others will be caught, hemmed in by dense scrub on two sides and at the end facing them, with us leaping straight out at them from the scrub sides and straight at their chests up from the dummy camp—others rushing straight down behind them from the mouth of the Trap. Even the boys' spears will have counted, whizzing in upon this narrow space from four directions! And now every nulla as we leap out from the darkness will be battering them. They will be stricken—

will seek only escape in the darkness from what is befalling them from every side—we should slaughter them almost as we have the wallabies. Well, Burradella, what do you think of the plan?"

"Good!" answered Burradella soberly. "Only the Red Chief could have thought of such a plan. Now, how about the women and children? They know how desperate our position is, but cling to the hope that Boobuk surely must return in time, since the enemy did not attack today. The women may not care to risk their children away from the Secret Camp. Remember, they love their babies and you are going to bring them right out from their only feeling of safety to here—where they are to be attacked!"

"They *must* come!" replied the Red Chief urgently. *"You* know very well we could not bait the Trap *without* the women—the enemy would smell a trap right away."

"That is so," agreed Burradella.

"We don't want them all," explained the Red Chief earnestly, "none who cannot look after themselves in their struggle back through the dark scrub, none with sick children—only the able-bodied ones and a few of the tough old women—I know *they* will gladly come. My young wives, Nareen and Naroo, will come too with their babies—I can depend upon them also."

"My three wives will come," answered Burradella promptly, "with their babies."

"I'm sure Weetah will come with her baby," said the Red Chief, "and she will bring her little brother Tuki. Every boy will be wild to come, anyway—we'll have no doubts with them. And most of the girls will come, too. Then there are the wives of your fourteen young guards, with babies most of them—I'm sure they'll come and join us here with their babies."

"You'll get all the women and children you want," agreed Burradella confidently. "And now—you mention the fourteen guards. That means there will not be a man left to guard the women remaining in the Secret Camp, and those women and children who will escape from here!"

"The guards must *all* come," replied the Red Chief desperately. "Even with every man we can muster we shall have only thirty-five spears—unless Boobuk's men come—against three times our number, perhaps even more! Our spearmen are from the youngest Bora lad warriors to greybeards, while the Cassilis warriors are the pick of the tribe. Every stripling, every greybeard, every boy *must* be ready in this Trap tonight—and must do his very best to save our tribe!"

Burradella nodded. "We will win," he said gravely.

"Good," replied the Red Chief earnestly, "and make every man confident when you muster them. Look, Burradella, it is not really as desperate as it seems. We know every *tree* of this scrub, every blade of grass in this great Wallaby Trap of ours, while to our enemy every yard is strange country. We have also complete surprise and darkness on our side. Then again, our spearmen lining the black scrub will be invisible to them, while we will have them out in the open Trap under the cold mist of the coming dawning. Our spears will rain into their massed numbers crammed into the narrow little space here. They will get the shock of their lives—they will lose their senses—helpless as the panic-stricken wallabies. And we need lose very few men—if only all know what to do, and do it when, and only when, the time comes."

Burradella nodded.

"If we lose—" the Red Chief shrugged—"then it is the end. They will kill us, then hunt the women and children at their leisure, hunt Boobuk and his men like dingoes. If we lose, then it means the end of the Gunn-e-darr tribe." Again Burradella nodded. "But I am *sure* we are going to win," went on the Red Chief eagerly. "I *know* it! We shall deal them such a crippling blow that the survivors will break away in terror. We should kill enough of them to bring their numbers down to the combined strength of our tribe, while their confusion and panic will then give us time to get all our men together and hunt them down."

"We are going to win!" declared Burradella. "What do I do now?"

"Get your men here," ordered the Red Chief. "Leave only four back there at the scrub edge to make the scouts think we are still waiting there. Put a hidden guard well out in front of the Trap here to scare off any Cassilis scouts that might come wandering this way too soon—we do not want them to see this opening in the scrub until we have baited it well. Send a runner to bring here ten of the old women—make sure there are some good, shrill-voiced fighters amongst them. Send a runner for all the boys. You prepare the Trap. Build the temporary gunyahs, set others collecting wood for the campfires. Make the Trap look perfectly natural while I hurry for the women and children and camp guard."

And the Red Chief was speeding back to vanish into the scrub. At the Secret Camp he told the guards and women his plan.

"So there you are," he ended. "We bait the Trap with your young wives, and mine, and Burradella's, and with all others willing and able to come, and with our babies and the tribe's children. That Trap is our *one* hope. Now, are you prepared to risk your wives and children in this one desperate surprise blow? Or would you rather have them stay here while the enemy kill us off one by one?"

"We follow where you lead, Red Chief," was the grave answer. The women silently nodded assent.

The Red Chief laughed delightedly.

"We *will* beat them," he cried enthusiastically, "when I have such warriors and women and children with me! Never fear, we shall beat them. Now, we do not need all of you—only the able-bodied, for we have a lot to do, and then, just before the attack comes at tomorrow's dawn, it is only the able-bodied who will be able to crawl away back through the scrub."

He selected twenty unmarried girls, forty of the younger married women with their children, and all girls and boys still in camp of from eight years onward. He then started back, urging all possible speed, with forty girls and young women and six guards, leaving the remaining eight guards to bring the others on at a slower pace to give the toddlers a chance of not becoming too tired to do their "play-acting" properly that night.

The Red Chief hurried his party

through the scrub to the summit of Porcupine Ridge, ordered them remain hidden there until he made sure that all was well, then raced down the spur leading from Black Hill and along the scrub edge to Burradella. With one relieved glance he saw that all was going very well; the lean-to gunyahs of bushes were already being erected down at the end of the Trap; the boys were very busy collecting bushes and firewood; the ten old women had just arrived and were choosing their camp-sites with matronly efficiency.

The Red Chief sent a boy runner to bring his boy scouts back from the ridges, then started to help "bait" the Trap with a smiling enthusiasm that spread from men and women to the youngest boy and girl.

Presently the strongest children with the women began to come in, guided close along the sheltering scrub edge by the guards. The other women with the toddlers were coming by easy stages.

Before sundown the Trap was perfectly arranged. Even Burradella nodded his satisfaction, his eyes roving round the shadowing Trap searching for any touch that might have been overlooked.

Just at sundown a scout came running to the Red Chief.

"Many fresh Cassilis warriors have come running into the Mullibah Lagoon camp, to be heartily greeted by the others," he panted. "We think they are all gathered together now!"

"We have got them!" said the Red Chief exultantly to Burradella. "I'm sure of it. They scouted all around the scrubs and are sure now they've got us cornered within the Big Scrub. They've all gathered together to hunt us out tomorrow. All we've got to do now is let their scouts discover the Trap, the camp they are seeking. We must do that very cunningly—and then we'll *cripple* them."

And the Red Chief with Burradella went again down both sides of the Trap with their thirty-five men—and the boys, too—to make sure each warrior and boy knew his exact stand, and exactly what he must do.

Satisfied at last, the Red Chief walked back along the darkening Trap to the mouth with Burradella. Far away out over the bushlands below, the screeching of cockatoos came up to them as they squabbled over their evening roosts.

"Everything is set!" said the Red Chief confidently. "It only remains for us to spring the Trap. But I do wish Boobuk and his twenty-nine would come." He sighed. "How we'd cut our enemies to pieces then!"

Though he did not dream it, if Boobuk and his carefree hunters had come dawdling back towards camp it would have spoilt all.

## CHAPTER XXXIII

### THE DEATH TRAP

That very morning out on the Breeza Plains Boobuk with his twenty-nine warrior hunters, loaded with meat, had started on the return to Mullibah Lagoon camp. They dawdled along, blissfully unaware of all that had happened during the last forty-eight hours, little dreaming how desperately they were needed by their hard-pressed tribe.

A glorious morning, a lazy man's day. At mid-sun they came across the largest mob of roos they had yet seen. Big fat roos that would hardly take the trouble to hop just out of spear-throw. The fun was too tempting to be missed. Boobuk's men put down their emu meat and started on the hunt again.

Several hours later and they had speared so many that it would be impossible to carry the meat. The elder warriors, as was their right, cut off the best meat from the kills and made heaps of it here and there upon the tussocky grass of the plains. They would send out the women to bring it in after they arrived in camp. They enjoyed a gossipy spell, then each man loaded himself heavily with meat and marched again for camp. But they had dawdled long. It was well into the night when they struck the Mooki only about two miles from Mullibah Lagoon.

They could just see a twinkle of fires away ahead in Mullibah Lagoon camp. So all was well. Feeling tired and hungry, Boobuk ordered a spell while they cooked some of the meat, which all did justice to, then stretched out round the little cooking fires.

And one of them did remark, "Seems a bit unusual—seeing a twinkle of the fires this distance away."

"Why not?" growled his mate lazily. "They're all in camp and perhaps old Mullionkale has some of them practising for the Fire Dance. Or the piccaninnies are playing a Fire Dance on their own." Which was a quite satisfactory explanation.

Boobuk yawned hugely, and decided to camp here the night on the Mooki. After all, there was no rush to get back to camp, anyway. They could sleep here, and be in camp at piccaninny daylight, just after dawn.

Setting guards, two at a time to be on duty one hour only through the night, Boobuk and his men settled themselves for a gossip on the recent hunt and the coming ceremonials, then, yawning, one by one began dropping off to sleep—the sleep of the innocent. Had Boobuk and his twenty-nine men come trudging into Mullibah camp loaded with meat they would have walked straight into the spears of eighty-one wide-awake Cassilis warriors.

Meanwhile, about the time Boobuk's lazy men began snoring, just down from the Black Ridge Red Kangaroo and seven men were anxiously watching for signs of enemy scouts who would see the little campfires within the trap. But no enemy scouts came. Red Kangaroo hurried back to Burradella.

"They are so sure they have us deep within the scrub," he said anxiously, "that they have hardly any scouts out. We must light a fire at the very mouth of the trap so that it *must* be seen—but only as if it is a fire that has flared up incautiously for a moment. Take three men along the Ridge until you can clearly see the enemy fires in Mullibah camp. Send a runner racing to me if the enemy see gleam of our fire from Mullibah. Then swiftly return."

The Red Chief craftily lit his fire at the mouth of the Trap framed by the dense blackness of the scrub edge. Lit it, then threw on light tinder to make a needle flame shoot up, then quickly die down. From away down in the bush outside it would look exactly as if some child, told to poke the firesticks together, had in temper thrown on an armful of dried grass or kindling.

In a short time a runner came racing from Burradella.

"All the fires down in Mullibah Lagoon camp suddenly went out!" he said.

"They have seen it!" laughed the Red Chief. "Their scouts will be here soon. Quickly, carry this hot wood back to the guards' fire. Dig a hole with your tomahawks, sweep the hot ashes into it. Be sure that not a hot stick or coal remains. Then stamp the dirt back flat and scatter loose grass over the dug-up ground. For when they come creeping in here, should a scout's foot touch heat where a fire has been he would look round—they would grow suspicious at the last moment."

He and Burradella then lay out from the edge of the scrub, anxiously waiting to see if that decoy fire would really bring the enemy scouts. Before them was the long strip of open forest land growing neither shrub nor tree, the open ground upon which the wallabies used to feed. To spy well upon this supposed camp, enemy scouts coming up the bush-clad ridge would finally have to cross this open, starlit space.

Half an hour later the Red Chief exultantly nudged Burradella. From where they were lying they saw in silhouette the feather-bedecked head of a Cassilis scout rising up above the grass. It stayed as if balanced upon the night skyline, then his shadowy arm beckoned to someone behind him. Presently there were two dark heads peering across the open from away back there. Soon Burradella had counted fifteen as one would rise to creep forward, or drop to earth to stare and listen. Or a shadow-glimpse of head or back as they came crawling along over the short grass. Like dimly glimpsed, long black snakes they came silently squirming nearer and nearer the mouth of the Trap, away down in which they presently could see guards occasionally outlined by dim firelight, and back in the black scrub behind them the women's fires that just illumined the gunyahs, women squatting before them, youngsters at play here and there. They saw, and heard small children laughingly chasing one another around the gunyahs, to be growled at occasionally by some cranky old woman. As night drew on, one woman after another called the boys to come to sleep. They were answered defiantly by the toddlers who had to be chased to their friends' gunyah before being dragged back, whimpering or struggling, to the home gunyah to sleep.

A score or so of unmarried young girls were dimly visible sitting or standing by the married people's gunyah fires, gossiping until well after the last rebellious boy had been sent to sleep. Presently, yawning, the camp owners began banking up their little fires, scraping the ashes over them to hold in the heat of the coals. Thus one by one the gunyah fires began to go out, and as they did so the young women strolled back to their own gunyahs.

Some old women in garrulous gossip presently became heated, their angry, shrill accusations bringing subdued, reproving growls from the guards. The tirade died down, suddenly to break out afresh. Then two old women jumped up, their voices rising to a frenzy of accusations as viciously they began belabouring one another with their fighting sticks, edged on by their howling sisters. Two of the guards jumped up and running down to the fighters seized them by the necks and savagely bumped their heads together, throwing one into one gunyah, the other into the farthest gunyah. With angry warnings, the two guards came striding back to their fires.

As the night drew slowly on, so the camp quietened. It began to grow very late. Some of the guards began to come strolling to their separate fires, barely glowing coals. Yawning, each of these stuck a spear upright in the ground, sat down by his fire, rolled his possum rug round him, and lay down to sleep. Here and there a guard sat wrapped in a rug, staring into his little fire, while others slowly strolled between the fires across the entrance way to his dark camp, or strolled down as far as the women's gunyahs to bank up a fire that was still glowing too brightly, or stood at the mouth-edge of the scrub leaning sleepily there, just a shadow only visible in the glow of some guard's fire.

Slowly the night drew on. Very quiet now, growing chilly, then cold. Those dim guards still crouching over the dying coals of their fires wrapped their possum rugs tighter round them.

The Red Chief gripped Burradella's arm; his fierce eyes could just see a shadow movement here and there out in front under the starlight.

"Some of the scouts are stealing back to their camp with the news," he whispered, "while others remain to watch."

Away back in the darkness within that narrow gap in the scrub a baby began to whimper, then cry and cry. The invisible mother must have crawled out of her gunyah, for a tiny flame flickered up away down there, showing the concerned face of young Naroo as, baby at breast, she made up the fire into a small glow, warming the baby at the fire, drawing her possum rug tightly round both herself and the crying baby. The outline of the young woman crooning over her baby could just be seen in the little fire glow she built up there in the black darkness.

Presently the baby ceased its crying. The enemy scouts were not to know that Naroo, so unwillingly, had been pinching it. The shadowy form of the young woman bent over the flame as she now smothered it with ashes before crawling back into her gunyah with the now sleeping baby. It had been perfectly done.

A deathly quietness settled over the dense black scrub. The night smelt cold. Presently another baby began crying. And again a young mother came creeping out of her gunyah, blew upon the coals of her fire until tinder burst into flame, then, wrapped in her possum rug, crooned over her wailing child as she warmed it over the fire.

This young mother was Weetah, and Giluram, standing invisible in his place with his back to a great tree towards the Trap mouth, gripped his weapons with a fierce strength. His eyes rolled, his teeth flashed as he watched that little figure down there outlined by the fireglow. Men would die tonight—Cassilis men—Giluram would kill and kill and kill until he himself was killed before they should snatch his Weetah from him.

Standing invisible along both walls of trees every man and lad gripped his weapons with the same fierce thought. When those Cassilis warriors did come, they surely would enter a death trap.

Away out past the scrub edge in the open, the enemy scouts murmured together. One pointed up to the Southern Cross and the Emu and Two Hunters. It was becoming late indeed, but they must remain to the last moment, though certain this *was* a sleeping camp. And now even those guards on duty were nodding by the fires, or sleepily leaning up against that big tree by the edge.

And now another piccaninny began crying. And again the scouts stared down into the darkness between those two black walls of trees. Again a little campfire blazed up away down there, showing another young mother making up her fire. The cry of the baby sounded high on the cold night air. He kept on crying. By the fire glow, the enemy scouts saw two old women creep out from their gunyah and come and sit beside the young mother and softly talk to her. They warmed something on the fire, put it on the baby's belly, crooning over him. Soon he stopped crying. The young mother then went back to her own gunyah. The two old women wrapped their possum-skin rugs round their cold old bodies, spread the ashes over the fire, then lay down side by side on the hot ashes. The camp lay in the depth of sleep.

The scouts waited but a little longer. Their leader pointed contemptuously to the guards huddled asleep round their dying fires. Barely taking the trouble to disguise their going, they crept away back and out into the night.

"They've gone," whispered the Red Chief exultantly, "and swallowed the bait! They'll hurry back to camp. Presently every man of them will come. They will crawl into the Trap with the dawn—and then—!" He clenched his fists in grim silent mirth. And the warrior Burradella smiled with him.

With nine warriors, he and Burradella scouted out after the enemy scouts. When certain they were all returning to their camp they came racing back.

"Quick!" hissed the Red Chief to the campfire guards, "every man to his task!"

The sleeping figures sprang up, the possum-rug bundles of grass and sticks were dragged from their hiding-places and cunningly arranged round the dying fires just as the sleepers' bodies had been. Those two guards leaning sleepily against the opposite trees at the mouth of the Trap replaced themselves with a log draped in a possum rug, looking for all the world like a shadowy man leaning sleeping against the scrub edge.

Burradella, with a few warriors and boys, hurried straight down the Trap to the women's gunyahs.

"Quick!" he whispered. "And go quietly. Don't let a baby whimper now *whatever* you do! Take the children and yourselves straight into the scrub, deep in.

Start to make your way back to the Secret Camp if you can manage it. These two boys will be guides, and these two will stay with the old women and help them along. Be deep within the scrub before dawn, out of our hearing. If any of you cannot manage it then remain still as death until you hear the fighting. Then go for your lives. Now go!"

Invisible as the darkness, with an unbelievable quietness those seventy women and all the children vanished into that dense black scrub.

Down toward the mouth of the Trap the Red Chief took his stand with his sixteen warriors spread out to either side of him, armed boys motionless between them. Facing him across the blackness of the other side waited Burradella with his seventeen men and the boys. Only thirty-five grown warriors all told. Two old warriors with a thin line of the older boys faced towards them at the narrow end of the Trap.

A deathlike silence now, oppressive smell of dank vegetation, cloying touch of drifting dew. Nothing to see but the blackness, except the dull embers of the "sleeping" guards' fires well down within the mouth of this cutting in the scrub.

The enemy came silently, just before the first chill greying of the dawn.

The Red Chief's men pushed noiselessly back against the undergrowth, and waited. With the first cold light the enemy sent their scouts creeping in. Satisfied by the still shapes of guards sleeping by the coals they crept back. Only then did the enemy come creeping to the very mouth of the Trap. They waited then until those little scrub birds that always begin their sleepy chatter with the first clear, grey light of dawn, began their chirruping. The Cassilis warriors leapt up with spears ready fitted to wommeras. Their shadowy forms seemed to stretch back, then lurch forward as one as they hurled a volley of spears full at the dim shapes of the sleeping guards. Then the scrub howled to the Cassilis war-cry as they leapt into the kill with the club.

The Red Chief's men stepped forward clear of the scrub, spears ready fitted. At close range they hurled their spears into the black mass of enemy smashing down with clubs at the forms of the supposed guards.

Sudden silence of that war-cry—screams of pierced men, then gasps, and the thud of falling bodies clawing at the grass. Those unhurt wheeled round in shocked terror, open-mouthed, amazed eyes, hands trembling at their weapons as another shower of spears came viciously biting into them. To agonized yells those still unhurt leapt amongst the clattering weapons back towards the mouth of the Trap. But from there came a roar as the gigantic figure of the Red Chief appeared, followed by his leaping men howling the Gunn-e-darr war-cry. The Cassilis men turned and raced blindly down the Trap. The roar of the Red Chief stopped his excited men in their tracks.

"Quick! Pull out your spears! Burradella, remain by the mouth of the Trap and kill any who run to get by—I'll deal with those who've run down to the end!"

The warriors leapt to pull their spears from the dead and dying, then the Red Chief's men ran with him down to the end of the Trap from which the enemy, bewildered by the yells of the boys and a flight of spears, were sneaking back to be again met by the howling charge of the Red Chief. They wheeled in despair to crash their way into the scrub at the end of the Trap. Three were speared here before they disappeared, with Red Kangaroo's men exultantly following the noise of their going. Burradella's men had run back to the Trap entrance, but, meeting no enemy, ran back down the Trap to beat their way to the Red Chief. Burradella had swiftly counted thirty-four dead and dying enemy within the first sixty yards of the Trap, with six badly wounded. And three more killed by the Red Chief's men where the enemy had rushed into the scrub at the Trap end. Forty-three enemy warriors already accounted for and not one Gunn-e-darr man yet lost! Burradella's men howled exultantly as they hurried into the scrub seeking sight or sound of enemy, but met no one coming against them from the direction of the Mullibah camp, nor did any enemy break out of the scrub to run across the open forest down the Porcupine Ridges. But presently war-cries of Gunn-e-darr and Cassilis warriors set them hurrying towards the east side of the Black Hill.

The Red Chief's men had kept hot on the sounds of seventeen warriors who had escaped the Trap and were pushing through the scrub in desperate haste. It turned out that they were trying to break through to join twenty-one warriors whom their chief had early sent round to the south of the Black Hill to cut off the escape of the women and children when he attacked the sleeping camp. The rally cries of the fleeing men attracted this party of twenty-one, who had hurried into the scrub to meet them, shouting their whereabouts. Now came Burradella's shouts, answering to the shouts of the Red Chief. As the enemy parties combined they turned back to attack the Red Chief, who fell back with his sixteen men, shouting to Burradella to hurry to attack from the rear.

When Burradella shouted he was in position the Red Chief roared so that his voice could be heard far through the scrub, "Now remember your *shield* when at close quarters!"

He then roared the order to attack and rushed straight at the enemy while Burradella's men came surging through the scrub straight behind the Cassilis men. They cut the thirty-eight in half and cunningly concentrated on the one half. There was no chance of using spears amongst this tangled undergrowth; the only weapons that could he used were nulla and tomahawk and shield, to fiendish yells and ripping of vines by stumbling men. But this body of the enemy, cut off from their mates, refused fight when two of their men fell. They leapt away into the scrub. The Red Chief turned against the other party, now close against him, but these, too, turned and fled when they heard their mates vanishing into the undergrowth.

"Stand together!" yelled the Red Chief as his men started to scatter in pursuit.

They stood there panting, listening to the noise of enemy scrambling away in all directions.

"We've beaten them!" laughed the Red Chief. "But we still must stick together. Remember, there were only thirty-five of us, and they still must have that number left!"

As a matter of fact, they had just thirty-six. Sixty men had entered the Wallaby Trap. Of these, only fifteen now survived, scattered in the scrub. Of the twenty-one who had been sent round Black Hill to cut off escape of the women, all were still alive. And they clung together, forced their way out of the scrub, and raced across the open ground and down into the bush, racing for Mullibah Lagoon camp to collect their spare weapons and prized possum rugs and belongings before making haste back into their own country. As they came racing into camp warriors leapt up out of the ground and hurled spears and boomerangs amongst them, to howls of the Gunn-e-darr war-cry. Three of their young warriors went crashing to earth, the remainder fled without throwing a spear. Any survivors who got back to their own country would never afterwards believe that the Gunn-edarr lands were not alive with warriors.

These Gunn-e-darr warriors were

Boobuk's men, only just arrived in camp at last, amazed and in great apprehension to find the camp deserted but sheltering the belongings of their dreaded Cassilis foes. The warrior Boobuk's ugly, "man-killing" face was comical in its wrath and bewilderment.

## CHAPTER XXXIV
## FRIENDS, MY TRIBAL LANDS, FAREWELL

Shortly afterwards the Red Chief and his men came running down into Mullibah camp. The Red Chief stood looking down at the three dead Cassilis warriors. The apprehensive Boobuk then growled out his story. Glad indeed then was the Red Chief that Boobuk had not come blundering into camp sooner than he did. Had he come earlier he and his men would not only have been hopelessly ambushed but would have spoiled the trap as well. And now the Gunn-e-darr party was reinforced by twenty-nine more warriors, while the enemy had lost half their number and were in full flight.

The warrior Burradella then came into camp, limping badly. During the chase he had trodden on a sharp stake that cut deep into the sole of his foot. He reported that none of the Gunn-e-darr men had been killed, and only three wounded.

With only thirty-five men and some staunch boys the Red Chief had tricked and attacked eighty-one able-bodied enemy in the most successful ambush ever known to the legends of the Gunn-e-darr tribe. News of this would make the name of the Red Chief and the Gunn-e-darr men feared far and wide, while giving them that greatly desired time to build up the tribe. Feeling happier than he had for many a long day, the Red Chief sat apart from his exultant men with Burradella, seriously debating what they should do next.

"We must run to earth those we can," declared the Red Chief vigorously. "Few must reach home. We shall carry straight on and attack *their* home camp—we shall steal *their* women, instead of their stealing ours. Their tribesmen will be expecting their victorious warriors' return. They will never dream that *we* shall come first! So we should attack, I say, for such a chance as this will never come again."

Burradella fully agreed, and the Red Chief shouted his orders. "Cook all the meat that Boobuk brought—we shall eat a strong man's meal. Then the fifteen oldest warriors and fifteen boys will carry a full load of meat to the women and children at the Secret Camp, and remain there under Burradella's orders as guards. Thirty-five picked men will come with me to chase the Cassilis warriors, then attack their home camp. Only the very fittest warriors can come with me, for we travel fast and far there and back and there may be much fighting. All the rest of the warriors will remain here with Burradella to protect the women and be ready with help should I have to fight my way back."

There was a rush then to build up the fires and cook, while soon fierce arguments broke out as to who were the fittest men to go with the Red Chief.

The Red Chief with his thirty-five

picked warriors, with Boobuk as second in charge, loaded themselves with their war weapons and cooked meat and set off swiftly on the tracks of the eighteen foemen who had fled from the camp when surprised by Boobuk.

Across the Porcupine Ridges the tracks kept together for some miles at racing pace, then slowed down. There the tracks deviated south towards the scrub near Carrowreer. Apparently the fugitives, finding that they were not pursued and realizing that a long and arduous journey lay ahead, had paused to hunt for food.

"They seek wallaby meat," said the Red Chief grimly, "and they know where to look for it. They will come out of the scrub to cook their meat—and we will be waiting to eat it for them!"

They rattled their weapons with guttural laughter at the grim joke. Almost as the chief spoke six Cassilis warriors, each with a wallaby on his shoulder, appeared striding down the mountain side. Twelve more followed. They came out to the forest land and climbed down into a deep gully.

With a wave of his hand the Red Chief nodded to Boobuk. The two parties separated and skirted widely out through the bush so that when they came together the enemy would be trapped between them. The Red Chief's men took the top end and began stalking stealthily down the tree-lined gully bank, while Boobuk's men began creeping up towards them. Soon both parties sniffed fresh smoke, then the smell of warm meat grilling on the coals. They crept closer until they were within spear-throw of one another, then crept to the gully bank and peered over.

Down there, huddled round a fire on the gully bottom midway between them, were the eighteen Cassilis warriors, now ravenously wolfing half-cooked meat.

The Gunn-e-darr men swept back their spear arms for the throw. As the spears hurtled from the wommeras they yelled their war-cry and sprang down into the gully. Seven Cassilis warriors leapt frantically for the gully bank. They got away, leaving their eleven friends writhing or dead among the gully stones. The young warriors were eager to pursue the escaping men, but the Red Chief called them back.

"We must not waste time chasing scattered runaways," he explained. "We must hurry straight to the Cassilis tribal lands before any of these men reach there so that we may surprise their guard and capture their women. Those seven men will take to the scrub and hide there until we are well on our way. We must now overtake or pass the party who broke away from the fight in the scrub this morning. If we pass them we keep straight on. If we overtake them, then not one must escape to carry the news back to his own country. Now pull out what spears are not broken in these dying men and we shall carry on at a steady run."

At mid-afternoon they stopped and ate, then with a strong guard circling them slept two hours. They travelled on again fast until midnight, when half the party kept guard while the other half slept. At dawn each ate a strong man's meal, then the Red Chief had them hurrying on again at the jog-trot. At midday they were lucky, for they ran upon a big mob of roos lazing under a patch of wilga-trees. They speared eight, which gave them a hearty meal again without having to waste time in the hunting of it. They carried on again, slowing down to the long, easy stride that takes the Australian aboriginal so far and fast.

"We have passed those that broke away from us in the fight in the scrub," said the Red Chief to Boobuk. "We've seen neither sight nor sound of them, neither track nor smoke nor cooee, and no sign from animal or bird to mark their passing or hunting."

"They're skulking in the scrubs away behind," growled Boobuk. "They got such a hiding, they're scattered like frightened dingoes. They'll only be game to sneak back to their own country under cover of night."

Which was correct. Those fifteen warriors, all that were left out of the sixty that had rushed into the Trap, had fled in panic, scattering in twos and threes as they raced across the open country to sheltering patches of scrub after scrub. And at the last scrub, with open bushland before them, they had lain hidden awaiting the cloak of night.

"We shall enter their lands before any of them return," said the Red Chief confidently. "We shall give our enemies the surprise of their lives. This proud tribe of the Cassilis will never forget their attack on the men of Gunn-e-darr."

And they never did.

Afternoon shadows were softly falling when they came to a prettily tree-lined creek. Noiselessly they disappeared amongst the foliage to peer down at the gurgling waters. One glance up and down the creek and they were down the bank to wade across. The Red Chief stopped with hand raised and they stood like crouching black statues, sinewy hands gripping weapons.

The Red Chief was staring down at fresh tracks—the tracks of five men on the wet sands of the creek. He glanced upstream. Boobuk stood with head upthrust—sniffing. They all sniffed the air from up creek. Their eyes rolled, teeth gleamed white as they glared one to the other with an upward thrust of the chin up creek.

Some had sniffed the fresh smoke of a newly lit cooking fire. Without a word they started upstream. They spread out, taut fingers gripping their weapons, crouching forward in a silence quiet as the approach of death. Around a bend in the tinkling creek five Cassilis men were sitting on the grass by the clean white sands of the creek, just spreading out the coals on which to cook nine fat fish. In hungry anticipation they were chuckling at some joke when the joker grunted sickeningly at a shattering blow from a club. Then clubs were smashing down upon them in a medley of struggling limbs. It was all over within seconds. The Gunn-e-darr men stood panting in the frenzied grip of their blood-lust.

But there were no more victims here. They carried swiftly on, wild eyed, urged by that terrible blood-lust as they entered their enemies' territory. They came upon a big camp an hour after sunrise. There were thirty guards, now scattered about the camp around the gunyah fires.

The Red Chief's men crept close up, Boobuk taking one side of the camp, the Red Chief the other. From the earth the Red Chief suddenly howled his war-cry, joined in full-throated roar by every warrior. The camp seemed stricken into stone. Open-mouthed, with fear-filled eyes, the women and children stood or crouched in motionless terror. Then the Red Chief roared again, and on the instant women and children were racing for the bush, mothers snatching up their babies, screaming to children, "Run! Run! Run!"

The guards snatched weapons and ran together for support. A shower of spears came hurtling amongst them as the howling Gunn-e-darr men came racing into the camp from all directions with tomahawk and nulla. The guards went down in the frenzied rush, except twelve who broke and ran, chased by howling men.

Immediately the chase was over the Red Chief yelled to his men to round up the women and children. To all points of the compass his men sped well out of camp, then, turning, they formed a far-flung circle of racing men. These drew in closer and closer as they circled back towards camp, flushing the women and children from bushes and hollows and under sheets of bark as dogs would flush quail from their hiding places. Soon from all directions wailing women and children were being herded within a rapidly dwindling circle, until the despairing-eyed, shivering mob were huddled back in camp again. A few of the young women and girls had made their escape, and nearly all the prized boys of from ten years onwards, while already they had started heavy smokes to warn their far-flung camps. The Red Chief's men rounded up forty young women and children and ten youngsters of from ten to eleven years of age. The warriors glanced at these young women with gleaming eyes. They would make fine wives to mother Gunn-e-darr braves, while the children would be adopted into the tribe to become in time as good Gunn-e-darr warriors and women and children as the tribe's children born.

None of the old people, the wounded or the sick and weakly were interfered with. The Red Chief cut short the death-wailing over the guards, ordered women to cook immediately all food in camp, ordered others to bring out every possum and kangaroo rug, and all their hunting and cooking tools and anything useful that they would need in the new future before them. All such things were to be wrapped into bundles for the carrying. While his men watched the prisoners the Red Chief made the sullen boys bring out all weapons from the gunyahs. Any good weapons his men took a fancy to they could have. The remainder—there were hundreds of spears, wommeras, boomerangs, nullas, tomahawks—were quickly broken and thrown on the fires.

The Red Chief then ordered everyone to eat well. After which the wailing women were ordered to load themselves with any belongings of theirs.

"Those who travel lightest, will travel the easiest," he shouted, "for we travel fast and far!" At a nod, his scouts ran out in front, heading back towards the beloved lands of the Gunn-e-darr. As he shouted to the captives to march a wailing immediately broke out, but his men were among them with the spear-point and there was a scurry to pick up bundles and march. Out into the open bush they went, for long followed by the dismal wailing of those left behind crouching over the cooking fires, throwing ashes over their heads. Just the wailing and the "Cark! Cark!" of the crows in dismal memory of those loved ones and loved Cassilis lands they were for ever leaving behind.

The sullen ones, and those who sought to lag behind, were hastened by a spear jab where it hurt. Thus to harsh urgency, to snarling threat of a battering death to the first who attempted escape, the swift, grim march back to the Gunn-e-darr lands began.

## CHAPTER XXXV

### THE RED CHIEF

The Red Chief and his exhausted captives arrived safely back to the lands of the Gunn-e-darr, to the great relief of Burradella and the joy of the tribe.

Thus, when he had been but two years chief Red Kangaroo not only saved his tribe from extinction but defeated its most feared enemies so disastrously that it took them years to recover. Not only so, but the news spread like wildfire and made such a reputation for the Gunn-e-darr men that other powerful tribes feared to attack them. Only just in time, for three large tribes were combining with the purpose of wiping them out, having at last come to the conclusion that the Gunn-e-darr tribe was not nearly as powerful as they had for long believed. The disaster to that picked band of Cassilis warriors immediately halted such plans. They feared now that the Gunn-e-darr must be even more powerful than they had believed in the first place. And this gave the Red Chief the greatly desired breathing space in which to build up his tribe.

But to tell of his long, exceptionally active and adventurous life, and all that he did for his tribe, would take another book even though only using the remainder of the story as left by old Bungaree. Suffice to say that before he was forty years of age he had absorbed six small tribes, built up his tribe to one hundred and sixty fighting spearmen, all able-bodied. Year followed year and more and more lads were trained to go through the Bora. The children were numerous now; he delighted in their numbers. Every young warrior had a wife, five-year warriors had two and three, older warriors more still. He led strong, swift raiding parties to as far away as Bingara, Warialda, Moree, Walgett, Coonamble, Narrabri, Tamworth, Quirindi, Murrurundi, Gulargambone, Gulgong, Wingen, Walcha, and Uralla, as those localities are named today. Thus, in a wide circle he kept enemies and would-be enemies busy and guessing, thus also keeping them away from his own tribal grounds.

A time came when his old enemy the Goonoo Goonoo tribe, and the Manilla River tribe, sought both peace and his aid. These two tribes had been badly mauled by the fierce Bundarra and Kingston tribesmen, and at last Ilpara, the chief of the Goonoo Goonoo, and Mooti the chief of the Manilla, sought the aid of the Red Chief of the Gunn-e-darr.

The Red Chief, though not keen on outright fighting against the Bundarra and

Kingston tribes, shrewdly saw how he could guide the problem to his own tribe's advantage. Also, he was uneasy at the heavy raids those two tribes were making, coming so close to his own tribal lands. They might cripple the Goonoo Goonoo and Manilla people, then eventually turn their attention to the rich lands of Gunn-e-darr. So here was a wonderful chance to cripple *them,* with the aid of eager allies. Far better than being forced to fight alone later on.

So terms were arranged. And soon then a combination of picked men of the Gunn-e-darr, Goonoo Goonoo, and Manilla tribes, ninety in number, set out to attack the Bundarra and Kingston in their own mountain haunts.

This fighting was both fierce and prolonged. Ilpara was killed by a spear through the throat. The Manilla chief, Mooti, was ambushed in a clump of heath scrub by two Bundarra warriors and tomahawked to death. The Red Chief's combined force lost eighteen men killed and twenty wounded in the first fight. In the next fight the Bundarra lost their war chief, Kibbi, killed by the Red Chief's spear as he raced across a flat to reach the cover of scrub.

This fighting ended in the defeat of the Bundarra and Kingston tribes with heavy loss of warriors, and loss by capture of thirty-four young women, and five boys and girls, besides a goodly number of women whom they had taken from the Goonoo Goonoo and Manilla in previous raids. The Red Chief insisted that these captive women should be returned before he would make peace.

In time the Red Chief built up the Gunn-e-darr tribe so that they could face the most powerful enemies with confidence. He never suffered a defeat, while in peace his tribe prospered as never before, enhancing the prophetic reputation of cunning old Nundoba the witchdoctor.

The Red Chief lived to be a very old man. The sorrow of his passing when he obeyed the call of Baia-me to his place in the skies was remembered in legend for as long as one solitary member of his tribe remained, just as old Bungaree has given it to us.

Thus lived and passed, the Red Chief.

He was buried under the big old box-tree by the Porcupine Ridges, near his beloved Mullibah Lagoon camp, which he had defended so well. And there his bones rested for many years, until long after the white man came. Little did he know that his bones would be dug up and, with what remained of the carvings on the box-tree stump, sent to the Sydney Museum.

It is well that the Red Chief, during all those long years that he thought and fought for and fiercely struggled to build up his beloved tribe so that it would last for ever, knew nothing of the future coming of the white man.

Only Baia-me knew that.

# APPENDIX

## Understanding the Aboriginal

Very, very few Australians indeed, probably barely a score, have ever come to a real knowledge of the Australian aboriginal. This is understandable, for from early settlement, in that antagonistic, forceful impact of the first settlers, advancing as rapidly increasing "civilizers" upon the scattered tribes of Stone Age men whose home was this isolated continent that we were so hungry to occupy, there was not the time, and but little inclination, for the "whites" to get to know the "blacks".

Even the overlanders and settlers who lived all their lives in the back country never came to know the real aboriginal, as he never came to know us. He was not given time, anyway. To the inlanders, the abo. was either a "good nigger", a "no-hoper", a "bad nigger", or a Myall, a wild bush black. He was a good boy, a bad boy, or a good-for-nothing, according to the degree in which he was willing to work, or not to work, or to be a "nuisance".

Even those settlers—and there were plenty of them—who were "very good to the blacks", never, with the rarest of exceptions, really came to know their inner life, their inner beliefs—understandably so. The puzzle was so well hidden in the first place, and the pioneers' days from dawn to dark were so laboriously occupied in knocking a living out of this so often harsh, strange land, handicapped by their own localized and individual problems of life and labour and isolation, transport, and the battle to survive despite the frugal, and sometimes non-existent, market for their heavy labours.

For instance, how could the new settlers coming to this strange land and people be expected to learn that the primitive "blacks" had long since developed command of three languages? These were their tribal language, a sign language with which they could converse perfectly amongst themselves, quite undetected even in the presence of the whites, and a Sacred Language, their Secret Language, only used among the fully initiated elder men and only on occasions of deep significance.

Easy for us to understand now why the settlers never got to know the real, inner lives and deep beliefs of the nomad primitives who haunted the lonely bush around them.

As for my own humble self, granted a wandering life in isolated localities under conditions very favourable to getting to know and understand "the old abo.", and with the keenest of interest from youthful days, only after years of wanderings amongst the semi-wild and still wild tribes, and of actually living at times with various tribes, did I pierce the veil of their real beliefs, to be slowly amazed by the fact that all the time many of their beliefs, their hopes and fears, were strangely akin to ours. It took me half a lifetime of roaming over the continent and northern coasts to realize there was such a lot I did not know, such a lot I had missed. Little wonder, then, that we have never got to know the real aboriginal.

Too late now The Stone Age man has vanished with the years. And a story of man going back to the mists of time has vanished with him.

## *Baia-me*

Baia-me, the Great Builder, Builder of All Things, the Great Spirit, was, under various tribal names, believed in with reverent secrecy among many tribes, if not by all. He represented one of their deep cultural beliefs, and was rarely mentioned except in the Secret Language, amongst the elders when alone, and to initiates undergoing the sacred ceremonies.

## *Wunda*

Wunda was a spirit with a white skin. So far as my experiences among aboriginals goes, this same spirit was believed in, under varying names, among numerous tribes over a vast area. It is my personal opinion that Wunda, under different names, was probably believed in by every tribe throughout the continent—certainly by tribes I have come in contact with across northern Australia from the east coast to the west, from Queensland's Cape York Peninsula to Western Australia's Kimberley coast.

Wunda, the pale-skinned spirit, was, amongst the aboriginals I knew, regarded as a very powerful spirit either for good or for evil—mostly for good. With the coming of the white man, I believe, the aboriginal belief that the white man was the Wunda spirit in reincarnated form became universal. Ridley and others found this belief in the south in the very early days. Many years later I—and of course other folk—found the same belief in our farthest north among still wild and semi-wild tribes.

The belief that Wunda, the white-skinned spirit was a force for good, great good, or evil, at times caused me to ponder whether this would be one cause for misunderstandings between black and white. In most areas the whites were greeted in friendly fashion, and experienced but little trouble in settlement amongst the blacks. In other areas there were suspicions and mutual misunderstandings, with, at times, immediate and brutal use of the gun by the whites or spear by the blacks. In such localities the aboriginals, of course, must have here believed that "Wunda" had come in a fury of evil, and they retaliated in the only way they knew. Had it not been for their superstitious fear of Wunda, greatly increased by the horses, the white men would not so easily have settled Australia.

It is interesting to remember the closely similar belief among the vastly more cultured people of those fascinating civilizations of the Aztecs and Incas. There, too, the white man was believed to be a spirit, a son of the Sun, unconquerable in his reincarnated spirit form, with his "thunder weapons" of fire and death. And his horse was a part of him, as Australian aboriginals believed. Had it not been for such beliefs Cortes and Pizarro, with their puny handful of Spaniards, would never have conquered the Aztec and Inca armies of Mexico and Peru.

## A Side-light on Totemism

The "destruction of totemism" by the whites in later years brought, in many instances, violent retaliation from the Australian aboriginals. And the whites utterly failed to realize the true reason why. They believed it to be "bloodthirsty hostility" on the part of the blacks, little realizing that when they themselves ruthlessly slaughtered animals, birds, and trees, or polluted sacred waterholes with their stock, they were "killing" part of the deep inner life of the aboriginal, some of his most sacred beliefs. For any of the tens of thousands of rotting animal carcasses left where they fell all over the continent meant to the aboriginal not only criminal waste of precious food, but in that decaying remnant of bones might be his father, his mother or brother or sister or baby, that had come back to earth reincarnated, only to be needlessly slain by the "white devil, Wunda". The early settlers, of course, could not know that many and many a tree they chopped down was sacred to the aboriginals as a totem, or as the abiding place of spirit babies awaiting their chance to enter a native mother to be born again. The destruction of such a sacred tree or grove meant to the local tribe that the abiding place of future babies for their tribe was gone for ever.

Little wonder that in their bewilderment, rage, and despair they sometimes retaliated in the only way they knew, by killing any white man they could.

This unwitting destruction by the whites was but one of the misunderstandings between white and black which helped make the relationship between the two so unhappy. It was Destiny, of course.

## The Chief Look-out Posts of the Gunn-e-darr Tribe

Sir Thomas Mitchell in his explorations to the north-west mentions Ydire or Nobby Rock. He was exploring the Namoi in search of the Kindur, a great and wonderful river according to the reports of George Clarke, the escaped convict called "The Barber", first white man to live on the Namoi with the blacks. In December 1831 Mitchell eventually pitched his camp near Nobby Rock. Almost twenty-five miles away he could see the sharp outline of Tangulda, Barber's Pinnacles. Mitchell, with Surveyor White, climbed Nobby Rock, where White took bearings of the principal summits, securing the aboriginal names from the natives. Mitchell was well pleased with the grandeur of the scene, and has left an interesting account of what the country looked like then as seen from these mountain look-outs.

## Place Names

I have used some place names of the present day so that the reader can see at a glance the localities where the events of the story took place. The country was very different then, of course.

## The Name of Gunnedah

There is some doubt as to the origin of the name of the present town of Gunnedah. Several of the old hands have left on record that the name came from Cumbo Gunnerah, which they believed was one of the aboriginal names of the Red Chief.

Others say—and Ridley has it in his

vocabulary of the Kamilaroi—that it is the same word as Gunida, meaning "place of the white stones".

There are no "white stones" in Gunnedah now. But until the eighties there was in Elgin Street, on the site of the present Intermediate High School, a small hill of white stones, probably crushed quartz or limestone. The stone was very friable and quickly crumbled, making it ideal for the making of roads. The hill was carted away and used in the formation of the streets.

## A Story of Bungaree

Old Bungaree, "King" of the Gunnedah blacks, was a well-known figure in the district in the nineties. He died at Pullaming Station, a very old man. A well-known yarn of old Bungaree was that one dark, cold night, having imbibed not wisely but exceeding well, he swam the Mooki River, crawled shivering up to a boundary rider's hut, and noiselessly got into bed between the sound asleep boundary rider and his wife. When the couple awoke in the morning to the grampus-like snores of their uninvited bedmate their feelings may be imagined.

## The Date of the Story

So far as could be ascertained, the Red Chief lived in the late seventeenth and early eighteenth centuries. Bungaree told of a great flood that apparently occurred about 1750, changing the course of the Namoi and Mooki rivers. The Red Chief appears to have died about twenty years before this flood.

## J. P. Ewing and S. C. Ewing

The late Sergeant J. P. Ewing was born on 28 December 1829 at Anderston, Glasgow. He was second officer on the ship *Curlew* when he landed in Victoria in May 1853. He joined New South Wales Police Force in 1856 and formed the first police station at Forbes. In 1865 he was transferred from Merlo Goldfields to Coonabarabran, and was Sergeant of

Police at Gunnedah in 1885. He died at Gunnedah in 1911. For forty years he led an active life in the New South Wales Police Force. A fine bushman, keenly interested in the country and particularly the mazes of the Warrumbungles, he was esteemed by the whites and particularly by the aboriginals, whom he befriended on every possible occasion.

Stanley Craig Ewing, son of the old sergeant, was born in Coonabarabran in 1878. With his brother Ernest, he inherited their father's love of roaming the country and his keen interest in the aboriginals of that period, the remnants of the local tribe whom he knew well from boyhood. It was said of him that no one in New South Wales knew more of the existing remnants of the Kamilaroi tribes than he. Quiet and unassuming, he has left a memory respected by all. He died as a result of wounds received in the 1914-18 War. His simple cross at Gunnedah bears the inscription: "Private S. C. Ewing, 764, 33rd Battalion. 18/10/38."

## The Lands of the Kamilaroi

The explorations of Mitchell and Cunningham drew attention to the magnificent lands of the Liverpool Plains. Settlers anxious to migrate from the Hunter River districts were warned by the Government of the dangers existing in that No Man's Land across the Great Dividing Range, and that no protection could be afforded against the very warlike and hostile tribes in the lands of the Kamilaroi. Murrurundi was then known as Page's River, and any settlers venturing past that outpost did so at their own peril—which they chanced, of course.

It was in 1818 that Oxley named the Liverpool Plains after Lord Liverpool. The Kamilaroi called the plains Corborn Comleroy. These fertile lands are supposed to have once been the bed of a great land lake.

*Vale*—tribe of the Gunn-e-darr, tribes of the Kamilaroi.

Dear Reader,

Bolinda Press is proud to present you with Large Print books that are easy to read, comfortable to the eye, and light and easy to handle. Read your favourite author or book of interest in a type-size that brings you pleasure and enjoyment. Remember you don't have to have trouble reading standard print books to ENJOY reading our Large Print books.

Bolinda Press is the only family owned and operated Large Print publisher in the Southern Hemisphere. All books are produced in Australia.

If you have enjoyed reading this book, check for the Bolinda Press name next time you are at your local library or bookshop. You are even more than welcome to call us Toll Free on 1800 335 364 (Australia) or 0800 44 5788 (New Zealand) to give us any feedback or suggestions.

We have endless hours of reading enjoyment for you and Remember: **Eyes love Large Print!**

Thanks for your support.

Rebecca Walshe (Publisher)

**rebecca@alpav.com.au**